Building Crafts Foundation

4th edition

Level 1&2

Peter Brett

Nelson Thornes

Published in 2011 by:
Nelson Thornes Ltd
Delta Place
27 Bath Road
CHELTENHAM
GL53 7TH
United Kingdom

11 12 13 14 15 / 10 9 8 7 6 5 4 3 2 1

A catalogue record for this book is available from the British Library

ISBN 978 1 4085 0888 6

Cover photograph © Kuzma/iStockphoto
Page make-up by Wearset Ltd

Printed in Croatia by Zrinski

Acknowledgements
Alamy p18 (qaphotos.com), p22 (Construction Photography), p41 (Frank Paul), p55a (Transtock Inc.), p55b (Alex Hinds), p55c (Tony Watson), p55d (Mike Abbot), p57c (Enigma), p62b (mambo), p62c (67photo), p62d (David Askham), p64a (Construction Photography), p64b (Sheldon Levis), p64d (T.M.O. Buildings), p70 (Alan Fern), p80 (Jack Sullivan), p189B (Paula Solloway), p201 (David Hoffman), p206 (Chris Pancewicz), p248 (Joe Fairs), p249T (Paul Williams), p250 (Arthur Gebuys); **Ancon Building Products** p217; **Art Directors** p76, p79T6, p86R; **Construction Photography** p43a (Jean-Francois Cardella), p43b (Cultura), p61 (Paul McMullin), p62a (Buildpix), p69 (Tristan Savatier), p186 (Buildpix), p237 (Chris Henderson), p249b (Buildpix); **Crown Copyright** p91; **Dormole Ltd** p57L; **Fotolia** p46 (mast3r), p50a (Lusoimages), p50b (Julián Rovagnati), p50c (theclarkester), p50d (kurhan), p51 (hartphotography), p75 (ibphoto), p79T5 (design56), p84M (Lisa F. Young), p196 (Diego Cervo); **Getty** p200 (Digital Vision); http://www.cscs.uk.com p17; **Instant Art/ NT** p42, p44, p52, p89; **iStockphoto** p29, p43c, p50e, p57, p64e, p76M, p79T1–4, p79T8, p85b, p90, p169, p189T, p189M, p199, p256; **Martyn Chillmaid** p76b, p86L; **Photolibrary.com** p1 (Keith Morris), p94 (HuntStock), p108; **Rozalex** p79T7; **Science Photo Library** p84T (Michael Donne), p85T (Cordelia Molloy).

Contents

Introduction v

Chapter 1 Safe working practices in construction **1**

K1 Health and safety regulations, roles and
responsibilities 2
K2 Accident and emergency procedures and how
to report them 22
K3 Hazards on construction sites 32
K4 Health and hygiene in a construction environment 40
K5 Handle materials and equipment safely 49
K6 Basic working platforms 55
K7 Work with electricity in a construction environment 72
K8 Using personal protective equipment (PPE) correctly 78
K9 Fire and emergency procedures 83
K10 Safety signs and notices 89

Chapter 2 Information, quantities and communicating with
others **94**

K1 Interpret and produce building information 95
K2 Determine quantities of materials and estimate
quantities of resources 121
K3 Relay information in the workplace and
communicate workplace requirements efficiently 166

Chapter 3   Building methods and construction technology   **196**

K1 Principles of building methods and construction
    technology   197
K2 Principles of internal building work   231
K3 Delivery and storage of building materials   253

Glossary   264

Index   270

Introduction

This book matches the learning outcomes and assessment criteria of the Construction Awards Alliance (CAA) Diploma core units at Levels 1 and 2, which are common to a range of construction crafts qualifications.

Each chapter in the book relates to a particular CAA Diploma unit and covers all the information you need to gain the level of knowledge and understanding required for each learning outcome.

Building Crafts Foundation also supports the learning outcomes of the core NVQ Diploma units, for construction craft apprentices who are working towards a competence-based qualification.

Each chapter contains features to help you successfully complete each unit:

- ⬡ *Learning outcomes*. At the start of each chapter there is an overview of the unit covered and a list of the learning outcomes (what you are required to know) for each level.

- ⬡ *Key terms*. Words and terms you may not have come across before are highlighted and defined. They can also be found in the glossary at the end of the book.

- ⬡ *FAQ*. Answers to common questions about the topic.

- ⬡ *Safety tips*. Key guidance on working safely.

- ⬡ *Remember*. Essential information to reinforce your knowledge.

- ⬡ *Did you know?* Fascinating facts about the topic.

- ⬡ *Example*. Worked examples to show how calculations have been carried out, as a helpful guide when answering questions and undertaking other tasks.

○ *Link*. Links to other sections of the book where further relevant information can be found.

○ *Activity*. Engaging activities which help you to gain useful information from other sources.

○ *Check Your Understanding*. Activities to check your understanding of the topic.

○ *Assessment check*. A list of the required assessment criteria (what you are required to do) at the end of each outcome to show what you should be able to do now you have completed this learning outcome.

○ *Revision Quiz*. Multiple choice revision quiz for each level to check your knowledge at the end of each chapter.

Good luck! Wishing you all the best for your studies and your future in the construction industry.

Peter Brett

Safe working practices in construction

1

Health and safety forms an essential part of your daily working life. Construction site safety is **paramount** for the **well-being** of all concerned. Ensuring that a site is as safe as possible is a shared responsibility between employers and the workforce. Employers have a duty to create safe working conditions and provide the workforce with training, which explains safety rules, procedures and regulations. You, as part of the workforce, have a major contribution to make in site safety by responding to safety instructions, complying with safety rules and developing the skills to identify potential safety **hazards** and reduce **risks**.

This chapter covers the following learning outcomes for Unit 1001:

K1 Health and safety regulations, roles and responsibilities

K2 Accident and emergency procedures, and how to report them

K3 Hazards on construction sites

K4 Health and hygiene in a construction environment

K5 Handle materials and equipment safely

K6 Basic working platforms

K7 Work with electricity in a construction environment

K8 Use personal protective equipment (PPE) correctly

K9 Fire and emergency procedures

K10 Safety signs and notices

This unit also supports the learning outcomes of the NVQ Diploma unit QCF 01 – Conform to general workplace safety.

KEY TERMS

Paramount: greatest in importance or significance.

Well-being: a good, healthy, or comfortable state.

Hazard: something with the potential to cause **harm**.

Risk: concerned with the severity of harm and the likelihood of it happening.

Harm: can vary in its severity, some hazards can cause death, others illness or disability or maybe only cuts or bruises.

KEY TERMS

Hazardous: something or a situation that is potentially very dangerous to people, animals or the environment.

Plant: describes all industrial machinery and vehicles used on a construction site.

Legislation: a law or set of laws written and passed by parliament.

Regulations: orders issued by a government department or agency that has the force of law.

Approved codes of practice (ACoP): a published document that contains guidance, examples of good practice and explanations of the law.

K1 Health and safety regulations, roles and responsibilities

Health and safety legislation

Working in construction can be very **hazardous**. Projects can involve working at height, in confined spaces, with construction **plant**, power transmissions, hazardous chemicals, materials, machines and a wide variety of tools. While at work, you must follow a wide range of **legislation**, **regulations** and supporting **approved codes of practice (ACoP)**. Health and safety legislation is there to protect all persons at work and others from the risks occurring through work activities.

DID YOU KNOW

Failure to obey legislation or a set of regulations is a criminal offence that could result in prosecution. Failure to follow an ACoP is not in itself an offence, but if a breaking of the associated regulations is alleged, failure to follow the ACoP will be accepted as evidence in a court of law.

The Health and Safety at Work Act 1974 (HASAWA)

HASAWA introduced the main statutory legislation in the 1970s, covering the health and safety of all persons at work and others from the risks occurring through work activities. As a member of the construction industry, you need to know about your responsibilities with regards to various safety legislations.

There are four main objectives of the HASAWA:

1 To secure the health, safety and welfare of everyone at work.

2 To protect the general public from risks due to work activities.

3 To control the use, handling, storage and transportation of explosives and highly flammable substances.

4 To control the release of noxious or offensive substances into the atmosphere.

These objectives can be achieved only by involving everyone in health and safety matters, including:

⬡ **employers** and management

⬡ **employees** (and those undergoing training)

⬡ the **self-employed**

⬡ **designers**, **manufacturers** and **suppliers** of equipment and materials.

Duties in legislation can be either 'absolute' or have a qualifying term added called 'reasonably practicable':

⬡ **Absolute** means that the requirement must be met regardless of cost or other implications, unless a qualifying term is added, such as 'whenever reasonably practicable'.

⬡ **Reasonably practicable** means that you are required to consider the risks involved in undertaking a particular work activity. However, if the risks are minimal and the cost or technical difficulties of eliminating the risks are high, it might not be reasonably practicable to do so.

KEY TERMS

Employer: a person, business, or organisation that engages and pays one or more employees.

Employee: a paid worker.

Self-employed: a person who earns a living by working independently of an employer, either freelance or by running a business.

Designer: a person who designs things.

Manufacturer: a person, factory, or company that produces finished goods from raw materials.

Supplier: a person or company that provides goods, materials or services.

Duty: something that a person or organisation is expected or required to do.

DID YOU KNOW

Responsibilities and duties under HASAWA

Employers' duties

Employers have a **duty** to ensure 'so far as is reasonably practicable' the health, safety and welfare of their employees, visitors and the general public. Therefore they must:

DID YOU KNOW

Under HASAWA, employers must provide a range of **personal protection equipment (PPE)**, such as a safety helmet, gloves and eye protection. Employers are not allowed to charge for equipment provided to meet any health and safety requirements.

- provide and maintain a safe working environment

- ensure safe access to and from the workplace

- provide and maintain safe machinery, equipment and methods of work

- ensure the safe handling, transport and storage of all machinery, equipment and materials

- provide all employees with the information, instruction, training and supervision to ensure safe working

- give employees an up-to-date written statement of the firm's safety policy

KEY TERMS

Personal protection equipment (PPE): equipment, additions or accessories designed to be worn or held by a person at work to protect against risk.

LINK

For more information on PPE, see:

- The Personal Protective Equipment at Work Regulations 1992 (PPER) on page 13 of this chapter

- K8 Use personal protective equipment (PPE) correctly on page 78 of this chapter.

BBS Construction Services

STATEMENT OF COMPANY POLICY ON HEALTH AND SAFETY

The Directors accept that they have a legal and moral obligation to promote health and safety in the workplace and to ensure the cooperation of employees in this. This duty of care extends to all personswho may be affected by any operation under the control of BBS Construction Services.

Employees also have a statutory duty to safeguard themselves and others and to cooperate with management to secure a safe work environment.

The directors shall ensure, so far as reasonably practicable, that:

- Adequate resources and competent advice are made available in order that proper provision can be made for health and safety.
- Safe systems of working are devised and maintained.
- All employees are provided with all information, instructions, training and supervision required to secure the safety of all persons.
- All plant, machinery and equipment is safe and without risk to health.
- All places of work are maintained in a safe condition with safe means of access and egress.
- Arrangements are made for safe use, handling, storage and transport of all articles and substances.
- The working environment is maintained in a condition free of risks to health and safety and that adequate welfare facilities are provided.
- Assessment of all risks are made and control measures put in place to reduce or eliminate them.
- All arrangements are monitored and reviewed periodically.

These statements have been adopted by directors of the company and form the basis of our approach to health and safety matters.

Ivor Carpenter, Finance Director

Christine Whiteman, Human Resource Director

James Brett, Managing Director

The Director with responsibility for Health and Safety

Peter Brett, Chief Executive

1.1 A typical construction company's 'safety policy'

⬡ involve trade union safety representatives (where appointed) with all matters concerning the development, promotion and maintenance of health and safety requirements.

Designers', manufacturers' and suppliers' duties

Designers, manufacturers and suppliers, as well as importers and hirers of equipment, machinery and materials for use at work, have a duty to:

⬡ ensure that their product is designed, manufactured and tested so that when used correctly there is no hazard to health and safety

⬡ provide information as to the correct use, without risk, of their product. Employers should ensure this information is passed on to their employees.

⬡ carry out research so that any risk to health and safety is eliminated or minimised as far as possible.

Employee's duties

HASAWA and other health and safety regulations exist to protect employees and visitors. As well as rights, the regulations give you, as an employee, certain responsibilities.

Therefore, employees must:

⬡ take reasonable care at all times and ensure that their actions or **omissions** do not put at 'risk' themselves or any other person

⬡ cooperate with their employers to enable them to fulfil the employers' health and safety **obligations**

⬡ use the equipment and safeguards provided by the employers

⬡ never misuse or interfere with anything provided for health and safety

⬡ report hazards, accidents and near misses.

DID YOU KNOW

You could be prosecuted if you interfere with anything provided for health and safety purposes.

Self-employed people and **sub-contractors** have the same duties as employees. If they employ other people, they must also work to the duties set out for employers.

KEY TERMS

Omission: something that has been deliberately or accidentally not done or has been left out.

Obligation: something that you must do because of a legal or moral duty or responsibility.

Sub-contractor: a self-employed person or a specialist company that is hired by a main building contractor to carry out a specific part of the building work.

DID YOU KNOW

LAs are the main enforcing authority for retailing, wholesale distribution, warehousing, hotel and catering premises, offices, and the consumer/leisure industries. However, responsibility for enforcement at certain premises may be transferred between HSE and LAs by agreement.

The Health and Safety Executive (HSE)

Roles and responsibilities

Under HASAWA, an enforcing authority was established, aimed at reducing death, injury and ill health. The HSE is a government body and, jointly with local authorities (LAs), is responsible for the enforcement of health and safety in the UK.

As enforcing authorities, both the HSE and LAs provide free advice and guidance on the law, conduct inspections and investigations, and take enforcement action where appropriate.

Inspectors appointed by enforcing authorities are given wide powers of entry, examination and investigation to enable them to enforce the HASAWA and other safety legislation. In addition to giving employers advice and information on health and safety matters, HSE inspectors can:

- enter premises to carry out investigations and take measurements, photographs, recordings and samples. The inspector may require the premises to be left undisturbed while the investigations take place.

- ask questions relevant to the investigation and require people to sign a declaration as to the truth of the answers.

- check records. All books, records and documents required by legislation must be made available for inspection and copying.

- give information. An inspector has a duty to give information about the safety of their workplace and details of any action they propose to take

- demand the seizure, dismantling, neutralising or destruction of any machinery, equipment, material or substance that is likely to cause immediate serious personal injury

- issue an improvement notice. This requires the responsible person (employer, manufacturer, etc.) to put right any minor hazard or infringement of legislation within a specified period of time.

- issue a prohibition notice. This requires the responsible person to stop immediately any activities that are likely to result in serious personal injury. This ban continues until the situation is corrected. An appeal may be made to an industrial tribunal.

Health & Safety Executive

Health and Safety at Work etc Act 1974,
Sections 21, 23 and 24

Prohibition notice

Serial number

P

Name

Address

Trading as*

Inspector's full name — I,

Inspector's official designation — one of Her Majesty's Inspectors of
Being an Inspector appointed by an instrument in writing made pursuant to section 19 of the said Act and entitled to issue this notice

Official address — of

Telephone number

hereby give you notice that I am of the opinion that the following activities namely:

Location of premises or place of activity

which are being carried on by you/likely to be carried on by you/under your control* at

Location of premises or place of activity

Involve, or will involve, a risk of serious personal injury, and that the matters which give rise/will give rise* to the said risk(s) are:

and that the said matters involve/will involve* contravention of the following statutory provisions:

because

and I hereby direct that the said activities shall not be carried on by you or under your control immediately/after*   unless the said contravention(s)* and matters have been remedied

I further direct that the measures specified in the schedule which forms part of this notice shall be taken to remedy the said contravention(s)* or matters.*

Signature   Date

* A Prohibition Notice is also being served on

of

related to the matters contained in this notice

Environment and Safety Information Act 1988 — This is a relevant notice for the purposes of the Environment and Safety Information Act 1988   YES/NO*
This page only will form the register entry*.

Signature   Date

LP2 (rev 12/88)   *See notes overleaf*   * delete as appropriate

1.2 Copy of a HSE prohibition notice

FAQ

What can I do if I think my employer is asking me to do jobs that put my health and safety at risk?

If you think your employer is putting your health or safety at risk, you should first raise your concerns directly with your supervisor or site health and safety representative.

If, as a result, no improvement is made and you consider that your health or safety is still at risk, you can report this in confidence to the HSE for them to look into.

○ prosecute anybody who fails to carry out their safety duty, through a magistrates' court or in the higher court system. Conviction can lead to unlimited fines, a prison sentence or both.

Contacting the HSE

It is a legal duty of employers, the self-employed and others in control of work premises to report to the HSE the following events or reportable incidents:

○ Deaths arising out of or in connection with work.

○ Major injuries, which include most fractures, amputations, loss of sight, loss of consciousness, acute illness requiring medical treatment or any other injury involving a stay in hospital.

○ Over three-day injuries, where a person is away from work or unable to perform their normal work role for more than three consecutive days.

○ Injuries to members of the public or people not at work who are taken away from the scene of an accident to hospital.

○ Work-related diseases, which include poisoning, skin diseases, lung diseases, infections, musculoskeletal disorders and hand–arm vibration syndrome (HAVS).

○ Dangerous occurrences, which include the collapse of a crane, hoist, scaffolding or building, an explosion or fire, or the escape of any substance that is liable to cause a health hazard or major injury to any person.

○ Certain near misses, where something happened that could have resulted in an injury but didn't. This is classified as a dangerous occurrence.

The Reporting of Injuries, Diseases and Dangerous Occurrences Regulations 1995 (RIDDOR)

This legislation states that employers, the self-employed and persons in control of premises must report to the HSE some accidents and incidents at work. These reports alert the HSE to individual incidents, provide data to indicate where and how risks arise and show up trends. This information enables the

Under the CDM regulations, the HSE must be notified where the construction work is expected to:

- last for more than 30 days

- involve more than 500 person days of work, for example 50 people working for over 10 days.

HSE form — Report of an injury or dangerous occurrence

Health and Safety at Work etc Act 1974
The Reporting of Injuries, Diseases and Dangerous Occurrences Regulations 1995

Report of an injury or dangerous occurrence

Filling in this form
This form must be filled in by an employer or other responsible person.

Part A

About you
1 What is your full name?

2 What is your job title?

3 What is your telephone number?

About your organization
4 What is the name of your organization?

5 What is the address and postcode?

6 What type of work does the organization do?

Part B

About the incident
1 On what date did the incident happen?
   /   /

2 At what time did the incident happen?
(Please use the 24-hour clock e.g. 0600)

3 Did the incident happen at the above address?
Yes Go to question 4
No Where did the incident happen?
   elsewhere in your organization – give the name, address and postcode
   at someone else's premises – give the name, address and postcode
   in a public place – give details of where it happened

If you do not know the postcode, what is the name of the local authority?

4 In which department, or where on the premises, did the incident happen?

F2508 (01/96)

Part C

About the injured person
If you are reporting a dangerous occurrence, go to Part F.
If more than one person was injured in the same incident, please attach the details asked for in Part C and Part D for each injured person.

1 What is their full name?

3 Was the injury (tick the one box that applies)
   a fatality?
   a major injury or condition? (see accompanying notes)
   an injury to an employee or self-employed person which prevented them doing their normal work for more than 3 days?
   an injury to a member of the public which meant they had to be taken from the scene of the accident to a hospital for treatment?

4 Did the injured person (tick the boxes that apply)
   become unconscious?
   need resuscitation?
   remain in hospital for more than 24 hours?
   none of the above?

Part E

About the kind of accident
Please tick the one box that best describes what happened, then go to Part G.

   Contact with moving machinery or material being machined
   Hit by a moving flying or falling object
   Hit by a moving vehicle
   Hit something fixed or stationary
   Injured while handling, lifting or carrying
   Slipped, tripped or fell on the same level
   Fell from a height
      How high was the fall
      _____ metres
   Trapped by something collapsing
   Drowned or asphyxiated
   Exposed to, or in contact with, a harmful substance
   Exposed to fire
   Exposed to an explosion
   Contact with electricity or an electrical discharge
   Injured by an animal
   Physically assaulted by a person
   Another kind of accident (describe it in Part G)

Part F

Dangerous occurrences
Enter the number of the dangerous occurrence you are reporting. (The numbers are given in the Regulations and in the notes which accompany this form)

For official use
Client number   Location number   Event number
                                                    INV REP Y

Part G

Describing what happened
Give as much detail as you can. For instance:
- the name of any substance involved
- the name and type of any machine involved
- the events that led to the incident
- the part played by any people

If it was a personal injury, give details of what the person was doing. Describe any action that has since been taken to prevent a similar incident. Use a separate piece of paper if you need to.

Part H

Your signature
Signature

Date
   /   /

Where to send the form
Please send it to the Enforcing Authority for the place where it happened. If you do not know the Enforcing Authority, send it to the nearest HSE office.

1.3 Report of an injury or dangerous occurrence

Remember, you should always wear the appropriate PPE for the work in hand.

KEY TERMS

Hazardous substances: substances that can cause ill health.

Risk assessment: the process of identifying hazards in the workplace or a particular work activity, assessing the likelihood of any harm arising and deciding on adequate precautionary control measures.

DID YOU KNOW

COSHH covers all hazardous substances except for asbestos and lead, which have their own regulations.

LINK

For more information on the control of hazardous substances, see:

○ Risk assessments and method statements on page 32 of this chapter

○ Hazardous substances on page 43 of this chapter.

HSE to focus on where there are issues and to advise employers on strategies to help prevent future injuries, ill health and accidental loss.

Deaths, major injuries and dangerous occurrences must be reported without delay. Over three-day injuries must be reported within 10 days. The quickest way to report an incident is to telephone the incident contact centre (ICC) where an advisor will help you make the report and send you a copy for your records. Alternatively, reports can be made by e-mail or post using the HSE 'Report of an injury or dangerous occurrence' form.

The Control of Substances Hazardous to Health Regulations 2002 (COSHH)

These regulations require employers to control exposure to **hazardous substances** in the workplace to prevent ill health and protect employees and others who may be exposed.

Hazardous substances can be found in most work environments and include:

○ substances used directly in work activities, such as adhesives, paints and cleaning agents

○ substances generated during work activities, such as the dust from sawing

○ naturally occurring substances, such as sand dust

○ biological agents (germs), such as bacteria and other micro-organisms.

COSHH requires employers to follow an eight-step procedure to control hazardous substances in the workplace:

Step 1: Assess the risks (carry out a **risk assessment**) to health arising from hazardous substances used in the workplace or created by work activities.

Step 2: Decide what precautions are needed.

Step 3: Prevent or adequately control exposure.

Step 4: Ensure that control measures are used and maintained.

Step 5: Monitor exposure.

Step 6: Carry out appropriate health surveillance.

Step 7: Prepare plans and procedures to deal with accidents, incidents and emergencies.

Step 8: Ensure that employees are properly informed, trained and supervised.

The Construction (Design and Management) Regulations 2007 (CDM)

Design and management legislation requires that health and safety is taken into account and managed during all stages of a construction project. The CDM regulations apply to all construction projects whatever their size. They require all duty holders, including the client, designers and site workers , to play their part in improving on-site health and safety.

CDM duty holders

- **The client**: the person or organisation for which the work is being done.

- **The CDM coordinator**: the person appointed by the client for **notifiable projects** to advise and assist them and ensure aspects of health and safety during all phases of the project.

- **The principal contractor**: the main contractor appointed by the client for notifiable projects to undertake the construction work – they may appoint other contractors and sub-contractors for specific parts of the work.

- **The designer**: the person who prepares drawings or specifications for a building including products to be used within it. These include architects, engineers, surveyors and other product designers.

- **Contractors**: the main contractor on **non-notifiable projects** and sub-contractors and self-employed people working on-site for all projects.

- **Workers and others**: everyone working on a building site or working for any of the above duty holders.

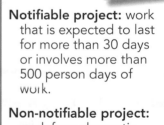

DID YOU KNOW

Under the CDM regulations, the client must ensure that the appointed CDM coordinator, designers, principal contractor and other contractors are competent. No person should accept an appointment unless they are competent. No person should instruct a worker or manage design or construction work unless the worker is competent or under the supervision of a competent person.

KEY TERMS

Notifiable project: work that is expected to last for more than 30 days or involves more than 500 person days of work.

Non-notifiable project: work for a domestic client or where it is expected to last less than 30 days and less than 500 person days of work.

Health and Safety Executive

HSE

Notification of construction project

1. Guidance notes for completion - Please complete in block capitals using black ink

What should this form be used for
- To notify the enforcing authority for the Construction (Design and Management) Regulations 2007 of any project that is likely to last longer than 30 days or involve more than 500 person days of construction work.
- Any day on which construction work is carried out (including holidays and weekends) should be counted, even if the work on that day is of short duration.
- A person day is one individual, including supervisors and specialists, carrying out construction work for one normal working shift.
- Construction work for a domestic client is not notifiable.

Who should use this form
- The CDM co-ordinator for the project.

Where to send the completed form
- F10 Scanning Centre, Health and Safety Executive, c/o Central Despatch, Redgrave Court, Merton Road, Bootle, Merseyside L20 7HS.
- If the notifiable work is on an operation railway, the notification should be sent to the Office of Rail Regulation. You can get the address by contacting HSE's Infoline, Tel: 0845 345 0055.

When to send this form
- As soon as practicable after the CDM co-ordinator for the project is appointed by the client.

2. Notification type

Is this the initial notification of the project or are you providing additional information not previously available?

☐ Initial Notification ☐ Additional Information

3. Date of forwarding this notification or provision of additional information?

☐☐ - ☐☐ - ☐☐☐☐

4. Name of the Local Authority where the site is located

☐☐☐☐☐☐☐☐☐☐☐☐☐☐☐☐☐☐☐☐☐☐☐☐☐☐☐☐☐☐☐☐☐☐☐☐☐☐

5. Address of the construction site (Mandatory fields are marked with an asterisk(*))

Are there multiple construction sites ☐ Yes ☐ No (Please give the main address below)

Address Name	☐☐☐☐☐☐☐☐☐☐☐☐☐☐☐☐☐☐☐☐☐☐☐☐☐☐☐☐☐☐☐☐☐☐
Street*	☐☐☐☐☐☐☐☐☐☐☐☐☐☐☐☐☐☐☐☐☐☐☐☐☐☐☐☐☐☐☐☐☐☐
District	☐☐☐☐☐☐☐☐☐☐☐☐☐☐☐☐☐☐☐☐☐☐☐☐☐☐☐☐☐☐☐☐☐☐
Town*	☐☐☐☐☐☐☐☐☐☐☐☐☐☐☐☐☐☐☐☐☐☐☐☐☐☐☐
County	☐☐☐☐☐☐☐☐☐☐☐☐☐☐☐☐☐☐☐☐☐☐☐☐☐☐☐☐☐☐☐☐☐☐

Country* ☐ England ☐ Wales ☐ Scotland Postcode* ☐☐☐☐ ☐☐☐

F10 (04.08)

1.4 Notification of a construction project

The Provision and Use of Work Equipment Regulations 1998 (PUWER)

PUWER requires the prevention or control of risks to people's health and safety from equipment that they use at work. Employers and the self-employed who provide equipment, or people who control or supervise the use of it, have the following duties under the regulations to ensure that it is:

⬡ suitable to use for the purpose and in the conditions that it is used

⬡ maintained in a safe condition

⬡ inspected by a **competent person** to ensure that it is and remains in a safe condition.

In addition, risks created by the use of equipment must be removed wherever possible or controlled by taking a combination of the following appropriate measures:

⬡ Hardware measures (guards, protection devices, warning devices, safety markings and PPE).

⬡ Software measures (safe systems of work and adequate operating information, instruction and training).

The Personal Protective Equipment at Work Regulations 1992 (PPER)

PPER requires that: all items of PPE must be suitable for purpose and provision must be made for PPE storage, maintenance, replacement and cleaning; where more than one item is being worn, they must be compatible; training must be provided in the correct use of PPE and its limitations; employers must ensure that appropriate items are provided and are being used properly; employees and the self-employed must make full use of PPE provided and any defect or loss must be reported to their employers.

KEY TERMS

Competent person: someone who has the experience, knowledge and appropriate qualifications, which enable them to identify the risks arising from a given situation and the measures that are required to lessen the risks.

⟨⟨⟨ REMEMBER

Using PPE should be the last, not the first, resort. The first step is to undertake a risk assessment to prevent or control any risk in the first place by making machinery or work processes safer.

In order to comply with health and safety regulations, employers must provide you with a range of PPE, such as a safety helmet, gloves and eye protection free of charge.

LINK

For more information on PPE equipment, see K8 Using personal protective equipment (PPE) correctly on page 78 of this chapter.

LINK

For more information on manual handling, see K5 Handle materials and equipment safely on page 49 of this chapter.

The Manual Handling Operations Regulations 1992 (MHO)

These regulations ensure that employers and the self-employed do not expose anyone to manual handling operations that might create a risk of injury. Where avoidance is not reasonably practical, employers have to make an assessment with the aim of removing hazards and minimising potential risk of injury in the following ways:

- ⭘ Avoiding all unnecessary manual handling.

- ⭘ Automating handling tasks (for example, by the use of cranes, conveyor belts and lifting/movement aids such as wheelbarrows and pallet trucks).

- ⭘ Arranging for heavy or awkward loads to be shared when finally lifting or moving into position by hand.

- ⭘ Ordering materials in easily handled sizes (for example, bagged sand, cement and plaster come in 25 kg bags).

- ⭘ Positioning all loads mechanically as near as possible to where they will be used so that carrying by hand is limited.

- ⭘ Providing employees with advice and training in safe lifting techniques and sensible handling of loads.

Employees are required to:

- ⭘ cooperate with their employer

- ⭘ follow the safe systems of work laid down by their employer

- ⭘ make full and proper use of any equipment provided

- ⭘ ensure others are not put at risk by their actions

- ⭘ report any identified hazards.

The Work at Height Regulations 2005

These regulations apply to any work at a height where there is a risk of a fall liable to cause injury, including work at a low level and below ground level. Access to a place of work via a ladder can also be considered as work at height. This legislation places a duty on employers, employees, the self-employed and anyone else who controls the way work at height is undertaken.

Duty holders must ensure:

○ all work at height is properly planned and organised

○ those involved in work at height are competent

○ the risks from work at height are assessed and appropriate work equipment is used

○ the risks from fragile surfaces are properly controlled

○ all equipment for working at height is properly inspected and maintained.

The HSE has set out a simple approach for managing and selecting equipment for working at height:

○ Avoid working at height wherever possible.

○ Where work at height cannot be avoided, use equipment to prevent falls, such as working platforms and guard-rails.

○ Where the risk of a fall cannot be eliminated, use equipment to minimise the distance and consequences of a fall, such as safety nets, harnesses and air bags.

Other sources of health and safety information

The HSE and the Health and Safety Commission (HSC)

The HSE and HSC were previously two government agencies responsible for health and safety in Great Britain. Both were established under the HASAWA to control the risks and exposure to hazards in the workplace and have now merged into a single organisation operating under the HSE name.

Construction Skills

Construction Skills (formally the Construction Industry Training Board – CITB) is the Sector Skills Council and Industry Training Board for construction. Led by employers, it works with them and the government in partnership to ensure a safe, professional and fully-qualified construction workforce. Construction Skills is funded mainly by the construction industry through a type of tax based on the employer's size and turnover. It also receives

LINK
For further information on work at height, see K6 Basic working platforms on page 55 of this chapter.

LINK
The HSE's website provides a vast range of safety-related news, information, guidance and support, ACoP, information sheets and other publications. Go to: www.hse.gov.uk.

ACTIVITY
Visit the Construction Skills website to research the sources of information and services the organisation provides. Go to: www.cskills.org. You will also find links to Cskills Awards, the awarding body for construction qualifications and the Construction Awards Alliance (CAA) which is also an awarding body and is an alliance between City & Guilds and Construction Skills or Cskills Awards.

income from the Learning and Skills Council, the European Social Fund and the sale of its own products and services. It uses this income to provide advice and financial support in the form of grants to employers who undertake training.

The Royal Society for the Prevention of Accidents (RoSPA)

RoSPA is a registered charity whose purpose is to provide information, advice, resources and training in the promotion of safety and the prevention of accidents in the workplace, at home, on the roads, in schools, during leisure activities and on or near water.

The Royal Society for Public Health (RSPH)

RSPH is an independent charity and is the oldest public health body in the world, with over 150 years experience in its field of protecting and promoting public health. It advises on policy development, provides education and training services, encourages scientific research, supplies information and certifies products, training centres and processes.

Manufacturer's and supplier's information

Manufacturers and suppliers have to provide workers and emergency personnel with procedures for handling or working with their product in a safe manner. This is normally published in the form of 'safety data sheets' that include information such as physical properties, toxicity, health effects, reactivity, first-aid treatment, storage and disposal guidance and the need for PPE and spill-handling procedures.

Health and safety testing in construction

In order to raise quality and safety standards in the construction industry, employers and their clients are demanding that all workers and visitors to sites have current membership of an appropriate, competence-based health and safety at work registration scheme.

The Construction Skills Certification Scheme (CSCS), administered by members of the construction industry, has the greatest uptake of all recognised schemes. A CSCS card proves that the cardholder is competent in the job and has up-to-date knowledge of appropriate health and safety legislation. There are various CSCS

LINK

The RoSPA website contains various sources of technical and practical information, guidance and support. Go to: www.rospa.com.

LINK

The RSPH website has further details and links to related information. Go to: www.rsph.org.uk.

LINK

A general web search for 'safety data sheets' will provide many links to sources of information. Alternatively, you can go direct to a particular manufacturer's website where you can normally view or download safety data sheets on their products.

cards available to suit all levels of industry qualifications (for example, trainees, craft operatives, management, site visitors and persons in a construction-related occupation).

1.5 Example of a CSCS card

To obtain a CSCS card, you need to pass the Construction Skills health and safety test. It involves answering up to 40 randomly selected multiple-choice questions on a touch-screen computer at either an accredited test centre or mobile testing unit.

Test results are either pass or fail. Where the result is not up to standard, the candidate will be able to retake the test on another occasion after undertaking revision. Construction Skills publish their bank of questions either as a book or CD-ROM, which you can buy for revision purposes.

Enforcing stringent guidance in health and safety

Health and safety legislation and guidance exist to protect all persons at their place of work and others from the risks occurring through work activities. Strict enforcement of health and safety legislation has seen a general reduction in the rate of accidents. Over the past 10 years, the rate of fatal injuries has been reduced by over 50 per cent. At the same time, the rate of reported major injuries to employees in construction has also fallen steadily.

Continued observance of all health and safety matters is required by everyone in order to continue the downward trend and make the construction industry a safer environment. In doing so, the industry as a whole is helping to prevent you and other people from becoming victims of accidents or ill health.

ACTIVITY

CSCS issues a range of cards depending on the status and occupation of the holder. Visit www. cskills.org to find out who the following card colours are intended for:

Red
Green
Blue
Gold
Black
White/yellow
Yellow
White/grey

DID YOU KNOW

Despite this falling trend, the rate of fatal, major and over three-day injuries is higher in construction than most other industries.

LINK

For more information on health risks and accident trends, see:

○ K3 Hazards on construction sites on page 32 of this chapter

○ K4 Health and hygiene in a construction environment on page 40 of this chapter

○ Key accident trends in the construction industry on page 25 of this chapter.

Inductions and toolbox talks

Site induction

1.6 A typical toolbox talk

SAFETY TIPS

In your working life, you may attend hundreds of site inductions. It is important that you attend each one as all sites are different and have a wide range of hazards that can change as the site develops.

When anyone comes to a site for the first time, it is important that they receive a site induction. This induction provides information about the site, its potential hazards and the procedures that are in place to control the risks.

Inductions will be specific to the site and provide you with information on the current site hazards and site rules. Some of the information they should cover includes:

○ introduction and purpose of the induction

○ outline of the scope of the work on the site

○ details of the site manager, safety officer and other supervisors on-site

○ details of the welfare facilities, such as canteen and toilets and any restrictions on their use

○ details of site access arrangements, such as signing in and out, details of the pedestrian routes on site and details of on/off-site parking arrangements

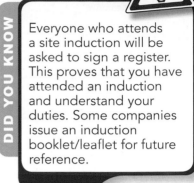

- emergency procedures – evacuation alarm, escape routes, designated assembly or muster points, name of nominated fire marshal and details of authorised re-entry to the site after an emergency

- first-aid procedures, including the location of the first-aid box, who the appointed first aider is and how to report accidents including near misses

- fire-fighting procedures in the event of a fire, including the location of equipment and the identity of approved fire-fighting personnel (fire wardens)

- details of how personnel will be advised of daily hazards, for example notices on the site notice board detailing the hazards of the day. These might include groundworks, working at height or planned material deliveries.

- details of the health and safety consultation procedures and sources of health and safety advice

- explanation of site rules.

DID YOU KNOW

Everyone who attends a site induction will be asked to sign a register. This proves that you have attended an induction and understand your duties. Some companies issue an induction booklet/leaflet for future reference.

REMEMBER

Site rules include:

- PPE requirements
- zero tolerance approach to health and safety risks, including violence and bullying
- no smoking/drug/alcohol policy
- use of equipment on-site is restricted to competent and authorised personnel
- alteration/construction/dismantling of scaffolds can only be undertaken by **carded scaffolders**
- the safe use of ladders, scaffolds and other access equipment
- keeping walkways around the site clear to reduce the risk of collision with moving vehicles and plant
- food and drink only to be eaten in the areas provided and these areas must be kept clean and hygienic at all times
- access to restricted areas.

KEY TERMS

Carded scaffolder: a person who holds a recognised skills card or certificate showing that they have been trained and assessed as being competent in the erection, alteration, dismantling and inspection of tubular scaffolding.

ACTIVITY

Various organisations produce toolbox talks, including Construction Skills and the HSE. Conduct a web search for 'construction toolbox talks' to see what you can find.

Toolbox talks

A toolbox talk is a short talk often on safety topics given by the site manager or safety officer during an induction before new personnel enter a site. It may also be given during lunch breaks to increase awareness of particular hazards on-site and how to try and minimise or control them. These talks form part of an employer's continual review of health and safety arrangements and training to make the workplace safer.

Toolbox talks are also used to deliver job specific skills training, such as how to use a new piece of equipment. Job specific toolbox talks should be relevant to the people attending. There would be little point in carpenters attending a talk on thin joint masonry techniques unless it directly affects them.

As with site inductions, a record of attendees to all toolbox talks should be kept to ensure that the appropriate people have received the talk.

CHECK YOUR UNDERSTANDING

- ✓ Name and explain the purpose of **three** pieces of health and safety legislation that affect the construction industry.
- ✓ Which organisation enforces health and safety legislation?
- ✓ State **two** duties under the Health and Safety at Work Act for both employers and employees.
- ✓ List **three** of the main powers of the HSE or other enforcing authority inspector.
- ✓ State **three** types of incident that must be reported under RIDDOR.

ASSESSMENT CHECK

Now that you have completed this learning outcome you should now be able to:

- identify key health and safety legislation relevant to and used in a construction environment
- state the key employer responsibilities under HASAWA
- state the key employee responsibilities under HASAWA
- state the roles and responsibilities of the HSE
- identify other sources of relevant health and safety information
- state when legislation would require the HSE to be informed
- state why there is a requirement for enforcing stringent guidance in health and safety
- state the importance of holding on-site safety inductions and toolbox talks.

K2 Accident and emergency procedures and how to report them

Types of major emergency

Emergencies are situations or events that require immediate action. In addition to accidents, workplace emergencies include:

⬡ fire

⬡ bomb threats/security alerts

⬡ leakage of chemicals or other hazardous substances.

Many of these examples are rare, but it is essential to know what to do if they occur. During a health and safety induction, individuals should be clearly briefed on what to do in the event of an emergency.

Injuries, diseases and other occurrences in the workplace

Reporting accidents

By law, all accidents must be reported and recorded. The key legislation that controls the reporting of accidents is the RIDDOR and CDM regulations.

The company's safety officer will regularly review the accident records to study reasons behind any occurrences and look at trends. This allows the company to make health and safety improvements in the workplace by preventing reoccurrences.

Accident or emergency records

A record should be made of all accidents, first-aid treatments and emergencies as soon as possible after the event. The accident record shown in Fig 1.8 is used as the basis of complying with RIDDOR and the CDM regulations.

1.7 A potential cause of an accident

REMEMBER ❯❯❯

Under RIDDOR, employers, the self-employed and persons in control of premises must report accidents and incidents at work to the HSE.

ACCIDENT RECORD

2 Report Number

1 About the person who had the accident

Name: JOHN WILSON
Address: 131 EASTWOOD LANE
EASTWOOD, NOTTS   Postcode: NG11 2DL
Occupation: JOINER

2 About you, the person filling in this record

▼ If you did not have the accident write your address and occupation

Name: PETER BATES
Address: 46 CHURCH ROAD
EASTWOOD, NOTTS   Postcode: NG11 2XB
Occupation: JOINERY TEAM LEADER

3 About the accident   Continue on the back of this form if you need to

▼ Say when it happened   Date 12 /APR / 11   Time 11:30 AM
▼ Say where it happened. State which room or place THE JOINERY WORKS
LONG EATON, IN THE JOINERY ASSEMBLY AREA
▼ Say how the accident happened. Give the cause if you can
TRIPPED ON AIR LINE WHEN STEPPING OFF SMALL HOP-UP

▼ If the person who had the accident suffered an injury, say what it was
SPRAINED WRIST ON LEFT HAND
▼ Please sign the record and date it
Signature Peter Bates   Date 12 /APR / 11

4 For the employer only

▼ Complete this box if the accident is reportable under the Reporting of Injuries, Diseases and Dangerous Occurrences Regulations 1995 (RIDDOR)
How was it reported?

Date reported   /   /   Signature

1.8 Accident record

The accident record should be completed by the injured person or, if this is not possible, a witness or someone representing the injured person. The first aider may also keep a record of first-aid treatments. To keep within the data protection act and confidentiality law, both records must be stored securely but separately.

Most companies will keep a record of accidents, incidents and emergencies in a site diary or 'incident' book, as well as a file containing photocopies of all reports to the HSE as required under RIDDOR. Organisations have to keep a record of any reportable injury, disease or dangerous occurrence for at least three years after it occurred.

REMEMBER

In addition to any accidents requiring treatment, near misses should be reported and recorded.

Dislocation: the displacement of a bone from its normal fitting in a joint.

Resuscitation: to revive someone from unconsciousness.

Hypothermia: dangerously low body temperature caused by prolonged exposure to cold.

Asphyxia: suffocation caused by a blockage of the airway or inhalation of toxic gases.

Biological agent: relating to living organisms that can cause detrimental heath effects.

Acute illness: extremely serious, severe or painful illness.

Toxin: a harmful substance that accumulates in the body.

Major, minor injuries and near misses

The HSE defines **major injuries** as those involving any of the following:

○ All fractures except to fingers, thumbs or toes.

○ Amputation – the loss of a limb or other body appendage.

○ **Dislocation** of the shoulder, hip, knee or spine.

○ The temporary or permanent loss of sight.

○ A chemical or hot metal burn to the eye or any injury penetrating the eye.

○ An injury from an electric shock or electrical burn, leading to unconsciousness requiring **resuscitation** or admittance to hospital for more than 24 hours.

○ Any injury leading to **hypothermia**, heat-induced illness or unconsciousness requiring resuscitation or admittance to hospital for more than 24 hours.

○ Unconsciousness caused by **asphyxia** or exposure to a harmful substance or **biological agent**.

○ An **acute illness** requiring medical treatment, or loss of consciousness arising from absorption of any substance by inhalation, ingestion or absorption through the skin.

○ An acute illness requiring medical treatment where there is reason to believe that this resulted from exposure to a biological agent or its **toxins** or infected material.

All other injuries may be classified as **minor injuries** and include cuts, burns and bruises.

A near miss can be seen as a lucky escape. These are accidents, incidents or occurrences that either nearly happened or did happen but did not result in an injury.

Key accident trends in the construction industry

2.2 million people work in the UK's construction industry. It is the country's biggest industry and also one of the most dangerous.

⬡ **Fatal injuries**: over the past 10 years, the rate of fatal injuries has been reduced by over 50 per cent from 5.9 people to 2.2 people per 100,000 persons engaged in the industry.

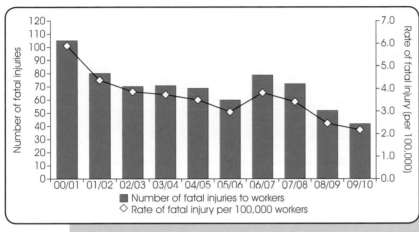

1.9 Number and rate of fatal injuries to construction workers

⬡ **Major injuries**: at the same time, the rate of reported major injuries to employees in construction has also fallen steadily, from nearly 400 to 230 per 100,000 persons engaged in the industry.

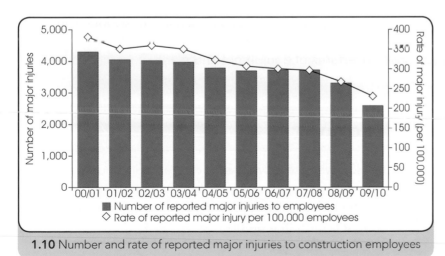

1.10 Number and rate of reported major injuries to construction employees

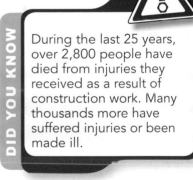

DID YOU KNOW

During the last 25 years, over 2,800 people have died from injuries they received as a result of construction work. Many thousands more have suffered injuries or been made ill.

⬡ **Three-day injuries**: in common with fatal and major injuries, the rate of over three-day injuries has also steadily declined over the last 10 years, from nearly 900 to just over 500 per 100,000 persons engaged in the industry.

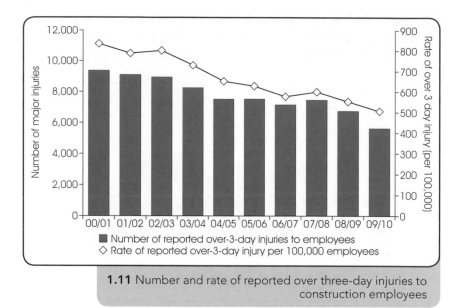

1.11 Number and rate of reported over three-day injuries to construction employees

Injury data

Despite falling numbers, the rate of fatal, major and over three-day injuries is still higher in construction than most industries.

The most common causes of industrial injuries are the result of poor handling or slips and trips. A higher proportion of reported injuries in construction are caused by falls from height, falling objects, contact with moving machinery and electricity, and collapses/overturns of equipment and plant.

ACTIVITY

Visit the HSE website (www.hse.gov.uk) and find out the main causes of fatal, major and over three-day injuries in the construction industry. Use the computer to record your findings in the form of a graph.

The effect of accidents and injuries on the employer

In addition to human pain and misery, accidents have other negative and financial implications for an employer, such as:

○ disruption and loss of production in the workplace

○ legal proceedings, costs and the possible closure of the workplace

○ costs associated with sickness pay, compensation awards and increased insurance premiums.

High accident levels create a poor image of both the employer and the industry to existing and future clients and the general public.

Minor accidents may affect profitability, as workers slow down to see what is happening or stop work to assist the injured person. Sick pay may have to be paid, as well as the cost of overtime or additional temporary staff in an attempt to keep the work on schedule.

More serious accidents will have high financial implications with workers absent and costs of HSE inquiries and possible compensation payments.

Companies with a poor accident record may find it difficult to gain new work contracts due to their poor 'health and safety' image. In addition, their insurance premiums will rise from the high number of injury compensation claims. Eventually, this may make the company uninsurable, causing it to go out of business.

Authorised persons

Many authorised persons could be involved in dealing with accident and emergency situations in the workplace.

○ First aiders will administer basic first aid and call an ambulance if required.

○ Supervisors, to whom accidents and emergency situations should be reported, will ensure the area is evacuated to prevent further injury and advise their site manager and safety officer of the incident.

SAFETY TIPS

Never ignore health and safety legislation or take short cuts. You will be putting yourself and others at risk.

REMEMBER

Under the CDM regulations, clients must ensure that the building contractor is competent to do the work and, thus, will be reluctant to work with companies with a poor health and safety record.

○ Having been informed of an incident, site managers and safety officers will first assess the area to ensure that it is made safe. They will then investigate the cause of the incident and prepare reports for company records and the HSE, if required.

○ The HSE must be immediately advised in the event of a death, major injury or a dangerous occurrence. For over three-day injuries, the HSE must be informed within 10 days.

○ The relevant emergency services – the police, ambulance, fire brigade or bomb disposal squad – will normally be called by a supervisor, site manager, safety officer or, in the case of an ambulance, the first aider.

First aid

First aid is the treatment of persons with the purpose of preserving life until medical help is obtained and also the treatment of minor injuries for which no medical help is required.

Employers and the self-employed are required under the Health and Safety (First Aid) Regulations to provide appropriate first-aid equipment, facilities and personnel. There should be an assessment of first-aid needs to determine the number of trained first aiders, contents of the first-aid box and whether a first-aid room is required. The minimum first-aid provision in any workplace site is:

○ a suitably stocked first-aid box

○ an appointed person or trained first aider

○ notices displayed in the workplace advising who and where the appointed person or first aiders are and the location of the first-aid room and/or first-aid box.

Only a trained first aider should administer first aid for all types of injuries, including minor ones. Send for the nearest first aider and/or medical assistance immediately.

Contents of the first-aid box will depend on the number of people and the type of work being undertaken. As a minimum, the box should contain:

○ a variety of sterile plasters and wound dressings

○ sterile eye pads

- triangular bandages

- disposable gloves

- notes on administering basic first aid.

The box should be checked regularly to ensure it remains well stocked and that the use-by date has not expired.

1.12 First-aid box

Emergency procedures, roles and responsibilities

In the event of an accident or emergency, the first action will be to ensure that the area is made safe. This will be followed by a call for assistance to the first aider, supervisor, site manager, safety officer or other nominated person. This person may then decide to evacuate the area to minimise the risk of further injury to other persons and also call the appropriate emergency service, if required.

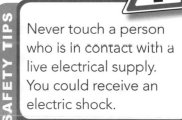
General emergency procedures

All personnel on-site should have been made aware of the following at their site induction:

- The type of evacuation alarm (for example, siren, tannoy or loud hailer). There may be a different form of alarm depending on the type of emergency.

LINK

For more information on working with electricity, see K7 Work with electricity in a construction environment on page 72 of this chapter.

FAQ

Can I go straight home in the event of an emergency, rather than reporting to the assembly point?

No, you must follow the evacuation procedures, which are there for everyone's safety. If you don't report to your designated assembly point, other people may be placed at risk trying to find you.

SAFETY TIPS

After an accident, make sure the area is safe before you restart work. Failure to do so may result in you becoming a casualty yourself.

- On the sounding of an alarm, you must proceed to your designated assembly point.

- Name of the nominated person to report to on arrival at the assembly point.

- What procedures are to be followed after reporting to the nominated person.

- The emergency services (fire, police or ambulance) will advise the nominated person when the emergency is over.

- You must remain at the assembly point until advised otherwise by the nominated person. Under no circumstances should you re-enter the site or building until the nominated person authorises you to do so.

Roles and responsibilities

Your role as part of the workforce in dealing with emergencies is restricted to the following:

- Raise alarm or report details of emergency to the nominated person.

- Report potential hazards and any near misses to the nominated person, who will arrange for the area to be made safe.

- Ensure that your own safety is not at risk.

- Follow the emergency procedures as instructed.

- Assist in the completion of accident records and reports.

If you are first on the scene, you may also be required to:

- ensure the area is safe (for example, by switching off the electric supply in the event of an electrocution)

- call for the first aider on-site or give emergency help yourself if you are a qualified first aider

- call for the fire warden on-site, or tackle the fire with an extinguisher if you have been trained and authorised to do so.

- make phone calls to summon the emergency services in the event of serious injury or fire.

CHECK YOUR UNDERSTANDING

- State why it is important to report all accidents, incidents and near misses.
- Name an item that should not be included in a first-aid box.
- Name the person who is normally responsible for entering details in an accident record.
- List **four** authorised persons who could be involved in dealing with accident and emergency situations in the workplace.
- State **three** actions an employee should take on discovering an accident or potential emergency situation.

ASSESSMENT CHECK

Now that you have completed this learning outcome you should now be able to:

- state the major types of emergencies that could occur in the workplace
- state the key legislation used for reporting accidents
- state the different types of injuries, diseases and occurrences in the workplace and the relevant current legislation
- state the main types of records used in the event of an accident or emergency
- state why it is important to report accidents and near misses
- state the difference between major and minor injuries and the meaning of a near miss
- list the key accident trends within the UK construction industry
- state the effects that common types of accidents and injuries could have on the employer
- list the authorised persons who could be involved in dealing with accident and emergency situations
- list the basic requirements of a complete first-aid kit
- state the actions to be taken on discovering an accident.

DID YOU KNOW

'Housekeeping' is a general term used for cleaning up after yourself. It is important that your work area is clean and tidy at all times.

K3 Hazards on construction sites

Housekeeping

It should be the aim of everyone to prevent accidents. As an employee, the main way you can prevent accidents is to work in the safest possible manner at all times, ensuring that your actions do not put anyone at risk.

A safe working area is clean and tidy. All unnecessary obstructions should be removed (for example, off-cuts of material, unwanted tools and disused items of plant). To maintain a good level of housekeeping, it is essential to:

○ regularly tidy your workbench/work area – off-cuts and shavings are potential tripping and fire hazzards

○ ensure walkways and stairways, and in particular emergency routes, are free of obstructions and tripping hazards such as trailing cables, building materials and waste

○ ensure that all combustible waste materials, such as packaging and timber off-cuts, are cleared away to reduce fire risks

○ keep internal floor areas clean and dry, ensure footpaths and pedestrian routes across the site are level, firm and clear of materials, plant and other obstructions.

Risk assessments and method statements

The Management of Health and Safety at Work Regulations (MHSWR) apply to everyone at work. Employers and the self-employed are required to plan, control, organise, monitor and review their work. They must:

○ assess the risks associated with the work being undertaken

○ have access to competent health and safety advice

○ provide employees with health and safety information and training

○ appoint competent persons in their workforce to assist them in complying with health and safety legislation

- ⬡ make arrangements to deal with serious and imminently dangerous situations

- ⬡ cooperate in all health and safety matters with others who share the workplace.

Employees' duties under the regulations are:

- ⬡ to use all equipment, dangerous substances and means of production safely and in accordance with the training and instructions given

- ⬡ to inform their employer or named competent person of dangerous situations and/or shortcomings in the health and safety arrangements.

Risk assessment and management are essential to put in place control measures. Employers need to identify the hazards involved in their work, assess the possible harm arising and decide on adequate control measures.

Risk assessment is a five-step process:

Step 1: Look for the hazards. Consider the job to be undertaken: How and where will it be done? What equipment and materials will be used?

Step 2: Decide who might be at risk and how. Employees? Visitors? The general public who may be near the job?

Step 3: Evaluate the risks and decide on the action to be taken. Can the hazard be completely removed? Can the job be done in a safer way? Can a different, less hazardous material be used? If any of the answers are yes, change the job to eliminate the risk. If risks cannot be eliminated, then ask: Can they be controlled? Can protective measures be taken?

Step 4: Record the findings. Employers should make a record of the risk assessment and pass it on to their employees. This is normally a safety method statement, which includes details of significant risks involved and the measures taken to remove or control them.

Step 5: Review the findings. There should be regular reviews to ensure that the findings are still effective. New assessments will be required if the risks or conditions change, or if there are new ones.

BBS Construction Services

RISK ASSESSMENT

Activity covered by assessment: MANUAL HANDLING OF PLASTERBOARD
(CARPENTER SEEN LIFTING SHEETS WITHOUT HELP)

Location of activity: DOMESTIC CONSTRUCTION SITE

Persons involved: CARPENTERS/SITE OPERATIVES

Date of assessment: 15 MARCH 2010

Tick appropriate box ☑

- Does the activity involve a potential risk? YES ☑ NO ☐

- If YES can the activity be avoided? YES ☐ NO ☑

- If NO what is the level of risk? LOW ☐ MEDIUM ☑ HIGH ☐

- What remedial action can be taken to control or protect against the risk?

1 WEAR PPE: BOOTS, HELMET AND GLOVES

2 PAIRED (2 PEOPLE) LIFTING OF TWO SHEETS ONLY

3 ENSURE CORRECT LIFTING TECHNIQUES ARE FOLLOWED AT ALL TIMES

4

5

MANAGEMENT SUMMARY

Priority for action: LOW ☐ MEDIUM ☑ HIGH ☐

Action to be taken: ENSURE ABOVE REMEDIAL ACTION IS FOLLOWED AT ALL TIMES

Date action to be taken by: 15 MARCH 2010 (IMMEDIATELY)

Date for reassessment: 19 APRIL 2010

Assessor's name and signature: _P.S. Brett_ P.S. BRETT

ASSESS THE RISK – PUT IN CONTROLS – CHECK THEY WORK

1.13 Typical construction company's risk assessment checklist

Method statements

A method statement is a key safety document that combines risks from a risk assessment with a job specification. It shows a practical and safe method of undertaking a work task with the smallest amount or no risk. Method statements should be specific to a task and detail the process and potential risks, the precautions to be taken and the PPE to be worn.

BBS: Shopfitting Services
33 Stafford Thorne Street
Nottingham NG22 3RD
Tel. 0115 94000

SAFETY METHOD STATEMENT

Process: **The re-manufacture of MDF panel products.** During this process a fine airborne dust is produced. This may cause skin, eye, nose and throat irritation. There is also a risk of explosion. The company has controls in place to minimize any risk. However, for your own safety and the protection of others, you must play your part by observing the following requirements.

General Requirements: At all times observe the following safety method statements and the training you have received from the company.
- Manual Handling
- Use of Woodworking Machines
- Use of Powered Hand Tools
- General House Keeping

Specific Requirements:
- When handling MDF, always wear gloves or barrier cream as appropriate. Barrier cream should be replenished after washing.
- When sawing, drilling, routing or sanding MDF, always use the dust extraction equipment and wear dust masks and eye protection.
- Always brush down and wash thoroughly to remove all dust, before eating, drinking, smoking, going to the toilet and finally at the end of the shift.
- Do not smoke outside the designated areas.
- If you suffer from skin irritation or other personal discomfort seek first-aid treatment or consult the nurse.

IF IN DOUBT ASK

1.14 Typical safety method statement

DID YOU KNOW

Hazard books and near miss reports are used by some companies to keep a record of the main hazards and near misses associated with particular tasks. These can be used to assist with risk assessments for similar tasks.

LINK

For more information on hazards in the workplace, see:

○ Safe lifting procedures on page 51 of this chapter

○ K7 Work with electricity in a construction environment on page 72 of this chapter

○ K9 Fire and emergency procedures on page 83 of this chapter.

Hazards in the workplace

Construction sites can be very dangerous places and workers and visitors should be made aware of the hazards. Below are some of the most common hazards:

○ **Falls from heights**: the single largest cause of workplace fatalities in the UK and a main cause of major injuries. Falls happen due to poor access to and from the workplace, or the workplace not being safe.

○ **Being hit by falling material**: material may fall from loads being lifted or material and equipment may roll or be kicked off scaffolds and other working platforms. People could be hit or buried by materials falling from collapsing excavations, structures or buildings.

○ **Slipping or tripping**: the most common causes of reported injuries on construction sites in the UK. Slips or trips are due to poor housekeeping. Most of these can be easily avoided by ensuring that the entire workplace is kept clean and tidy.

○ **Chemical spills**: cause slipping and environmental hazards as well as the risk of burns and skin problems. Prompt action is required to contain hazardous chemicals and clean them up if they spill.

○ **Fires**: cause burns, breathing problems due to smoke inhalation, as well as damage to materials and buildings.

○ **Burns**: also caused by materials containing chemicals such as cement and solvents. Contact with electricity can result in burn injuries.

○ **Electricity**: electric shocks and burns occur when unsafe equipment is used or contact is made with live wires, overhead power lines and buried cables.

○ **Manual handling**: lifting heavy or awkward loads can result in back and other injuries. An injury can result from a single lift, but more commonly long-term injuries develop on from repeated minor injury due to repetitive lifting.

○ **Noise and vibration**: high levels of noise can cause hearing loss and the repeated use of vibrating equipment can result in HAVS due to nerve and blood vessel damage.

Storing combustibles and chemicals

Safeguards must be put in place for the safe on-site storage of all **combustible** materials, **flammable** liquids, gases and chemicals in order to minimise the risk of fires and personal injury.

Combustible materials

Fire risk can be reduced by controlling the amount of combustible material stored on-site at any one time. Phased deliveries to suit the planned construction programme should be considered, as this will minimise the fire risk and prevent unnecessary long periods of storage and the need for large storage areas.

Flammable liquids and gases

White spirit, methylated spirits, cellulose, some paint thinners and strippers, petrol and liquefied petroleum gas (LPG) and some formwork release agents are among the flammable materials used in construction. These give off a vapour that can ignite at room temperature.

Flammable materials require special consideration and storage requirements in order to minimise the risks of fire and explosion. You should carry out a risk assessment, consider the use of **non-combustible** or **non-flammable** substitutes and implement control measures:

- Up to 50 litres may be kept in a fire-resistant cupboard or bin in the main store.

- Due to the increased risks, larger quantities should be placed in a special fire-resistant store, normally located away from any other buildings, stored materials, workplaces and site boundaries.

FAQ

What should I do if I smell something that I think may be flammable?

You should report the situation to your supervisor immediately and don't turn on any electricity or light any naked flames.

KEY TERMS

Combustible: a solid material that is able to catch fire and burn.

Flammable: a gas or liquid that quickly and easily sets on fire and burns.

Non-combustible: a solid material that is not able to catch fire and burn.

Non-flammable: a gas or liquid that is not able to catch fire and burn.

DID YOU KNOW

Rags used to mop up a spillage must **never** be left in the store. Rolled up dirty rags start to generate heat and can eventually burst into flames (spontaneous combustion). This creates an ignition source for the entire stored contents.

Hazardous products may be used directly from their container or a smaller amount decanted into a 'kettle' for convenience. The surplus should be returned to the main container after use.

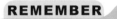

SAFETY TIPS

Never store any substance in an unmarked container, as this removes it from its user and safety instructions and makes the contents unknown. If you are unsure of the contents, don't use the substance.

- Ensure all storage vessels and containers are suitably marked with their contents and safety requirements.

- Maintain a cool temperature – high temperatures can cause the containers to erupt.

- Fire-resistant cupboards and bins should be sealed to ensure any vapours given off from a spill or leak are contained.

- Provide good ventilation in separate storerooms so that any vapours resulting from spills or leaks are rapidly dispersed.

- Eliminate all ignition sources and use special electric lights and switches that do not cause sparks.

- Provide suitable fire extinguishers to deal with a potential hazard.

- Keep the fire-resistant cupboard, bin or storeroom secured with limited access to authorised personnel only.

Decanting hazardous products

Consult the manufacturer's instructions on the container before pouring out as certain substances **must not** be used or stored in another container for safety reasons.

To pour from container to kettle:

- dust the top of the container

- remove the lid with an opener

- thoroughly stir the contents with a mixing knife to achieve an even consistency

- pour the required quantity into the kettle, from the side opposite the manufacturer's instructions

- use a brush to mop up the surplus on the rim or side of the container

- scrape the brush on the edge of the kettle to remove any surplus

- firmly replace the container lid to prevent vapours escaping and dust and dirt getting in.

Chemicals

Certain chemicals used on-site, such as acids, lime, some adhesives, paints, solvents, curing compounds and formwork release agents may be classed as hazardous chemicals. As few of these as possible should be stored on-site, in a locked compound or appropriate storeroom, to minimise any hazard and prevent misuse or risk of cross-contamination.

CHECK YOUR UNDERSTANDING

- List **three** ways in which you can contribute to maintaining good levels of housekeeping in the workplace.

- State the purpose and main stages of undertaking 'risk assessments'.

- List **five** types of hazard that may be encountered in the workplace.

- Explain the purpose of a 'method statement'.

- State the reason why 'hazardous products' should only be stored in their original containers.

ASSESSMENT CHECK

Now that you have completed this learning outcome you should now be able to:

- state the importance of good housekeeping

- state the purpose of risk assessments and method statements

- list the major types of hazards in the workplace

- state the importance of the correct storage of combustibles and chemicals on-site.

K4 Health and hygiene in a construction environment

Welfare facilities

Employers must provide employees with welfare facilities, such as toilets, to ensure health and safety in the workplace. Providing proper welfare facilities is a good motivator to employees, who in return will feel valued and respond by working better.

Toilets

Suitable and sufficient toilets must be provided or made available and accessible and, as far as is possible, shall be adequately ventilated, lit and kept clean. Separate toilets should be provided for men and women; however they may share the same facility if each toilet is in a separate room/cubicle with a lockable door. Adequate supplies of toilet paper should always be available.

Washing facilities

Wash basins with hot and cold water are to be provided immediately near the toilets and changing rooms. These must include soap, towels or other cleaning and drying facilities. Where the work is particularly dirty or involves exposure to **toxic** or **corrosive** substances, showers may be required. Unisex facilities are suitable for the washing of hands, faces and arms; otherwise a shower must be in a separate room that is used by one person at a time and can be locked from the inside. Rooms containing washing facilities must have adequate ventilation and lighting, and be kept clean and tidy.

Drinking water

Drinking water must be readily accessible in suitable places and clearly marked as such. Bottled drinking water must be protected from possible **contamination** and changed frequently to prevent it from becoming stale. Cups must be provided, unless the water is supplied via a drinking fountain.

Storage and changing of clothing

Secure rooms must be provided for normal clothing not worn for work and for protective clothing not taken home. Separate lockers may be required where there is a risk of protective

KEY TERMS

Toxic: a poisonous substance that is capable of causing an injury, ill health or death.

Corrosive: a substance that can destroy or damage another surface or substance on contact.

Contamination: the presence of an unwanted harmful substance that pollutes a material, physical body, natural environment or workplace, etc.

DID YOU KNOW

When working in existing buildings, arrangements can be made to use welfare facilities provided by the building owner. These should be of a similar standard to the above requirements and be readily accessible to the workforce.

clothing contaminating normal clothing. This accommodation should include changing facilities, seating and a means of drying wet clothing. Separate rooms for men and women are required where appropriate.

Rest facilities

Heated accommodation must be provided for taking breaks and meals. These facilities must include tables and chairs, a means of boiling water and preparing food.

Health effects of noise

Exposure to loud noise can permanently damage hearing, resulting in **deafness** or **tinnitus**. Noise levels are measured in decibels (dB) with a sound meter. Typical examples of noise levels on a construction site are:

- conversation 50–60 dB
- dumper truck 75–85 dB
- power drill 80–90 dB
- concrete breaker 90–100 dB
- chainsaw 100–110 dB.

Under the Control of Noise at Work Regulations, manufacturers, suppliers, employers and employees have to reduce the risk of hearing damage to the lowest level reasonable for that situation.

Manufacturers/suppliers have a requirement to provide low-noise machinery and information concerning the level of noise likely to be generated along with the potential hazards.

1.15 A typical toilet facility

KEY TERMS

Deafness: the temporary or permanent impairment or loss of hearing, caused by prolonged exposure to noise over many years or caused immediately by sudden, extremely loud noises.

Tinnitus: a ringing in the ears caused by exposure to loud noises.

DID YOU KNOW

Most people will notice a rise of 3 dB in noise level, but with every 3 dB rise the noise level actually doubles. What might seem like a small rise in number terms can be very significant. As a practical guide, if you are working in an area where you have to raise your voice to be heard by a person 2 m away, it would indicate that the noise level is too high.

SAFETY TIPS

Never put wet or damp clothing directly on to a heat source. If the clothing is left too long, it can cause overheating, which can result in a fire.

Employers have a responsibility to: advise people of the hazards and risks in their workplace, carry out risk assessments and issue method statements, display warning signs and create zones where hearing protection must be worn at all times, provide suitable ear protection and ensure that all persons entering the zone wears them.

The HSE safe action guidelines are as follows:

- 80 dB: employers should assess the risk, advise employees and provide protection on request.

- 85 dB: employers should designate the work area as an ear protection zone and suitable PPE must be provided and worn at all times.

- 87 dB: this is the maximum exposure limit, after taking into account the reduction in exposure provided by wearing PPE.

Employees have a duty to use the noise control equipment, wear hearing protection and report any defects.

Reducing the risks of exposure to noise

Employers can reduce noise and noise exposure by using a combination of the following control methods:

- **Change** the way work is done to a quieter way.

- **Replace** whatever is causing the noise with something that is less noisy.

- **Remove** the source of loud noises.

- **Move** noisy equipment and noise sources further away from people.

- **Enclose** or **surround** noisy equipment with soundproof material or screens.

- **Isolate** noisy equipment and processes from quieter areas.

- **Limit** the time people spend using noisy equipment or working in noisy areas.

- **Provide** hearing protection aids for people who are exposed to noise. This should be in addition to the above control measures.

Ear protection zone
ear protectors must be worn

1.16 Ear protection zone

Never use radios or music players whilst you are at work. They can cause a loss of concentration as well as interfere with general communications and make emergency warnings harder to hear.

SAFETY TIPS

1.17 Hearing protection aids

Hazardous substances

The use of chemicals and other hazardous substances is a major risk to people's health on construction sites and other workplaces. Hazardous substances can be found in most work environments and include adhesives, paints, cleaning agents, sawdust and biological agents such as bacteria.

People may be exposed to risks either because they handle a hazardous substance or because, during their work, a hazardous substance is created. Manufacturers and suppliers of such substances are required to provide safety data sheets for reference purposes.

In addition, most hazardous substance containers carry a warning sign to indicate the nature of the contents.

Assessment
A risk assessment must be undertaken by employers. Employers must look at the ways people may be exposed to hazardous substances in their particular type of work, such as breathing in dust, swallowing or eating contaminated materials or their skin or eyes coming into contact with them.

Prevention
Where harm from a substance is likely, the first course of action should be prevention of exposure by either doing the job in a different way so that the substance is removed or not created, or by using a less hazardous substitute substance.

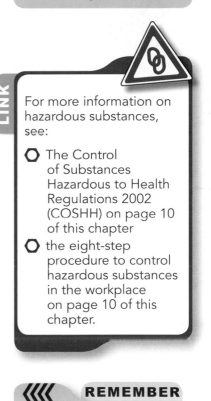

LINK

For more information on hazardous substances, see:

○ The Control of Substances Hazardous to Health Regulations 2002 (COSHH) on page 10 of this chapter

○ the eight-step procedure to control hazardous substances in the workplace on page 10 of this chapter.

《《《 REMEMBER

COSHH requires employers to control exposure to hazardous substances in the workplace to prevent ill health and protect both employees and others who may be exposed.

1.19 Typical hazard warning label displayed on packaging

BBS: Panel Products
33 Stafford Thorne Street
Nottingham NG22 3RD
Tel. 011594000

SAFETY DATA SHEET

Chemical Name:	Interior Medium Density Fibreboard (MDF)	
Trade Name:	MeDFit	
Chemical Family:	Wood Based Panel Product	
Formula:	Mixture	
Ingredients:	Mixed Softwoods	82%
	Urea Formaldehyde Resins	8–10%
	Paraffin Wax	0.5%
	Water	6–8%
	Silica	<0.05%
	Free Formaldehyde	<0.04%

Physical and Chemical Characteristics:
Specific Gravity: 0.65–0.99
Appearance/Colour: Cream to light brown, solid wood texture.

Fire and Explosion Hazard:
Extinguisher Media: Water
Explosion Hazard: None for the sheet material. However airborne dust produced during re-manufacturing operations may cause an explosion hazard. Dust should be continuously removed from processing machinery. Smoking should not be permitted in the working area.

Health Hazards: During re-manufacture wood dust may:
- increase mucosal output
- cause reddening and itching of the skin
- irritation of the throat and eyes.
Most of the effects are readily reversible after the end of exposure.

Personal Protection: During re-manufacturing operations:
- wear dust mask and eye protection
- apply a barrier cream (replenish after washing)
- wash before eating, drinking, smoking and going to the toilet.

Special Controls: During re-manufacturing operations the use of high efficiency dust collection equipment is strongly recommended to ensure compliance with the COSHH regulations.

First Aid:
Inhalation of Dust: Clean nasal passages, take in plenty of fresh air.
Contamination of Eyes: Flush with an approved eye wash solution for a prolonged period.

1.18 Typical manufacturer's safety data sheet

Control

Where a hazardous substance is unavoidable, perhaps because there is no choice or alternatives also present equal risks, exposure must be controlled in the following ways:

⬡ Using the substance in a less hazardous form (for example, use a sealed surface glassfibre insulation quilt rather than an open fibre one to reduce the risk of skin contact or breathing in fine strands).

⬡ Using a less hazardous method of working with the substance (for example, wet rubbing down of old lead-based painted surfaces rather than dry rubbing down, which causes hazardous dust; or applying solvent-based products by brush or roller rather than by spraying).

- Limiting the amount of substance used.

- Limiting the amount of time people are exposed.

- Keeping all containers closed when not in use.

- Providing good ventilation to the work area. Mechanical ventilation may be required in confined spaces.

- When cutting or grinding, using tools fitted with exhaust ventilation or water suppression to control dust.

Protection

If exposure cannot be prevented or adequately controlled, you should:

- wear protective clothing, such as overalls, gloves, boots, helmets, ear protection, eye protection and dust masks

- use barrier and after-work creams; this is recommended to protect skin from contact dermatitis

- ensure items of PPE are kept clean, so that they do not themselves become a source of contamination

- maintain items of PPE, checking for damage and storing in clean, dry conditions

- replace items of PPE and ensure spares are readily available.

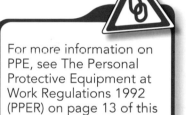

LINK

For more information on PPE, see The Personal Protective Equipment at Work Regulations 1992 (PPER) on page 13 of this chapter.

Monitoring and health surveillance

The workplace should be monitored to ensure exposure to hazardous substances is being adequately controlled and limits are not being exceeded (for example, regular checks on noise levels and dust concentrations). Health surveillance is a legal duty for a limited range of work exposure situations (for example, asbestos). However, many employers operate a health surveillance programme for all their employees. This gives medical staff the opportunity to check the general health of workers, as well as giving early indications of illness and disease. Simple, regular checks can be made, including blood pressure, hearing and eyesight and lung peak flow. Any deterioration over a time indicates the need for further action.

Information

Employers must provide employees who are or may be exposed to hazardous substances with safety information and training for them to know the risks involved, a safe working method statement, including precautions to be taken or PPE to be worn, and results of any monitoring and health surveillance checks.

Personal hygiene

Personal hygiene is as important as physical protection. Some building materials can irritate the skin, which can result in dermatitis and other disorders. Some substances are poisonous if swallowed, while others can result in a state of unconsciousness (narcosis) if their vapour or powder is inhaled. Exposure to dust, such as asbestos, can cause breathing problems and lung cancer. Contact with water infected by rats' urine can result in Weil's disease or leptospirosis. Early signs are cold or flu-like symptoms and muscular pains and, if untreated, the disease can be fatal. These harmful effects can be avoided by taking proper precautions:

1.20 Always wash hands

- Follow the manufacturer's instructions and safety data sheets.

- Look at the warning labels that are displayed on packaging.

- Follow the safety method statement.

- Avoid inhaling fumes or powders.

- Wear the appropriate PPE, as well as a barrier cream.

- Always wash hands before eating, drinking, before and after going to the toilet and also at the end of the working shift to prevent swallowing hazardous substances and reduce the risk of skin infections.

- Never eat, drink or smoke when working with hazardous substances or when near to the site of exposure.

- Change out of contaminated work wear into normal clothes before travelling home.

- Have contaminated work wear regularly laundered.

Hazards of drugs and alcohol

KEY TERMS

Substance abuse: the general term used to refer to the taking of and dependence on an addictive substance, such as drinking alcohol, taking drugs or inhaling solvents.

Your physical condition when at work must always be considered. Taking medicines, **substance abuse** and drinking alcohol must be avoided at work as they can reduce levels of concentration and raise the risk of accidents.

- Many prescription drugs and over-the-counter painkillers contain warnings such as 'do not drive or operate machinery' or 'may cause drowsiness'.

- The taking of other drugs or the inhaling of solvents is not only illegal, but also results in concentration problems and may lead to mental health problems in the long term.

- Drinking alcohol, even in small quantities, leads to slower reflexes and reduced concentration levels. Excessive drinking in the long term can result in alcoholism and kidney damage.

Health risks in the workplace

The construction industry has a high rate of ill health. Some health issues are not always immediately visible. In some cases, it can take years for symptoms to be noticed and diagnosed, but they can have the same devastating results as accidents and may result in long-term health problems. Some health problems associated with construction include:

- respiratory and breathing problems, such as asthma from exposure to asbestos and other hazardous substances

- skin diseases, such as dermatitis from exposure to paint and other hazardous chemicals

- biological infections, such as leptospirosis, from exposure to bacteria and other micro-organisms

- **musculoskeletal disorders (MSDs)**, such as back pain and pulled muscles usually from excessive manual handling

- noise-induced hearing loss, tinnitus and deafness

- eye infections and damage to sight, from exposure to dust

- head injuries, which can result in blackouts and, in the long term, epilepsy

- burns, from contact with heat, electricity and materials containing chemicals such as cement and paint solvents

- HAVS and vibration white finger from frequent operation of hand-held power tools and other vibrating machinery

DID YOU KNOW

Being under the influence of drugs or alcohol in the workplace places you and everyone you are working with in danger. You also have a duty to follow the instructions on prescription drugs and stop work immediately if you feel affected in any way.

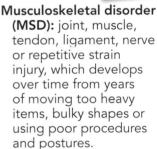

KEY TERMS

Musculoskeletal disorder (MSD): joint, muscle, tendon, ligament, nerve or repetitive strain injury, which develops over time from years of moving too heavy items, bulky shapes or using poor procedures and postures.

DID YOU KNOW

Managing health risks in construction goes beyond site safety inductions and the provision of first aid and welfare facilities. It involves an effective system where everyone is aware of the risks and works as a team toprevent them, while still obeying health and safety legislation.

O skin cancer, from over-exposure to sunlight

O minor cuts and abrasions, which, if untreated, can result in infections and diseases

O occupational stress, arising from excessive workload, job insecurity and the more risky nature of construction work in general.

CHECK YOUR UNDERSTANDING

⊘ Produce a list of **five** essential welfare facilities that should be made available for workers on all construction sites.

⊘ Explain why personal hygiene is considered to be important when working on construction sites.

⊘ State how a person may be exposed to a hazardous substance at work.

⊘ State how you might recognise that noise levels are too high.

⊘ Explain why the taking of medicines, substance abuse and the drinking of alcohol must be avoided at work.

ASSESSMENT CHECK

Now that you have completed this learning outcome you should now be able to:

⊘ list the requirements for welfare facilities in a construction environment

⊘ state the health effects of noise and the appropriate precautions that can be taken

⊘ identify the various substances hazardous to health under the COSHH and the appropriate precautions

⊘ state the importance of personal hygiene

⊘ state the types of hazards linked to drugs and alcohol

⊘ list possible consequences of health risks in the workplace.

K5 Handle materials and equipment safely

Manual handling

Manual handling refers to the lifting or movement of materials and equipment from one place to another without the use of mechanical equipment. It is a major cause of workplace MSDs. Therefore, it should only be undertaken as a last resort.

Before undertaking any manual handling operation, you should ask yourself the following questions:

○ Can I avoid moving the material or equipment?

○ Can it be moved by mechanical means?

○ Can I use manual aids, such as a wheelbarrow or pallet truck?

○ Can I break the load down to make it lighter or more manageable? The maximum load that one person should move is 25 kg.

○ Do I need another person to help? Two or more people are required to move heavier or larger items.

○ How much can I lift? Although the maximum load that one person should move is 25 kg, everyone's build and competence is different.

○ How far do I have to move the load? As a general rule, you should take a break to recover if the load has to be moved for more than about 20 m.

○ Do I need to twist or turn to the side whilst lifting? If so, this will reduce the load that you can safely move without the risk of back injury.

○ Is the intended route safe, with solid ground that is clear of obstacles? Ensure excavations and inspection chambers on your route are protected by a barrier or covered. All working platforms or exposed edges that you have to move along should be protected by guard-rails, toe boards and mesh guards.

REMEMBER

The key legislation that controls manual handling is The Manual Handling Operations Regulations 1992 (MHO).

SAFETY TIPS

Depending on the situation, hazards along the route may need to be protected by safety nets and fall bags. Alternatively, you may be required to wear a safety harness and lanyard.

○ Is there somewhere to put down the load when I get there?

○ Have I received suitable training for the manual handling operation in question?

○ Are there any specific method statements and manufacturer's instructions for the manual handling operation? These will give the safe manual handling procedure, identify any hazards associated with the particular material, and list suitable items of PPE that should be worn.

1.21 Mechanical and manual handling aids

FAQ

What should I do if there's not time to get the correct items of PPE before undertaking manual handling operations?

Make time. You should never do any task unless you are wearing the correct items of PPE. The time it takes to get the correct PPE will be much less than the time you could be off work with an injury or illness as a result of not wearing it.

Safe lifting procedures

Follow these practical tips when lifting materials and equipment:

Think first: can I use an aid? Do I need help? What PPE is appropriate? Are there splinters etc. on the items to be moved?

Take up the correct position: always lift with your back straight, elbows tucked in, knees bent and feet slightly apart.

Get a good grip: hands should be placed under the load and, on lifting, the load should be hugged as close as possible to your body.

Lift the load: use your leg muscles and not your back.

Move smoothly: avoid any twisting and leaning. Keep the load close to your body and look straight ahead.

Place the load down: keep hands and fingers out of the way before sliding the load into position on a suitable platform. Where the load has to be lowered to the floor, do the same as for moving it.

Your training should give you the opportunity to practise the safe handling of a range of materials and equipment in accordance with the relevant legislation and organisational requirements.

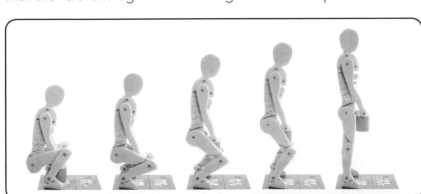

1.22 Correct lifting technique

DID YOU KNOW

Manual handling is the cause of over a third of all over three-day injuries reported each year to the HSE. Poor manual handling can result in MSDs, with back pain and pulled muscles being the most common. Most MSDs occur as a result of heavy manual labour, use of awkward postures and the manual handling of materials. People with previous or existing injuries are particularly at risk.

LINK

For more information on the Manual Handling Operations Regulations, see page 14.

For more information on the safe handling and storage of materials, see Handling and storage requirements on page 257 of Chapter 3.

SAFETY TIPS

Always think before undertaking any manual handling! Most manual handling injuries are the result of many years of poor technique, but it is possible to cause serious damage to the back with just one poorly executed movement. Even light or less bulky loads can cause injury, especially if you need to twist or turn to the side while lifting.

Carcinogenic: capable of causing cancer.

KEY TERMS

Materials

Materials you may practice handling include plasterboard, bagged cement/plaster, fluids, treated and untreated timber, bricks, blocks, bagged and loose aggregates.

Equipment

Equipment you may practice handling includes all power tools, wheelbarrows, ladders, scaffold boards, transformers and generators, sharp and manual cutting tools, pressurised painting vessels and equipment and compressed air and hydraulic powered equipment.

Waste

The Environment Protection Act places a duty of care on persons concerned with waste to:

○ prevent the unauthorised or harmful disposal of waste

○ prevent the escape of waste

○ ensure waste is only transferred to authorised persons.

Waste classification

Waste is any substance or object that you throw away, intend to throw away or are required to throw away, whether in a solid, liquid or gaseous form. Waste can be further classified as either:

○ **controlled waste**: all commercial and industrial waste other than that which is classified as hazardous

○ **hazardous waste**: all substances classified, marked or known to be explosive, oxidizing, flammable, toxic, harmful, irritant, corrosive, dangerous to the environment, poisonous or **carcinogenic**.

1.23 Common packaging labels

Waste disposal

The construction industry in the UK has a major role to play in improving the quality of the environment. Traditionally, the bulk of waste has been disposed of in landfill sites. However, the rapidly increasing costs of waste disposal, along with government and European pressure, mean that waste management on construction sites has to change. To minimise the amount of waste, all concerned must give priority to the following factors in the order stated:

These actions will minimise the environmental impact of waste disposal and, at the same time, help to improve site safety and reduce construction costs.

DID YOU KNOW

Over 70 million tonnes of waste is generated annually by the construction industry in the UK (around four times the amount of household waste). Approximately, 13 million tonnes of this total is estimated to be materials that have been delivered to sites and then thrown away unused.

Eliminate waste wherever possible	– Avoid over-ordering of materials – Order in the lengths required – Arrange suitable storage areas to avoid damage and loss
Reduce the amount of waste created	– Keep all materials in their protective packaging until required, to protect them from damage – Avoid as much double handling as possible, to result in less effort, damage and waste – Return unused materials back into storage, to aid site safety as well as reducing waste – Keep significant off-cuts for later use – Check that old stock of a material has been fully used before starting on a new batch
Reuse materials that are potential waste	– Use off-cuts where possible, e.g. off-cuts of plasterboard for repairs; off-cuts of timber for pegs and profile boards, etc. – Reuse materials as many times as possible until they are no longer fit for purpose, e.g. formwork and site hoardings etc. – Reuse materials for alternative purposes, e.g. broken bricks, stonework and tiles can be used as hardcore below concrete slabs
Recycle waste materials wherever possible	– Group waste on-site into different types and clearly mark separate skips or containers for potential recycling – Bricks from demolition works can be cleaned and recycled – Timber from demolition works can be recycled into new products, e.g. reclaimed oak and pine is in particular demand for recycling into furniture – Timber that can't be reused can be recycled for use in the production of chipboard and medium density fibreboard (MDF) – Surplus concrete can be crushed and recycled for use as a concrete aggregate (RCA) – Broken glass can be recycled for use in brick manufacturing, grit blasting, cement and concrete, fibreglass insulation and the manufacture of new glass – Plasterboard and other gypsum products can be recycled for use in the manufacturing process – Scrap metals can be recycled for use in new materials – Packaging materials can also be recycled for use in new materials
Dispose of any remaining waste to a landfill site	– Only do so after all of the above have been implemented

Waste separation

Dividing waste into different types can aid recycling, help minimise the cost of waste disposal and reduce the environmental impact of waste. Waste containers and skips should be labelled with the standard signs shown in Fig 1.24 to encourage and improve the separation of waste.

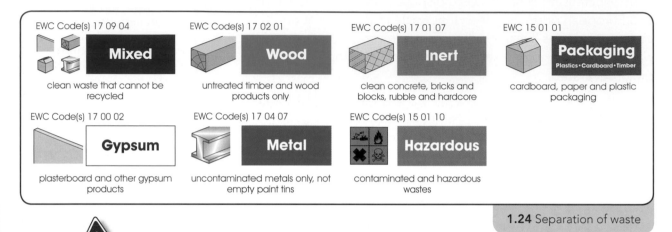

1.24 Separation of waste

CHECK YOUR UNDERSTANDING

- Explain what the term 'duty of care' means.
- Name **three** lifting aids.
- State the safe procedure to follow when manually lifting an object from the floor.
- State **three** factors that can help to minimise the amount of waste material in construction.
- State **three** duties of an employee under The Manual Handling Operations Regulations 1992.

ASSESSMENT CHECK

Now that you have completed this learning outcome you should now be able to:

- state the procedures for safe lifting in accordance with guidance and legislation
- state the importance of using site safety equipment when handling materials and equipment
- identify the key legislation relating to the safe handling of materials and equipment
- state the importance of waste control procedures in the workplace.

K6 Basic working platforms

Working at height

Each year in the construction industry numerous falls take place during the use of working platforms and access equipment, such as scaffolding and ladders. Therefore, it is important that clients, designers and building contractors make every effort at the early stages of a construction project to reduce the time that workers need to work at height. The legislation that applies to any work at height situation is The Work at Height Regulations 2005.

LINK

For more information on The Work at Height Regulations 2005 and what, as a duty holder, you are required to undertake, see K1 Health and safety regulations, roles and responsibilities on page 2 of this chapter.

DID YOU KNOW

The Work at Height Regulations 2005 also applies to holes in the ground. Excavations and inspection chambers should be either protected by a barrier or covered over completely to prevent people carelessly falling into them.

1.25 Protection of holes in the ground

Ladders

Ladders should only be considered where a risk assessment has shown that the use of other more suitable work equipment is not appropriate because of the low risk, short duration of the task or other considerations such as where the work is located. There are two main types of ladder: **standing ladder** and **stepladder**.

Standing ladders

Ladders are made from timber, aluminium or fibreglass and consist of two long stiles which support rungs at about 250 mm centres.

Timber standing ladders were traditionally made from Douglas fir, redwood, whitewood or hemlock, with half-round or rectangular stiles and round or rectangular rungs. Although timber ladders are still available, the majority of ladders used today are made from aluminium.

Aluminium ladders are used in preference to timber ladders as they are lighter, stronger and rot-proof. In addition, they will not warp, twist or burn. However, they should not be used near overhead electric cables.

Fibreglass ladders are favoured by electricians. They are safer because they will not conduct electricity in the event of a fault occurring or contact with a source of electricity.

Pole ladders are single-section ladders made from wood or metal. They are only suitable for scaffold access and not for working off. The length of pole ladders typically ranges from between 3 and 10 m.

Extension ladders consist of two or more interlocking sections, which can create a range of lengths. Latching hooks are fitted at the bottom of the extending sections and guide brackets to the top of the lower sections. Lengths of extension ladders vary from about 2.5 to 7.5 m when closed, extending up to approximately 20 m.

Roof ladders incorporate a hook and wheels at the top. The ladder is pushed up a pitched roof slope on the wheel side. After it reaches the ridge, the ladder is turned over so the hook rests on the other side of the roof and locks it in place. A standing ladder will also be required to access the roof and this should extend around one metre above the base of the roof ladder. A ladder standoff device should be attached to the access ladder to prevent it bearing on weak plastic guttering.

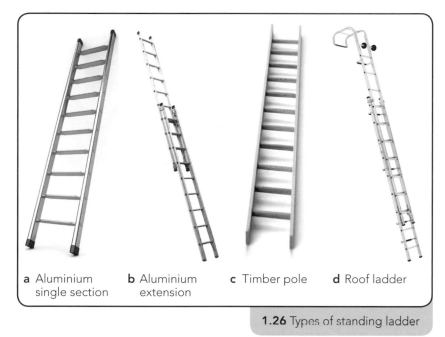

a Aluminium single section   **b** Aluminium extension   **c** Timber pole   **d** Roof ladder

1.26 Types of standing ladder

Using, moving and erecting standing ladders

The following points must be considered when determining the suitability of a ladder for a particular task:

- Standing ladders should only be used for tasks of up to 30 minutes in each position.

- Standing ladders should not be used for heavy or strenuous tasks.

- Any work done off a ladder should not require the use of both hands and should not require leaning out or stretching.

- Sufficient space must be available to erect a ladder at its correct working angle and it should be secured.

An alternative working platform should be considered if any of the above points can't be fulfilled.

Pre-use checks for ladders

Ladders should be inspected on a daily basis by the person intending to use them. Before use, you should check that:

○ they are maintained and stored in accordance with the manufacturer's instructions

○ wooden components show no signs of rotting, splits, cracks, warping or other significant damage

○ wooden ladders have not been painted, as this may hide defects

○ rungs are in good condition and not missing, bent, loose or otherwise damaged

○ stiles are not bent, twisted or dented, as this could lead to the ladder collapsing

○ non-slip feet of the stiles are not worn or missing

○ rungs and ladder feet are clean, to provide adequate grip.

If after undertaking the above checks any defects are found, the item must be taken out of use immediately, labelled with 'DO NOT USE' and reported to your supervisor.

Moving and erecting ladders

○ Extension ladders should only be moved with the sections in the closed position.

○ Small ladders may, over short distances be carried by one person almost vertically over the shoulder.

○ For longer ladders or greater distances, two people are required to carry a ladder, one towards each end with the ladder at shoulder height.

○ Extensions are raised one at a time ensuring each latching hook is engaged before progressing.

○ The feet of the ladder should be positioned on a solid, level, non-slip base. The use of packers under the foot of a stile to level the rungs is not recommended, however on soft ground you may use a scaffold board under the feet to spread the load.

○ Extension ladders need sufficient overlap between each section for strength; this is normally at least two rungs for short ladders and up to four for longer ones.

DID YOU KNOW

In addition to the daily pre-use checks undertaken by the person intending to use a ladder or stepladder, ladders should also be regularly visually inspected by a competent person and a record kept. Access ladders that are part of a scaffold system have to be inspected along with the scaffold every seven days.

REMEMBER ❯❯❯❯

When using ladders or other types of equipment, always refer to the manufacturer's instructions before use.

○ When erected, the working angle should be 75 degrees (a ratio of 1:4). In other words, the foot of the ladder should be one horizontal unit out for each four vertical units in height. This gives a comfortable angle at which to ascend, descend and work vertically with arms extended. It also reduces the possibility of the feet slipping.

○ Both stiles of the ladder should be securely tied at the top or part way down. Where a fixing at the top is not possible, an alternative is the stake and guy rope method. This prevents ladders slipping outwards from the base and the top sliding sideways.

○ A ladder stand off device should be attached to prevent a ladder bearing on weak surfaces such as glazing or plastic guttering.

○ The top of a ladder used to access a working platform must extend above the stepping off point by one metre. This provides you with a handhold and also reduces the risk of the ladder slipping off the edge.

○ Where the base of a ladder is exposed, it should be protected by a barrier or cones so that it is not knocked or walked into. As a last resort, a person should be positioned to guard the base.

○ When finished with, ladders should be lowered and locked away. The lower rungs of fixed access ladders to scaffolds should be covered with a tied scaffold board to prevent out-of-hours access.

REMEMBER

'Reasonably practicable' means that you are required to consider the risks involved in undertaking a particular work activity. However, if the risks are small and cost or technical difficulties of actions to remove the risks are high, it might not be reasonably practicable to carry out those actions.

SAFETY TIPS

Remember the footing of a ladder is the last resort to secure a ladder and other access equipment should be considered. Where the risk assessment justifies the use of a footer, it is essential that they pay attention to the work in hand at all times.

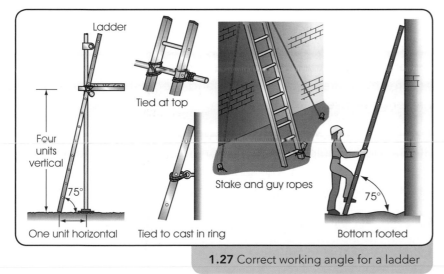

Ladder

Tied at top

Four units vertical

75°

One unit horizontal

Tied to cast in ring

Stake and guy ropes

75°

Bottom footed

1.27 Correct working angle for a ladder

Using ladders

○ Wear non-slip footwear and clean the soles of your footwear if dirty.

○ Keep the rungs clean and in good condition.

○ Don't exceed the maximum weight limit on the ladder. This includes your weight and that of tools and equipment.

○ Take each rung one at a time when going up or down a ladder.

○ Both feet and one hand should be in contact when working on a ladder.

○ Never carry heavy or awkward-shaped objects up or down a ladder. Anything over 10 kg should be avoided.

○ Always keep your body centred within the ladder.

○ Never overreach when working on a ladder, always move the ladder closer to the work position.

○ Never stand on the top three rungs.

○ Never use a ladder in poor weather conditions.

Stepladders

These are used mainly for short duration internal work on firm, flat surfaces. Like standing ladders, stepladders are available in timber, aluminium and fibreglass, consisting of stiles supporting flat treads at about 250 mm centres. A back frame hinged at the top and secured towards the base with cords or locking bars ensures the correct working angle and checks the opening to prevent collapse.

Pre-use checks for stepladders

Stepladders should be inspected on a daily basis by the person intending to use them. The same pre-use checklist can be used as for ladders, but for stepladders you should also check that:

○ there are no loose screws, nuts, bolts and hinges

○ tie cords are not rotten or that the locking bars operate correctly.

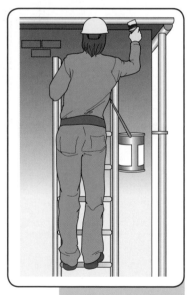

1.28 Using ladders

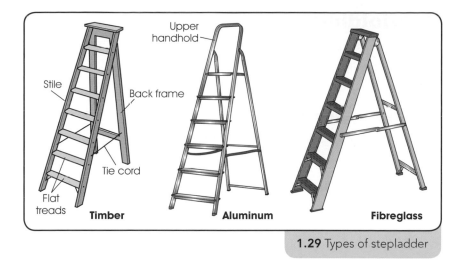

1.29 Types of stepladder

1.30 Using stepladders

Using stepladders

The safe use of stepladders is the same as ladders, with particular emphasis on the following:

○ Only use a stepladder on a flat, firm, non-slip surface. Do not use the stepladder if it is not level, sinks into the ground or slips on the surface.

○ Always open the steps fully so that the tie cords are taut or the locking bars are fully engaged.

○ Avoid working sideways-on, especially when applying force such as when drilling as this greatly increases the risk of the steps tipping over.

○ Don't use the top two or three treads unless they have a raised upper handhold.

○ Always ensure that your knees are below the top tread to enable a third point of contact.

○ Never use stepladders as a means of access to a working platform.

○ Never use stepladders off another working platform to gain additional height.

○ Consider tying tall stepladders to a suitable point in order to reduce the risk of slipping and tipping.

SAFETY TIPS

For your own safety and that of those working or passing below, when using ladders and stepladders **never**:

○ try to move them while standing on the rungs/steps

○ slide down the stiles

○ stand them on another working platform or moveable object, such as a pallet, stack of brick or the back of a van.

Scaffolding

Scaffolding is a temporary structure that is used in order to carry out certain building operations at height. It must provide safe access to heights and a safe working platform.

Tubular scaffolding

Tubular scaffolding is the most common scaffolding used in the construction industry. There are two forms of tubular scaffolding:

Putlog scaffolds: these are often known as a single or bricklayer's scaffold, as they are normally used when constructing new brick buildings. They consist of a single row of vertical tubes known as standards, which are connected by horizontal tubes known as ledgers. Putlogs, which are short tubes with a flattened end, are joined at right angles to the ledgers at intervals and are either built into the wall as the brickwork progresses, or are fitted into raked out bed joints left by the bricklayer. This type of scaffold obtains most of its support and stability from the building. It must be tied to the building through door and window openings, as putlogs could easily work loose in green newly-laid brickwork.

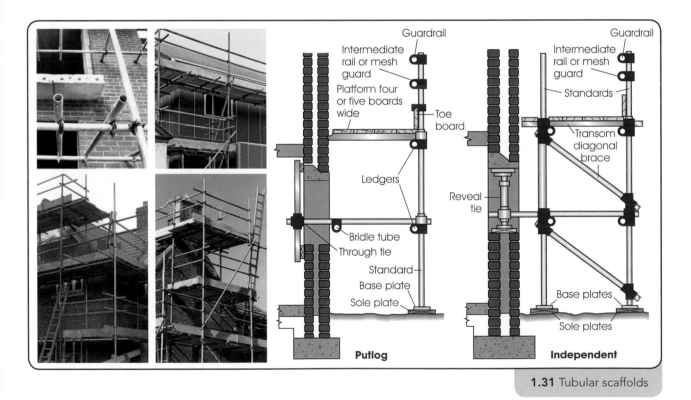

1.31 Tubular scaffolds

Independent scaffolds: these are also known as double scaffolds, as they are constructed using a double row of standards. Each row is connected by ledgers, which are in turn joined at right angles using ledgers. Bracing tubes both hold the scaffold into the building and resist sideways movement. This type of scaffold carries its own weight and the full weight of the loads imposed on it. However, it's not completely independent, as it must also be tied to the building through door and window openings to prevent any movement away or towards the building.

Scaffolding must only be erected, altered or dismantled by a trained, competent carded scaffolder but it is essential that you know how to work safely on one.

A written record of all inspections must be made and kept in the health and safety file.

Working safely on scaffolds

For your own safety and that of others, make note of the following:

⬡ Carry out a check before you use a scaffold:

   – Is there a sign attached saying that it's incomplete or unsafe?

   – Are all components present and in good condition?

   – Are there base plates and sole plates at the base to spread the load of the standards?

   – Is the base undermined or too close to excavations?

   – Is the working platform fully boarded over with no gaps or traps?

   – Is the edge protected with toe boards, guard-rails and mesh guards?

   – Is the platform overloaded or partially blocked by stacked or waste materials?

   – Is there a suitable access ladder, which is tied at the top and extends beyond the step-off point by at least one metre?

   – If in doubt about anything, do not use and report to your supervisor immediately.

⬡ Never remove or adjust any part of a scaffold, as you may be responsible for its total collapse.

⬡ Never use a scaffold in poor weather conditions.

⬡ Never block a working platform with your tools or materials.

DID YOU KNOW

Scaffolds must be inspected by a carded scaffolder or other competent person to ensure its safety on the following occasions:

⬡ After erection, before it is used for the first time.

⬡ At least once every seven days.

⬡ After cold weather, frost and snow, heavy rainfall or high winds.

Proprietary system: one that has been designed and manufactured by the owner of the patent, brand name, or trademark associated with the system.

○ Never use a ladder or a stepladder on a working platform to gain additional height.

○ Always clear up your mess as you work and also before leaving a working platform.

○ Never push or throw your mess over the edge; it should be safely lowered using a hoist or via a chute into a covered skip.

Tower scaffolds

These may be either mobile or static and are suitable for both external and internal use. Most are '**proprietary systems**' made from interlocking aluminium components; however they may also

1.32 A hoist or chute should be used to safely lower waste materials from a height

be constructed using standard tubes and fittings. Aluminium and thin-wall steel towers are fairly lightweight and can easily overturn if used incorrectly.

Proprietary system towers can be erected by trained competent persons following a safe method of work as set out by the manufacturer.

Towers can be used inside and outside. However, they must only be erected on firm, level ground with the wheels or feet fully supported. Their stability depends on the height and size of the base – taller towers are more likely to become unstable than lower ones. For internal use, the height should not exceed three and a half times the shortest base dimension. For external use, this figure is three times. The height can be increased by the use of outriggers fitted to each corner of the tower to increase the base dimension. However, it may also require tying into the building.

Working safely on tower scaffolds

For your own safety and that of others, you should ensure that:

○ the wheels or base plates of the tower are resting on firm, level ground and the brakes are engaged

○ the working platform is fully boarded out with no traps or holes

○ the working platform is provided with suitable edge protection and toe boards on all four sides

  – guard-rails are fitted at a minimum of 950 mm high above the working platform

  – intermediate guard-rails are fitted, leaving a maximum unprotected gap of 470 mm

○ the tower has been erected with an internal ladder or steps to gain access to the working platform.

○ you never use a tower:

  – in high winds or other poor weather conditions

  – with any missing or damage component parts

  – as a support for a ladder, stepladder or other access equipment

  – to hoist materials or support chutes.

SAFETY TIPS

Always lower waste material safely to the ground. It should never be thrown or dropped from scaffolds and window openings, as even a small bolt or fitting dropped from a height can penetrate a person's skull, and almost certainly lead to brain damage or death.

EXAMPLE

If the base of a tower scaffold is 2 × 3 m, the maximum height would be 7 m for internal use, which is reduced to 6 m for external use.

DID YOU KNOW

Proprietary towers rely on all of the component parts being in place to ensure sufficient strength and they are likely to collapse during use if any sections are left out or removed.

○ a tower is never overloaded with tools and materials, or people

○ you never climb up the outside end frames of a tower

○ when moving a tower, ensure:

- its height is reduced to a maximum of 4m

- there are no overhead obstructions such as power lines, etc.

- the surface is firm, level and free from potholes

- it's moved manually from the base and never by a powered vehicle

- all tools, materials and people have been cleared

- it's never done in windy conditions.

○ the brakes are re-engaged after moving

○ when working in public areas, ensure:

- work is undertaken in the least busy periods

- the area around the tower is isolated with a barrier and hazard warning signs displayed

- the storage of material and tools is kept to an absolute minimum

- there is no unauthorised access via steps or ladders.

Other working platforms

There is a wide variety of other working platforms that you may use during your construction work, including hop-ups, ladder platforms, split-head platforms and platforms based on A-frames or folding trestles. Each has its own range of uses and safe working procedures and suitable training must be provided.

○ This type of equipment is generally suitable for internal use, at restricted heights and for short durations.

○ Before use, a check must be made to ensure that all equipment is in good order and that it is only erected on a firm, flat and level surface.

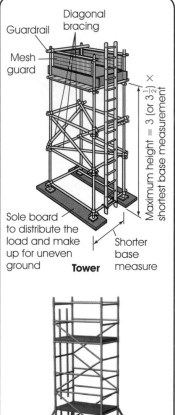

Guardrail — Diagonal bracing

Mesh guard

Maximum height = 3 (or 3½) × shortest base measurement

Sole board to distribute the load and make up for uneven ground

Tower

Shorter base measure

1.33 Tower scaffolds

⬤ Guard-rails and other edge protection may be required when working on these platforms. However, this will depend on the nature of the work and will have been identified by a risk assessment.

Hop-ups or step-ups provide an ideal isolated working platform for reaching low level work that is just out of reach. They can be either purpose made or obtained as a proprietary item.

Split-head platforms consist of tripod supports used in conjunction with timber joists and scaffold boards. They are intended for use internally to board out a whole room for work on ceilings, such as plastering and painting.

Ladder platforms are proprietary items consisting of two short ladders, which are spanned by a braced staging board. The board can normally be fixed at differing heights to enable it to provide a level platform for work on stairs. In most types, the ladders can also interlock to provide a short multi-section extension ladder.

A-frames are used in pairs in conjunction with scaffold boards or a proprietary staging board, and they can be simply adjusted in height to suit the work in hand. The width of the working platform must be at least 450 mm wide and should overhang the supports by at least 50 mm, but not more than four times the board's thickness. This prevents the board slipping off the rungs or flipping up if someone steps on the end.

Folding trestles are, again, used in pairs in conjunction with scaffold boards or a proprietary staging board. Height adjustment to suit the work in hand is achieved by resting the board on the relevant rung. However, the upper third of the trestles should always remain above the working platform, to provide a handhold and reduce the risk of toppling. Again, the width of the working platform must be at least 450 mm wide and should overhang the supports by at least 50 mm, but not more than four times the board's thickness.

SAFETY TIPS

Never attempt to use items such as milk crates, saw stools and chairs as an alternative to a hop-up. They are not designed for this purpose and may overturn or collapse.

SAFETY TIPS

Never use folding trestles as a substitute for a stepladder, as they are not designed for this purpose and present a greater risk.

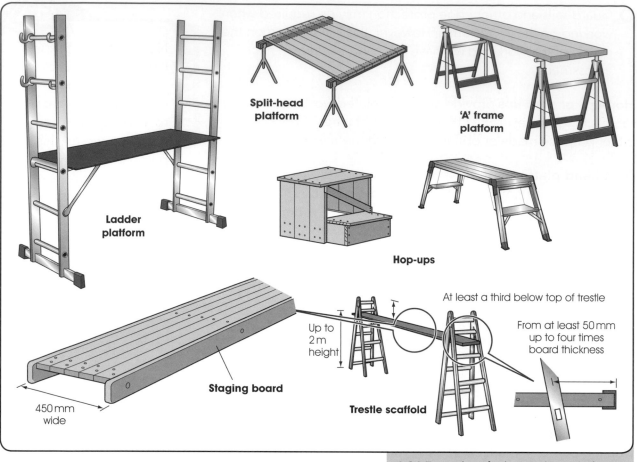

Split-head platform

'A' frame platform

Ladder platform

Hop-ups

Staging board

450 mm wide

Up to 2 m height

At least a third below top of trestle

From at least 50 mm up to four times board thickness

Trestle scaffold

1.34 Examples of other working platforms

Scaffold boards are also called 'battens'. They are available in different thicknesses, which will have an effect on the spacing of supports: 32 mm boards can span 1 m; 38 mm boards can span 1.5 m; 50 mm boards can span 2.5 m. A scaffold board's maximum span is normally indicated on its metal end bands.

Proprietary staging boards are designed to span greater distances than scaffold boards and are available in widths of 450 mm and 600 mm. They are available in both timber and lightweight aluminium with a non-slip plywood decking.

Fall protection

With any work at height, there is always the risk of injury from falls and falling objects. Where work at height cannot be avoided, equipment and other measures should be used to prevent falls, such as working platforms and guard-rails. It is not always possible to provide adequate protection using these measures and some form of fall protection equipment must be in place to minimise the height and consequences of a fall.

Harnesses and lanyards: a type of personal fall-arrest system. The worker wears the harness and the lanyard is attached to a suitable fixing point. In the event of a slip, the worker will only fall the length of the lanyard, rather than falling to the ground. However, as the person will be left swinging on the end of the lanyard, suitable emergency procedures must be in place for their safe rescue. Typical uses are work near the edge of flat roofs and on tall ladders.

Air bags: a collective soft landing system that minimises the consequences of a fall. These consist of interlinked air mattresses that, when inflated, expand to form a continuous soft surface. In the event of a slip, these provide a cushioned soft landing to minimise the risk of serious injury. Typical uses are under areas to be joisted or roofed over.

Safety nets: a collective fall-arrest system that minimises the height a person can fall. The nets are under slung at high level and secured to joists or beams above, to catch any person in the event of a slip. However, as the person will be left suspended, possibly entangled in the net, suitable emergency procedures must be in place for their safe rescue. Typical uses are during the erection and cladding of steel-framed buildings.

Fall protection working platforms: provide a combination of a temporary working platform and a collective fall-arrest system that minimises the height a person can fall in the event of a slip. Most are proprietary systems that are erected internally just below areas to be joisted or roofed over.

1.35 Fall protection equipment

The dangers of working at height

Apart from the obvious risk of a person falling from a height, there is the added risk that tools, materials and waste could fall from the edge of the working platform. This presents a risk of serious head and other injuries to the people working or passing below. A safe system of work that minimises the risk of anything or anyone falling is the best way of protecting people working or passing below. This includes the following:

○ Avoid working at height wherever possible.

○ Undertake a risk assessment before working at height.

○ Produce method statements and suitable training for the safe use of access equipment and working platforms.

○ Ensure that working platforms are fully boarded over and have suitable guards in place.

○ Monitor work at height against the method statements.

○ Ensuring that good housekeeping procedures are followed.

When working in public places, members of the public must be protected from the work area by the erection of barriers at ground level. Working 'out of hours' must also be considered as fewer people will be around.

1.36 Safe access to roofs

FAQ

How high do you have to be working for it to be considered as 'work at height'?

A working place is considered to be 'at height' where there is a risk of a fall liable to cause injury, including work at a low level and below ground level.

Is it correct that 'risk assessments'' only need to be carried out if the work is over 2 m above ground level?

No, risk assessments must be carried out before any work at height is undertaken.

I don't always ask questions if I'm unsure in case the person thinks I'm stupid! Is this OK?

No, there are no stupid questions with regards to safety. If you are unsure, it can put everyone at risk.

ACTIVITY

Either in a small group or on your own, consider the following real-life scenario:

Jim and Claire have been working on a scaffold to complete the eaves of a pitched roof on a two-storey house. They both know the importance of good housekeeping and the need to leave the working platform clear on completion. To speed up the task, Jim suggests that that they remove a section of the toe board and sweep the debris over the edge into a wheelbarrow they have positioned below at ground level.

a What do you think of Jim's suggestion?

b Is it safe? If not, why?

c Is there a safer way that Jim and Claire could clear the working platform? If so, what?

CHECK YOUR UNDERSTANDING

⊘ Explain the reason that wooden ladders should not be painted.

⊘ Explain why the stacking of materials on a working platform must be kept to a minimum.

⊘ State the purpose of fitting guard-rails and toe boards to high-level working platforms.

⊘ State the procedure to be followed on finding a ladder with broken rungs.

⊘ State **four** good practice points that should be observed when using ladders.

ASSESSMENT CHECK

Now that you have completed this learning outcome you should now be able to:

⊘ state the safe methods of use and appropriate parts of working platforms

⊘ state good practice methods in the use of working platforms

⊘ identify the dangers of working at height when using basic working platforms.

- For more information on risks and precautions, see Risk assessments and method statements on page 32 of this chapter.
- For more information on PUWER, see Provision and Use of Work Equipment Regulations 1998 (PUWER) on page 13 of this chapter.

LINK

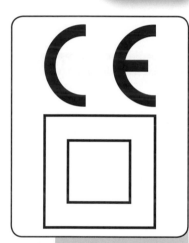

1.37 CE and double insulation marks

KEY TERMS

CE mark: indicates that it has been manufactured to European standards.

Double insulation mark: indicates that the motor and other live parts are isolated from the user.

K7 Work with electricity in a construction environment

Risks and precautions when working with electricity

Electricity can kill. Around 30 deaths a year resulting from an electric shock or burns at work are reported to the HSE, with many more non-fatal accidents resulting in severe and permanent injury. In the construction industry, many of these accidents are as a result of the following:

- Coming into contact with live parts causing shocks and burns.
- Falls from scaffolds and ladders as a result of receiving a shock.
- Burns in fires or explosions caused by electrical faults.

Employers have a duty under the Electricity at Work Regulations to assess the risks and hazards in the workplace. They must eliminate or reduce them as far as is practicable and provide information and training to combat any remaining risk.

Employers and the self-employed who provide equipment for use, or persons who control or supervise the use of equipment, have a duty under the PUWER to prevent or control risks to people's health and safety.

Safety precautions for power supplies and tools

- Always select the correct equipment for the work in hand. If in doubt, consult the manufacturer's instructions.
- In wet or damp conditions, use battery powered or compressed air equipment.
- Ensure that the power tool and supply are compatible.
- Ensure that all equipment has a **CE mark**.
- Ensure that mains and reduced voltage power tools have the **double insulation mark**.

- The use of a **residual current device (RCD)** provides increased protection to the operator from electric shock.

- Always follow the workplace rules and method statements concerning electrical equipment.

- Ensure all electrical equipment is isolated or unplugged from the power supply before leaving it unattended.

- Ensure cables and any extension leads are kept as short as possible and routed safely out of the way to prevent the risk of tripping and damage. Ensure they are not lying in damp conditions.

- Ensure that extension leads stored on a drum are fully unwound before use, in order to prevent overheating within the drum when supplying power.

- Ensure all electrical power tools, battery chargers, portable lighting and similar have a current **portable appliance testing (PAT)** pass certificate, issued by a competent person.

- Ensure that the cable or any extension lead is free from knots and damage, firmly secured at all connections and unable to come into contact with the cutting edge or become damaged during the tool's operation.

- Ensure that all electrical equipment is properly maintained and serviced at regular intervals by a suitably trained person.

- Never use power tools for extended periods of time, especially those that cause vibration, such as sanders, hammer drills and pneumatic tools, as this may result in HAVS.

- Never service or repair electrical equipment yourself. If it's not working correctly or looks unsafe, return it to the store.

- Never use an electric tool where flammable liquids or gases are present.

- Never use damaged items of electrical equipment. If anything is incomplete, damaged, frayed, worn or loose, do not use it and return it to the store for attention.

REMEMBER

Always wear the correct PPE for the job, including working with electricity.

DID YOU KNOW

Water is a very good conductor of electricity. The risk of receiving an electric shock in damp or wet situations is greatly increased.

KEY TERMS

Residual current device (RCD): monitors the flow of electricity in the live and neutral wires of the circuit. In the event of a fault, an imbalance in the flow occurs causing the device to trip, cutting off the electrical supply almost immediately.

Portable appliance testing (PAT): testing in addition to in-house testing and inspection, which is normally carried out on an annual basis but can be varied depending on the frequency of use.

Dangers and effects of electricity

Sparks and heat from faulty or overloaded electrical equipment can provide an ignition source, causing fires or explosions. Bodily contact with electricity can cause a range of injuries:

○ **Electric shock**: if electricity is allowed to flow through the human body it can block the electrical signals between the brain and the muscles, which can cause the heart to stop beating properly, stop or restrict breathing and cause muscle spasms. The amount of current, parts of the body involved, how damp the person is and the duration of contact all affect how serious it would be.

○ **Electrical burns**: as electricity passes through the body, the tissue along the length of the current flow heats up, causing deep internal burns. Again, the amount of current and the duration of contact affect how serious the result would be.

○ **Loss of muscle control**: electric shock can cause violent muscle spasms that can dislocate joints, break bones and also 'lock-up' the person so that they can't let go or escape from the electricity.

○ **Contact burns**: faulty or overloaded electrical equipment can get extremely hot; some electrical equipment even gets hot during normal operation. The skin will burn and blister if it comes into contact or gets too near hot objects and surfaces.

Electrical injuries can be caused by a wide range of currents but, in general, the risk of injury is greater with higher levels. However, effects are also dependent upon the individual:

○ **Low levels** of current may only cause an unpleasant tingling sensation. However, the resulting lack of concentration may cause accidental contact with moving parts or falling from a working platform.

○ **Medium levels** of current passing through the body may result in muscular tension and burning, in addition to loss of concentration as above.

○ **High levels** of current passing through the body, in addition to the effects above, may also affect the heart and can result in death or serious injury.

Voltages in the workplace

Mains supply electricity is 230 volts and normally supplied via a 13 amp three-pin plug and a two or three-core flexible cable that can be plugged directly into a standard outlet. The live wire (brown sheathing) is protected by a fuse, which should be matched to the ampere rating of the equipment being used. If a fault occurs, the earth wire (green and yellow banded sheathing) carries the current safely to earth. As a result of a fault, an increased flow of electricity passes through the fuse, causing the fuse to 'blow' (burn out) and cut off the electrical equipment being used.

Reduced voltage at 110 volts is the norm in the workplace. This is supplied by reducing the 230 volts mains supply via a step-down transformer with a centrally tapped earth. In the event of a fault, the maximum shock an operator could receive would be 55 volts. Reduced voltage equipment operating at 110 volts is the specified voltage for use on building sites, as this greatly reduces the risk of death as a result of an electrocution.

In addition to 230 volts and 110 volts, you may also come across 415 volts. This voltage is used to supply the power for large machines.

LINK

For further information on dangers and effects of electricity, see K2 Accident and emergency procedures and how to report them on page 22 of this chapter.

Colour coding

The electrical supply cables to portable appliances are colour coded to show their purpose and the voltage they are carrying.

- Black flexible supply cables are suitable for general use.
- Arctic flexible cable is designed to work at lower temperatures and remain more flexible than standard black flexible cables: blue is used for 230 volt supplies; yellow is used for 110 volt supplies.

In all cases, the outer protective covering of flexible cables contains three separate solid or stranded copper conductors, each with PVC insulating sheathing. The live and neutral wires carry the alternating current and the earth wire acts as a safety device. A standard European colour coding is used for the conductors, so that any person working with them knows which conductor is used for what purpose:

- Brown sheathing is used for the live wire.
- Blue sheathing is used for the neutral wire.
- Green and yellow striped sheathing is used for the earth wire.

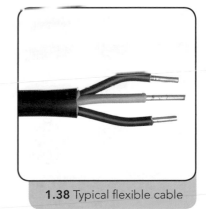

1.38 Typical flexible cable

1.39 Twin and earth cables

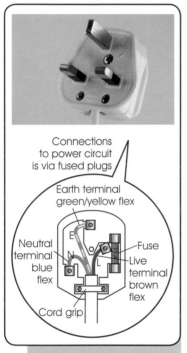

Connections to power circuit is via fused plugs

Earth terminal green/yellow flex

Neutral terminal blue flex

Fuse

Live terminal brown flex

Cord grip

1.40 Domestic three-pin plug

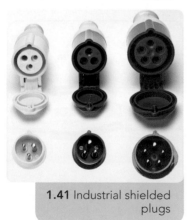

1.41 Industrial shielded plugs

Mains wiring to fixed power and lighting circuits is often installed using 'twin and earth' cables. These normally have a grey, flat outer protection and contain a blue sheathed live wire, a brown sheathed neutral wire and a non-sheathed earth wire. At connections, the earth wire should be covered with a separate piece of green and yellow striped sheathing. Alternatively, separate blue, brown and green/yellow wire may be run in a protective metal or plastic conduit. Some older properties will have been wired using the older colour code, which used red for the live and black for the neutral, however the earth was still green and yellow striped.

Domestic equipment operating at 230 volts is normally connected to a circuit using a fused square three-pin plug.

Building sites and some workplaces may be wired using colour-coded round pin industrial shielded plugs and sockets:

- Yellow 110 volts for reduced voltage equipment.
- Blue 230 volts for mains equipment.
- Red 415 volts (three phase) for large machines.

The position of the key and pin layout is different, making it impossible to plug into the wrong power supply.

Storing electrical equipment

When not in use, all electrical equipment should be stored safely in a locked store or site box to protect it from potential damage, theft and unauthorised use.

- Power tools, leads and plugs must be stored in dry conditions.
- After use, power tools are best returned to their carry case for additional protection.
- Leads should be unplugged and coiled before storage.
- Leads must not be stored or coiled where there is a risk of damage, for example coiling them around a portable circular saw where they could come into contact with the blade.
- Hot equipment, such as a glue gun, should be allowed to cool before storage to prevent the risk of fire.

ACTIVITY

Either in a small group or on your own, consider the following real-life scenario:

Sanjay has been working on a large housing contract as an apprentice carpenter for the last 18 months.

On the day in question, it had been warm and dry in the morning, but there were rain showers during lunch. After lunch, whilst plugging a 110 volt portable power drill into a transformer, Sanjay received an electric shock and burns to his fingers, which required hospital treatment and time off work.

After the accident, Sanjay's supervisor returned the drill to the stores, where on inspection it was found that the lead was damaged near the plug and a conductor wire could just be seen.

a   What do you think was the cause of Sanjay's accident?

b   Whose fault was the accident?

c   Write a method statement to highlight the main points of safety when working with electrical equipment.

CHECK YOUR UNDERSTANDING

⊘ What colour is used to denote 110-volt leads, plugs and sockets?

⊘ Explain why reduced voltage equipment operating at 110 volts is the specified voltage for use on building sites.

⊘ State the possible effects that high levels of electrical current passing through the body can have.

⊘ State the reason why electrical supply cables to portable appliances are colour coded.

⊘ Explain why extension leads that are stored on a drum must be fully unwound before use.

ASSESSMENT CHECK

Now that you have completed this learning outcome you should now be able to:

- state the precautions to be taken to avoid risks to yourself and others when working with electricity
- state the dangers and effects of those dangers associated with the use of electricity
- state the different voltages that could be used in the workplace
- state why there is a need for cables and wiring to be colour coded
- state the requirements for working safely with differing electrical voltages
- state the methods and importance of storing electrical equipment correctly.

K8 Using personal protective equipment (PPE) correctly

The importance of PPE

PPE is the equipment and clothes a worker needs to wear, or use, to protect them from risks to their health and safety that cannot be eliminated or adequately controlled in other ways

There are different types of injuries that can be caused by a person either not using PPE or using inappropriate or damaged PPE. Obvious injuries include punctures, cuts or amputations where safety gloves or safety boots are not worn, head or brain injuries from no safety helmet and severe injuries caused by a faulty harness. It is not just injuries that can occur; ill health and industrial diseases are also commonly caused by a lack of PPE or using inappropriate or damaged PPE. If an item of PPE is lost or damaged, it should be reported to your supervisor and a replacement obtained before undertaking or re-starting work.

Types of PPE
Some items of PPE must be worn at all times, other items relate to the work in hand and the body parts at risk. All items of PPE should be 'CE' marked to show that they meet safety requirements.

REMEMBER

PPE should be used as a last resort and any risk to health and safety should be avoided completely if at all possible.

Employers are required to provide employees with all necessary items of PPE free of charge.

The following table details the various types of protection and suitable items of PPE.

Type of protection	Item of PPE	Description
Head	Safety helmet	Provides protection from falling objects and bumps. Some have attachable eye and ear protection.
		Bump caps are for internal use in confined spaces to protect against accidental bumping of the head.
Hearing	Ear defenders	Help to prevent damage to the ears. They cover the entire ear and have a band that fits over the head. These should be used where noise levels are more excessive.
		Ear plugs are small, disposable fibre plugs that fit into the ear canal. They are suitable for use where noise is not too loud.
Eye	Goggles	Provide protection from dust, dirt, flying particles and chemical splashes.
		Protective glasses don't fully enclose the eyes and thus only provide protection from flying particles.
		Face shields provide full-face protection from flying particles.
Foot	Safety boots	These should have a steel toe-cap and mid-sole to protect the feet from heavy objects and also sharp objects, such as protruding nails from puncturing the sole and injuring the foot.
Respiratory	Dust mask	Respiratory protective equipment known as RPE is used to prevent the breathing in of dust and toxic fumes.
		Dust masks are lightweight, disposable masks that are moulded to fit over the mouth and nose and are suitable for use when non-toxic 'nuisance' dusts are present.
		Respirators offer protection against hazardous dusts, fumes and vapours.
Hand	Safety gloves	Gloves of various types are available to protect the hands from abrasive materials, sharp edges, chemicals, extremes of temperature and vibrating equipment.
		Gauntlets are longer gloves used to protect the hand and lower arm.
Skin	Barrier cream	This can be applied to the hands to offer protection from dust and chemicals, which can result in dermatitis.
		After work cream can be applied to the hands after cleaning to re-moisturise them.
		Sun protection cream provides protection from the sun's ultra-violet rays, which can cause skin burns and also lead to skin cancer.
		Wearing a shirt also provides protection from the sun, as well as creating a better impression of the workforce to visitors and passers-by.
Whole body	High-visibility jacket	Overalls can be worn as a protection from dirt, irritant dusts and the possibility of minor cuts and abrasions. In certain circumstances, waterproof or chemical-resistant overalls may be required.
		High-visibility jackets or vests are worn to ensure that individuals are easily visible at all times. They also provide protection against wet, cold and other poor weather conditions.

1.42 Site safety notice

Maintaining and storing PPE

All items of PPE must be stored in clean, dry conditions when not in use, kept clean, regularly checked for damage and maintained. Simple maintenance can be carried out by the trained wearer, but more intricate repairs should only be done by specialists. Damaged items must not be used and should be replaced immediately. Suitable replacement PPE and spare parts should always be readily available.

ACTIVITY

Visit the HSE website to find out further details on the use and maintenance of PPE. Go to: www.hse.gov.uk.

PPE legislation

As well as **PPER** and **PUWER**, other pieces of legislation govern the use of PPE.

COSHH requires you to wear appropriate PPE (for example, overalls, gloves, eye protection goggles and dusk masks) and to use barrier and after-work cream on skin.

The Construction (Head Protection) Regulations requires employers and the self-employed to provide and ensure that suitable head protection is worn on-site unless there is no foreseeable risk of injury to the head. Site rules should be displayed, giving guidance to employees, the self-employed and site visitors on the use of head protection.

- Safety helmets are normally required to be worn on-site at all times, but must be used when there is a danger of falling objects.

- Bump caps can be worn when there is a need to protect against accidental bumping of the head on overhead piping or other fixed obstacles.

The Noise at Work Regulations:

- Manufacturers/suppliers have a duty to provide low-noise machinery and information to purchasers concerning the level of noise likely to be generated and its potential hazard.

- Employers have a duty to reduce the risk of hearing damage. Specific actions are triggered at daily personal noise exposure levels of 80 and 85 dB.

- Employees have a duty to use the noise-control equipment and hearing protection that is provided and report any defects.

LINK

For a reminder on what PPER, PUWER and COSHH say about PPE, see K1 Health and safety regulations, roles and responsibilities on page 2 of this chapter.

REMEMBER

Not using PPE can result in serious health risks including dermatitis, skin cancer, cuts and infections, eye damage, head injury, burns, hearing damage, respiratory failure.

LINK

For more information on health consequences, see Health risks in the workplace on page 47 of this chapter.

ACTIVITY

Either in a small group or on your own, consider the following real-life scenario:

James has just reported to a construction site on his first day of employment. As part of his induction, he is issued with the following items of PPE: safety helmet; high-visibility jacket; safety boots; gloves; and a pair of goggles.

Whilst putting on the equipment, James looks at the date stamp on the safety helmet. It indicates that the helmet had been manufactured four years ago.

a   What effect does this date have?

b   What should James do?

c   Can the helmet still be used?

d   Is James safe to start working on the site?

CHECK YOUR UNDERSTANDING

⊘ List **three** items of PPE that are normally to be worn on-site at all times.

⊘ Name **two** pieces of legislation that are concerned with PPE.

⊘ List **three** possible consequences of not using PPE.

⊘ Explain the difference between a dust mask and a respirator.

⊘ State the action to be taken if an item of PPE is lost or damaged.

ASSESSMENT CHECK

Now that you have completed this learning outcome you should now be able to:

⊘ state the different types of PPE used in the workplace

⊘ state why it is important to store and maintain PPE correctly

⊘ state the importance of PPE, and why it is important to use it

⊘ state the legislation governing PPE

⊘ list the possible consequences of not using the correct PPE.

K9 Fire and emergency procedures

The fire triangle

Three essential elements are required for a fire to ignite and burn:

⬡ **Fuel**: any combustible or flammable material, which can be a solid, liquid or gas.

⬡ **Oxygen**: normally from the air, but can also be given off by certain chemicals.

⬡ **Heat** or an **ignition source**, such as a naked flame, cigarette end, electric spark, overheating equipment, welding or burning activity.

These make up what is called the fire triangle. If any one of the elements is missing, a fire will not start. If any one of the elements is removed from a fire, it will stop burning. This principle is used to tackle and extinguish fires in the event of an emergency.

1.43 The fire triangle

The spread of fire

It is not the actual material that burns when combustible or flammable materials are subjected to a fire, it is the vapour they give off when heated to their **ignition temperature** or **flashpoint**. These vary widely – timber, for example, has an ignition temperature of around 300°C, whereas many flammable liquids have a flashpoint well below normal internal temperatures.

Building fires can start from a small source of heat, such as a spark or discarded cigarette end. This can ignite a small fuel source, such as an armchair or waste paper in a rubbish bin, which in turn preheats other materials near them. This cycle of events will increase in scale, with more flammable vapours being given off as each different material in a room or building is heated above its ignition temperature or flashpoint, causing a **flashover** to occur.

KEY TERMS

Ignition temperature: the lowest temperature at which a combustible material will give off enough vapour to ignite when exposed to a flame.

Flashpoint: the lowest temperature at which a flammable material will give off enough vapour to ignite when exposed to a flame.

Flashover: the simultaneous ignition of flammable vapours from a number of sources, causing an intense fire involving all the contents of a room or building.

1.44 House fire

Methods of fire prevention

Employers should carry out a risk assessment to establish the type and number of fire extinguishers required in the event of an emergency. This will depend initially on the nature of the workplace or site, materials being used or stored, type of operations being undertaken and machinery and equipment being used. Ongoing health and safety risk assessments should take into consideration the following hazards:

○ General housekeeping and the disposal and nature of waste materials.

○ Storage and use of flammable substances.

○ Storage and use of potentially dangerous substances, such as petrol, propane and butane gases (LPG) and solvents.

○ Accumulation of dust and vapour, which create a high-explosive risk.

You will find the five-step process of a risk assessment on page 33 of this chapter.

All staff should know what to do in the event of a fire in the workplace and be given clear guidance. Everyone needs to understand the fire emergency procedures, including whether or not they should use fire extinguishers and in what circumstances.

DID YOU KNOW

Employers must take action in order to eliminate or reduce the risks in the workplace, such as:

○ establishing procedures to be followed in the event of an emergency

○ providing signs and audible alarms

○ providing information and training to employees on emergency responsibilities

○ conducting regular emergency evacuation practice drills.

1.45 Undertaking a risk assessment

Designated staff who are permitted to operate fire-fighting equipment should be given hands-on training in the use of fire extinguishers.

In the event of a fire, follow these guidelines to assess whether or not it's safe to fight a fire:

DON'T:

O put your own and other people's safety at risk

O use a fire extinguisher if the fire is in its late stages or it's blocking your escape route

O attempt to fight a large or well-established fire

O fight a fire that has already produced lots of smoke and fumes, as they are poisonous and can overcome and kill you

O use a fire extinguisher if you are not sure what is burning, as you won't know the correct fire extinguisher to use

O allow the fire to come between you and your exit route.

DO:

O have someone else with you if possible, in case you need assistance or someone to go for help

O leave if the fire is starting to rapidly spread

O make sure you have a safe escape route before tackling any fire.

1.46 Using a fire extinguisher

1.47 Emergency assembly point sign

Emergency evacuation procedures

If you are first on the scene of a fire, you may be required to:

O use a fire extinguisher (if trained) to tackle a small fire in its early stages or where it's blocking your escape route

O make a phone call to summon the emergency services, if people are injured or there is a threat to life

O call for the first aider on-site or give emergency help yourself if you are a qualified first aider.

LINK

For more information on emergency procedures and responsibilities, see K2 Accident and emergency procedures and how to report them on page 22 of this chapter.

SAFETY TIPS

Take extra care if you tackle a fire with a fire blanket as you will be very close to the fire.

DID YOU KNOW

Using a water fire extinguisher on:

○ an electrical fire can result in electrocution as the electrical current can travel back along the water jet

○ petrol, burning oil or fat can result in serious injury as the fire will explode.

REMEMBER ⟫⟫

Fire extinguisher label or band colour:
    Red = water
  Cream = foam
   Black = carbon dioxide
    Blue = dry powder
Yellow = wet chemicals.

ACTIVITY

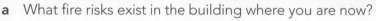

a   What fire risks exist in the building where you are now?
b   Where is the nearest escape route?
c   What is the emergency evacuation alarm?
d   Where is your assembly point?
e   Who do you have to report to?
f   What fire-fighting equipment is available?

Types of fire extinguisher

There is a range of fire extinguishers and fire blankets for tackling a fire in its early stages. It is essential to use the correct type depending on the class of fire; using the wrong type can make the fire spread or cause injury to the user. All fire extinguishers are red in colour and have a different coloured label or band to indicate the substance they contain. They may also have pictures and instructions on the type of fire they are suitable for.

1.48 Various fire extinguishers and a fire blanket

Fires are divided into six classes according to the type of materials involved, as shown in Fig 1.49.

Fire classification

Class A:
Wood, paper, textiles and any other carbonaceous materials

Class B:
Flammable gases such as petrol, oils, fats and paints

Class C:
Flammable gases such as propane, butane and natural gas

Class D:
Metals such as aluminium, magnesium and titanium

Class E:
Electrical equipment

Class F:
Cooking oils and fats

1.49 Classes of fire

Fire extinguishers

Remember: three essential elements are required for a fire to ignite and burn:

◯ A combustible or flammable fuel.

◯ Oxygen.

◯ Heat or a source of ignition.

All fire extinguishers work by removing one or more of the elements, without which a fire will stop burning. They are used to apply an agent to the fire that:

◯ cools down the fuel so that it can no longer burn

◯ removes or pushes away the oxygen to prevent the fuel igniting.

Fire extinguisher safety

PASS will help you to remember the basic safety rules for using a fire extinguisher (see Fig 1.50):

◯ **P**ULL out the pin from the top of the fire extinguisher.

◯ **A**IM the hose or nozzle at the base of the fire. Stand about 2 to 3 m from the fire.

◯ **S**QUEEZE the fire extinguisher lever to discharge the agent.

◯ **S**WEEP the agent back and forth across the lower part of the fire. Keep watch after extinguishing a fire in case it re-ignites.

1.50 PASS

If in doubt:

◯ don't put your own and other people's safety at risk

◯ only consider using a fire extinguisher if the fire is in its early stages or it's blocking your escape route

◯ ensure the emergency services have been informed and everyone reports to the assembly point.

The following table can be used as a guide when selecting the correct type of equipment:

Contents:	Label or band colour	Suitable for use on the following classes of fire:
Water	RED	A
Foam	CREAM	A and B
Carbon dioxide	BLACK	B, C and E
Dry power	BLUE	A, B, C, D and E
Wet chemicals	YELLOW	A and F

CHECK YOUR UNDERSTANDING

- What are the **three** elements that make up the fire triangle?
- What class of fire can water fire extinguishers be used on?
- What can happen if a water fire extinguisher is used on an electrical fire?
- What does PASS mean in relation to fire extinguishers?
- How do the contents of a fire extinguisher put out a fire?

ASSESSMENT CHECK

Now that you have completed this learning outcome you should now be able to:

- list the three elements essential to creating a fire
- state the ways in which a fire could spread and identify methods of fire prevention
- state the actions to be taken on discovering a fire
- state the correct fire evacuation procedures
- state the different types of fire extinguishers and their correct uses.

K10 Safety signs and notices

Legislation

The Health and Safety (Safety Signs and Signals) Regulations requires employers to provide information or instruction about health and safety in the workplace by displaying signs, sounding signals, making hand signals and verbal communication.

Types of safety sign

Each sign has a certain shape, colour, symbol or picture and may be supported by words to ensure that health and safety information is presented to employees in a consistent, standard way.

There are five main types of safety signs in general use containing pictograms or symbols and some with text, plus a sixth supplementary sign with text only:

1 Prohibition sign: a round sign with a white background, red circular border and a red diagonal line through it, and a picture in the centre. This tells you that something must not be done.

2 Mandatory sign: a round sign with a white picture on a blue background. This means that a special course of action is required; it tells you that something must be done.

3 Warning sign: a triangular sign with a black picture on a yellow background and black border. This gives a warning of a certain hazard. Yellow and black diagonally striped tape can be used to mark the perimeter of hazards.

4 Safe condition sign: a square or rectangular sign with a white picture and text on a green background. This provides information about safe conditions, such as escape routes and first-aid facilities, etc.

5 Fire-fighting sign: a square sign with a white picture on a red background identifies fire-fighting equipment or indicates the location of a fire extinguisher and fire alarm. Red and white diagonally striped tape can be used to mark obstacles and 'keep clear' areas.

1.51 Shapes and colours used for safety signs

1.52 Typical examples of safety signs in use

REMEMBER >>>

Safety signs are displayed in the workplace for number of reasons and it is your duty to follow the information and instructions they contain at all times.

As part of your induction to a site, you should be made aware of the safety signs used and their meaning.

DID YOU KNOW

1.53 Site safety poster

If you are unfamiliar with any safety sign displayed in the workplace, you should ask your site health and safety representative or supervisor to explain its meaning.

SAFETY TIPS

6 Supplementary information sign: text on a white background. This can be used in conjunction with a safety sign to provide additional information and instruction.

The following points are also highlighted in the regulations:

O In order to avoid confusion, too many signs should not be placed together.

O Signs should be removed when the situation they refer to no longer exists.

O Traffic routes should be marked out using yellow.

O Acoustic fire evacuation signals must be continuous and sufficiently loud enough to be heard above other noises on-site.

O Hand signals can be used to direct hazardous operations, such as crane and vehicle manoeuvres. Anyone giving hand signals must be competent, wear distinctive brightly-coloured clothing (hi-viz) and use the standard arm and hand movements.

O Verbal signals can also be used to direct hazardous operations. These can be spoken by a person or given by a recorded artificial voice. For example, lorries are often fitted with a record message that activates when reverse gear is engaged: 'warning this vehicle is reversing'.

Other safety signs and notices

A workplace will normally display a range of other pictorial and written information, such as:

O safety posters displayed at the site entrance to inform the general public, as well as authorised personnel entering the site, of potential dangers and site safety requirements

O legal notices, for example a certificate of insurance is normally displayed in the site manager's office

O the Health and Safety law poster. This should be displayed in an obvious position in each workplace or provided to each worker with a copy of the leaflet outlining British health and safety laws. The approved poster contains phone and web contact details for the HSE and also includes a space where details of any employee health and safety representative or other health and safety contact can be added.

Health and Safety Law
What you need to know

All workers have a right to work in places where risks to their health and safety are properly controlled. Health and safety is about stopping you getting hurt at work or ill through work. Your employer is responsible for health and safety, but you must help.

What employers must do for you

1   Decide what could harm you in your job and the precautions to stop it. This is part of risk assessment.

2   In a way you can understand, explain how risks will be controlled and tell you who is responsible for this.

3   Consult and work with you and your health and safety representatives in protecting everyone from harm in the workplace.

4   Free of charge, give you the health and safety training you need to do your job.

5   Free of charge, provide you with any equipment and protective clothing you need, and ensure it is properly looked after.

6   Provide toilets, washing facilities and drinking water.

7   Provide adequate first aid facilities.

8   Report injuries, diseases and dangerous incidents at work to our Incident Contact Centre:
0845 300 9923

9   Have insurance that covers you in case you get hurt at work or ill through work. Display a hard copy or electronic copy of the current insurance certificate where you can easily read it.

10 Work with any other employers or contractors sharing the workplace or providing employees (such as agency workers), so that everyone's health and safety is protected.

Your health and safety representatives:

Other health and safety contacts:

What you must do

1   Follow the training you have received when using any work items your employer has given you.

2   Take reasonable care of your own and other people's health and safety.

3   Co-operate with your employer on health and safety.

4   Tell someone (your employer, supervisor, or health and safety representative) if you think the work or inadequate precautions are putting anyone's health and safety at serious risk.

If there's a problem

1   If you are worried about health and safety in your workplace, talk to your employer, supervisor, or health and safety representative.

2   You can also look at our website for general information about health and safety at work.

3   If, after talking with your employer, you are still worried, phone our Infoline. We can put you in touch with the local enforcing authority for health and safety and the Employment Medical Advisory Service. You don't have to give your name.

HSE Infoline:
0845 345 0055

HSE website:
www.hse.gov.uk

Fire safety
You can get advice on fire safety from the Fire and Rescue Services or your workplace fire officer.

Employment rights
Find out more about your employment rights at:

www.direct.gov.uk

HSE

Health and Safety Executive

1.54 Health and safety law poster

○ employers have a legal duty under the Health and Safety Information for Employees Regulations (HSIER) to display the Health and safety law poster in a prominent position in each workplace or provide each worker with a copy of the equivalent leaflet outlining British health and safety laws. The approved poster contains contact details for the HSE and also includes a space where details of any employee health and safety representatives and other health and safety contacts can be added.

○ other safety posters, notices, site rules and site 'dos' and 'don'ts'. These are often displayed in the site canteen or other communal area.

CHECK YOUR UNDERSTANDING

⬡ What is the purpose of a round, blue safety sign with a white picture?

⬡ Name and state the meaning for each of the following safety signs:

⬡ State why it is important to report all accidents and incidents.

⬡ State why too many signs should not be placed together.

⬡ Employers have a legal duty to advise employees of Health and Safety Law. State the two forms this may take.

ASSESSMENT CHECK

Now that you have completed this learning outcome you should now be able to:

⬡ list the different signs and safety notices used in the workplace.

REVISION QUIZ

Q1 Which one of the following abbreviations refers to the main umbrella legislation that deals with health and safety in all workplaces?

a HASAWA

b COSHH

c RIDDOR

d PUWER

Q2 The purpose of a triangular safety sign with a yellow background and black border is to:

a Tell you something you must do

b Tell you something you must not do

c Warn you of a specific hazard

d Identify safe conditions

Q3 Why is it important to report a near miss, even if no one is hurt?

a Lessons can be learned, which help to prevent future accidents

b It should be recorded in the accident book

c You may be able to get compensation

d Someone may have to be disciplined

Q4 What is the major cause of fatal accidents on construction sites?

a Contact with moving machinery

b Struck by a falling object

c Falls from a height

d Contact with electricity

Q5 What colour sheathing is used to denote the live wire in modern electrical circuits?

a Red

b Black

c Blue

d Brown

Q6 Which one of the following is not an employer's responsibility under the Health and Safety at Work Act?

a Provide employees with the necessary information, instruction, training and supervision to ensure safe working

b Provide employees with safe transportation to and from work

c Provide and maintain a safe working environment

d Ensure safe access to and from the workplace

Q7 Legislation is:

a A law or set of laws that must be followed by all

b An approved code of practice that gives explanations of the law

c A guide to explain best health and safety practices

d Something that only applies to employers

Q8 Which one of the following regulations deals with the control of hazardous substances?

a COSHH

b PUWER

c RIDDOR

d PPER

From this chapter you should have gained a good understanding of:

K1 Health and safety regulations, roles and responsibilities

K2 Accident and emergency procedures and how to report them

K3 Hazards on construction sites

K4 Health and hygiene in a construction environment

K5 Handle materials and equipment safely

K6 Basic working platforms

K7 Work with electricity in a construction environment

K8 Use personal protective equipment (PPE) correctly

K9 Fire and emergency procedures

K10 Safety signs and notices

Q9 A fire extinguisher containing water can be used on:

a Class A fires

b Class B fires

c Class C fires

d Class E fires

Q10 The purpose of a method statement is to:

a Advise the HSE that construction work is going to be carried out

b Detail a practical and safe way of undertaking a work task

c Avoid the need to undertake risk assessments

d Identify situations where PPE is required to be worn

2 Information, quantities and communicating with others

Working in the construction industry involves working with and interpreting a wide range of information to suit the needs of a project. It also involves working within a team and communicating effectively with other people.

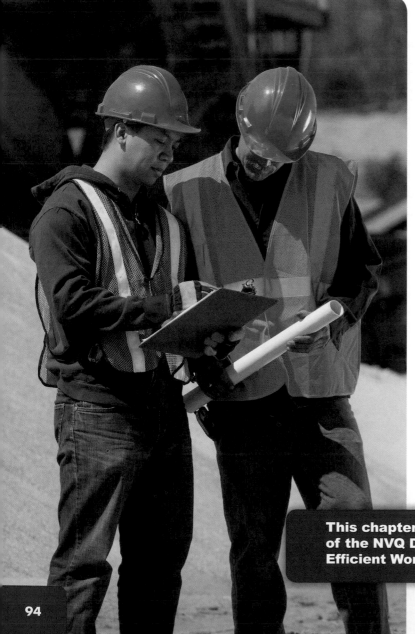

This chapter covers the following learning outcomes for Unit 1002K level 1:

K1 Interpret building information

K2 Determine quantities of materials

K3 Relay information in the workplace

This chapter also covers the following learning outcomes for Unit 2002K level 2:

K1 Interpret and produce building information

K2 Estimate quantities of resources

K3 Communicate workplace requirements efficiently

This chapter also supports the learning outcomes of the NVQ Diploma unit QCF 02 Conform to Efficient Work Practices.

K1 Interpret and produce building information

Most of the information used in the building industry is presented as written documents and drawings. Collectively, they are known as the contract documents and include:

- working drawings
- specification
- schedule
- bill of quantities
- form of building contract.

These documents are kept on-site for the duration of the contract. They should be locked in filing cabinets or plan chests in the site office, especially overnight and at weekends. The exception to this would be the signed form of building contract, which normally remains off-site and is kept secure in the contractor's head office. At the end of the contract, it is standard practice to **archive** the contract documents, paperwork and records for at least three years. Estimators and quantity surveyors often find it valuable to refer to them when estimating and reviewing costs of similar works.

Today, storage is easy as many documents are electronic and can be stored on computers. Even hard copies of forms, notes and sketches can be scanned and stored electronically. This reduces the storage space and makes access to information easier.

Drawings

Drawings are the key way to communicate technical building information between all parties involved in the building process. They must be clear, accurate and easily understood by everyone who uses them. In order to achieve this, architects and designers use standardised methods for scale, line-work, layout, symbols and abbreviations.

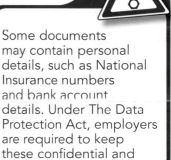

KEY TERMS

Archive: the term given to both a collection of records and documents, as well as the place in which they are located.

DID YOU KNOW

Some documents may contain personal details, such as National Insurance numbers and bank account details. Under The Data Protection Act, employers are required to keep these confidential and only use them for the purpose they were provided for.

2.1 Scale drawings

KEY TERMS

Scale: a way of reducing an object in size to fit on a drawing sheet.

Ratio: used in scale drawings to show the relationship between the drawing and the actual object: a **1:5** ratio means that 1 unit on the drawing represents 5 units in the actual object.

Scales and lines

Scales use **ratios** that permit measurements on a drawing or model to relate to the real dimensions of the actual job. It is impractical to draw buildings, plots of land and most parts of a building to their full size as they wouldn't fit on a sheet of paper. Instead, they are drawn to a smaller size, which has a known scale or ratio to the real thing. These are called scale drawings.

The main scales (ratios) used in the construction industry are:

1:1; 1:5; 1:10; 1:20; 1:50; 1:100; 1:200; 1:500; 1:1250; 1:2500

1:10 is a ratio or scale of '1 to 10' or sometimes '1 in 10'. The ratio shows how much smaller the plan or model is to the original. (See Fig 2.2 for a one-metre length drawn to various scales.)

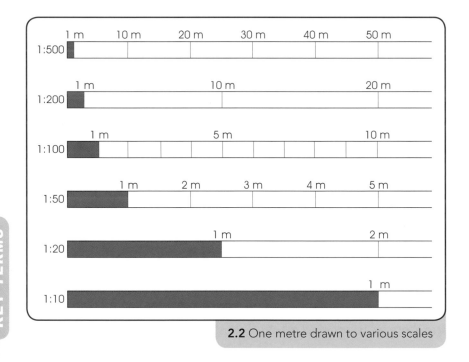

2.2 One metre drawn to various scales

Multiplying the scale measurement by the scale ratio determines the actual size to which it relates.

○ In a drawing to a scale of 1:10, 5mm would stand for 50mm on the actual job and 50mm would stand for 0.5m (500mm).

○ In a drawing to a scale of 1:20, 5mm would stand for 100mm on the actual job and 50mm would stand for 1m (1000mm).

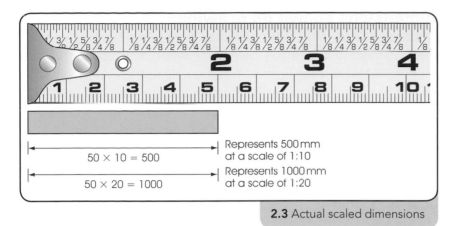

Represents 500 mm at a scale of 1:10
$50 \times 10 = 500$

Represents 1000 mm at a scale of 1:20
$50 \times 20 = 1000$

2.3 Actual scaled dimensions

Scale rules

A scale rule has a series of scales on it so that actual dimensions can be read directly from it.

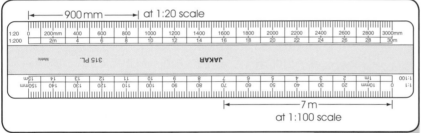

2.4 A scale rule

Preference should always be given to written dimensions shown on a drawing. Mistakes can be made as paper size can change if it gets damp for example or a fold in the paper might make it impossible to get an accurate size. The opening size shown in Fig 2.5 can be accurately determined by taking away the length of the stud partition from the overall width of the room, rather than trying to scale it with a rule.

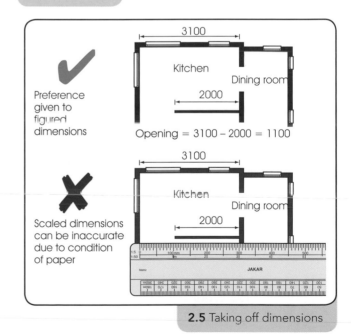

Preference given to figured dimensions

Opening = $3100 - 2000 = 1100$

Scaled dimensions can be inaccurate due to condition of paper

2.5 Taking off dimensions

Dimensions shown on drawings

Dimensions shown on scale drawings include the symbol for the measurement units used. A lower-case letter 'm' is used for metres and lower-case letters 'mm' for millimetres. Units should not be mixed on drawings; 2½ metres can be shown either as 2.5 m, 2.50 m, 2.500 m or 2500 mm. On some drawings, to avoid confusing or missing the position of the decimal point, an oblique stroke may be used to separate metres from millimetres, for example 2/500 for 2 m 500 mm or 2.500 m. Where the dimension is less than a metre, a '0' is added before the stroke, 0/750 for 750 mm.

Sequence of dimensioning

The recommended sequence for expressing dimensions is shown in Fig 2.6. Length is normally expressed first, followed by width and then thickness:

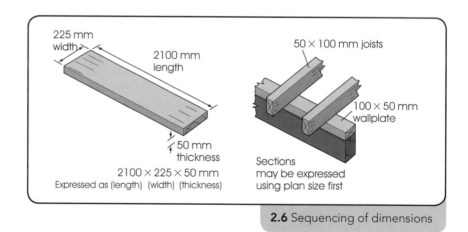

2.6 Sequencing of dimensions

$$L \times W \times T = 2100 \times 225 \times 50\,mm$$

Where only the sectional size is quoted, width is normally stated before thickness:

$$W \times T = 225 \times 50\,mm$$

Be aware that the sectional size on drawings may be stated with the size seen in plan first; a 100 × 50 mm section may be shown as 50 × 100 mm when used as a joist or 100 × 50 mm for a wall plate.

Lines used on drawings

A variety of different line types and thicknesses or 'weights' is used on drawings for specific purposes.

⬡ **Solid lines** show the actual parts of an object that can be seen. Thick or dark lines for the outside border; medium or lighter lines for internal borders and general detail; thin or light lines for construction and dimensioning.

⬡ **Break-lines** in a zig-zag pattern show a break in the continuity of a drawing. End break-lines indicate that an object has not been fully drawn. Central break-lines indicate that the object has not been drawn to its full length.

⬡ **Chain lines** in a long/short or dot/dash pattern are used for centre lines and services.

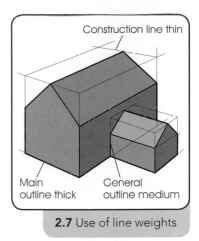

Construction line thin

Main outline thick

General outline medium

2.7 Use of line weights

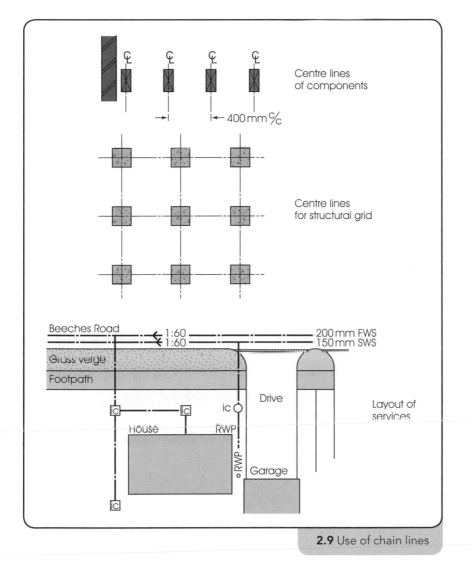

Centre lines of components

400 mm ℄

Centre lines for structural grid

Beeches Road

1:60
1:60
200 mm FWS
150 mm SWS

Grass verge

Footpath

Drive

ic

Layout of services

House

RWP

Garage

2.9 Use of chain lines

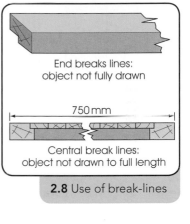

End breaks lines: object not fully drawn

750 mm

Central break lines: object not drawn to full length

2.8 Use of break-lines

○ **Section lines** indicate an imaginary cutting plane at a particular point through an object. Pointers or arrows on the line indicate the direction of view that will be seen on a separate section drawing. Where more than one section is shown, these will be labelled as A–A, B–B, and so on, according to the number of sections. The section drawings themselves may be included on the same drawing sheet or be cross-referenced to another drawing.

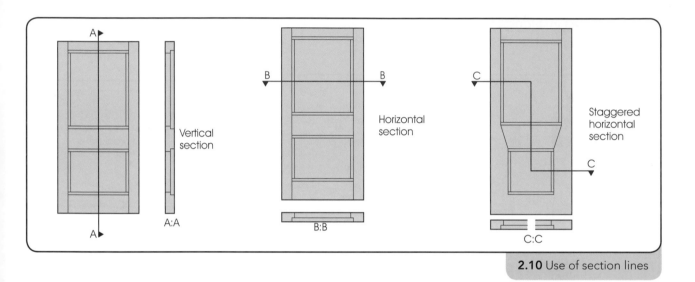

2.10 Use of section lines

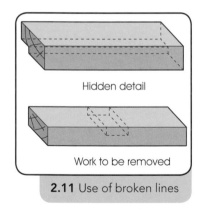

2.11 Use of broken lines

○ **Broken lines** indicate hidden details that cannot be seen on the object as drawn, or for work that is to be removed.

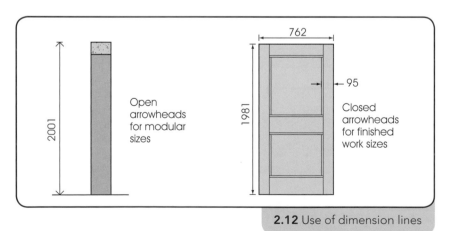

2.12 Use of dimension lines

⬡ **Dimension lines** indicate the distance between points on a drawing. These are lightly drawn solid lines with arrowheads terminating against short cross-lines. Open (birdsfeet) arrowheads are often used for the basic/modular 'unfinished' distances in a drawing. Closed (solid) arrowheads are the preferred method for general use and 'finished' work sizes.

Separate and running dimensions

The actual figured dimensions on a drawing may be shown as either separate or running dimensions.

⬡ Separate dimensions are normally written above and centrally along the line; figures on vertical lines should be written parallel to the line, so that they are read from the right.

⬡ Running dimensions are shown cumulatively commencing with zero from a fixed point or datum. These are often written on the cross-line at right angles to the dimension line.

Be careful not to confuse separate and running dimensions when reading them off a drawing.

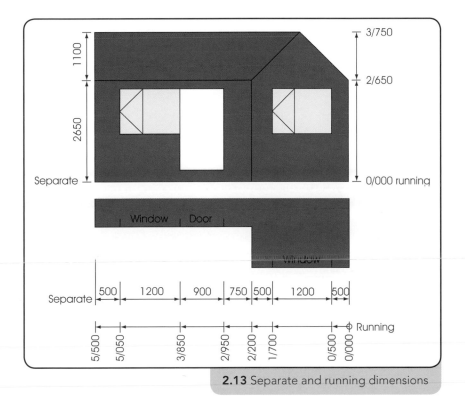

2.13 Separate and running dimensions

Symbols and abbreviations used on drawings

Symbols and abbreviations are used on drawings instead of words to allow as much information as possible to be given without taking up too much space. Symbols are pictures used to

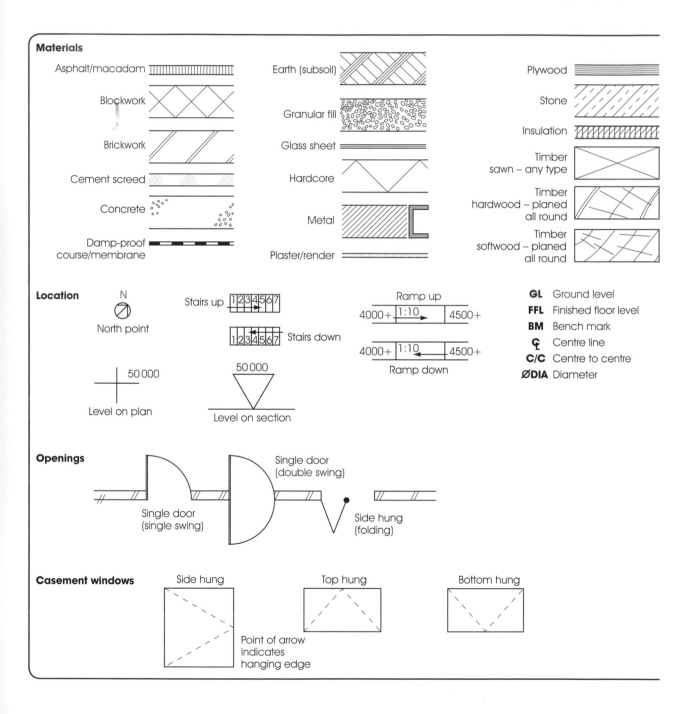

represent different materials and components in building drawings. Abbreviations are a short way of writing a word or group of words. Fig 2.14 shows some of the symbols and abbreviations commonly used in the construction industry.

Aggregate	agg	Column	col	Joist	jst
Air brick	AB	Concrete	conc	Mild steel	MS
Aluminium	al	Copper	Copp cu	Pitch fibre	PF
Asbestos	abs	Cupboard	cpd	Plasterboard	pbd
Asbestos cement	absct	Damp proof course	DPC	Polyvinyl acetate	PVA
Asphalt	asph	Damp proof membrane	DPM	Polyvinylchloride	PVC
Bitumen	bit	Discharge pipe	DP	Rainwater head	RWH
Boarding	bdg	Drawing	dwg	Rainwater pipe	RWP
Brickwork	bwk	Expanding metal lathing	EML	Reinforced concrete	RC
BS* Beam	BSB	Foundation	fdn	Rodding eye	RE
BS Universal beam	BSUB	Fresh air inlet	FAI	Foul sewers	FS
BS Channel	BSC	Glazed pipe	GP	Sewers surface water	SWS
BS equal angle	BSEA	Granolithic	grano	Softwood	swd
BS unequal angle	BSUA	Hardcore	hc	Tongue and groove	T & G
BS tee	BST	Hardboard	hdbd	Unglazed pipe	UGP
Building	bldg	Hardwood	hwd	Vent pipe	VP
Cast iron	CI	Inspection chamber	IC	Wrought iron	WI
Cement	ct	Insulation	insul		
Cleaning eye	CE	Invert	inv		
*BS = British Standard					

2.14 Some standard symbols and abbreviations used on drawings

Projection used in drawings

Drawings of objects can be produced either as a series of plan or elevation views called orthographic projection or in a form that looks like the three-dimensional appearance called pictorial projection.

Orthographic projection

This method is used for working drawings, plans, elevations and sections. A separate drawing of each face of all the views of an object is produced on the same drawing sheet. Each view is at right angles to the face:

⬡ **Plan view** shows the surface of an object when looking down on it vertically. Floor plans in building drawings are normally drawn as a section taken just above windowsill height.

⬡ **Elevation view** of an object details the surface from side, front or rear.

⬡ **Section view** details the cut surface produced when an object is cut through with a saw.

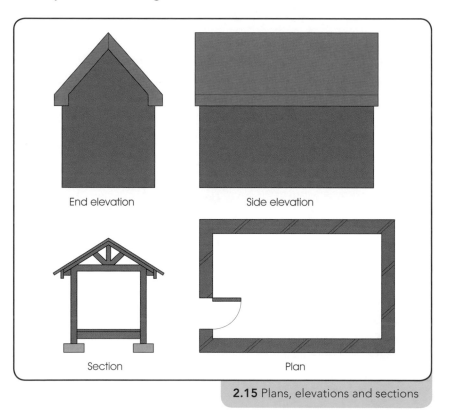

End elevation   Side elevation

Section   Plan

2.15 Plans, elevations and sections

The actual position of the plan, elevation and section on the drawing sheet will vary depending on whether first or third angle projection is used. The viewing position in relationship to the object is the same for both methods as shown in Fig 2.16.

First angle projection

This is used for building drawings where, in relation to the front view, the other views are arranged as follows:

○ The view from above is drawn below.

○ The view from below is drawn above.

○ The view from the left is drawn to the right.

○ The view from the right is drawn to the left.

○ The view from the rear is drawn to the extreme right.

○ A sectional view may be drawn to the left or the right where space permits.

Third angle projection

This is a form of orthographic projection used for engineering drawings. In relation to the front elevation, the other views are arranged as follows:

○ The view from above is drawn above.

○ The view from below is drawn below; the view from the left is drawn to the left.

○ The view from the right is drawn to the right.

○ The view from the rear is drawn to the extreme right.

○ Again, a sectional view may be drawn to the left or the right where space permits.

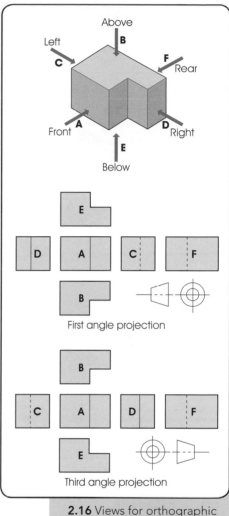

2.16 Views for orthographic projection

DID YOU KNOW

Pictorial projection is often used for design and marketing purposes, as showing the finished appearance of the object makes it easier for the general public to appreciate it. A range of views are shown by changing the angles of the base lines and the scale of the side projections.

Pictorial projection

This is a method of drawing objects in a three-dimensional form.

○ **Isometric**: the most common form of pictorial drawing where all vertical lines are drawn vertical and all horizontal lines are drawn at an angle of 30 degrees to the horizontal. Length, width and height are all drawn to the same scale.

○ **Planometric**: a form of pictorial drawing where all vertical lines are drawn vertical, horizontal lines on the front elevation are drawn at 30 degrees to the horizontal and those on the side elevation at 60 degrees to the horizontal, giving a true plan shape. Length, width and height are all drawn to the same scale.

○ **Axonometric**: similar to planometric, except that the horizontal lines in both the elevations are drawn at 45 degrees to the horizontal, again giving a true plan shape. Length, width and height are all drawn to the same scale.

○ **Oblique**: a pictorial projection, which uses a true front elevation; the side elevation can be either cabinet or cavalier. All vertical lines are drawn vertical and all horizontal lines in the front elevation are drawn horizontal, while all horizontal lines in the side elevations are drawn at 45 degrees to the horizontal. In **cavalier**, these 45-degree lines are drawn to their full or scale length, while in **cabinet** they are drawn to half their full or scale length to give a less distorted view.

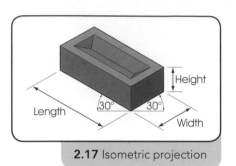

2.17 Isometric projection

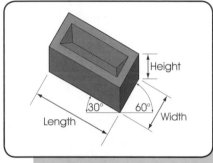
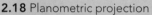

2.18 Planometric projection

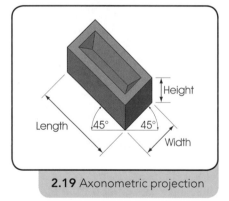

2.19 Axonometric projection

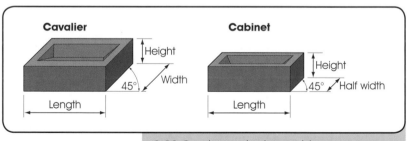

2.20 Cavalier and cabinet oblique projection

○ **Perspective**: a pictorial projection where the horizontal lines disappear to one or more points on the imaginary horizon. These disappearing points are called VPs or 'vanishing points'. **Parallel perspective** has a true front elevation with the sides disappearing to one vanishing point (one-point perspective). **Angular perspective** is drawn with the elevations disappearing to two vanishing points (two-point perspective). All upright lines in both forms are drawn vertically. Sloping lines such as the pitch of the roof are best first drawn in a rectangular box, with the ridge being positioned midway across the box.

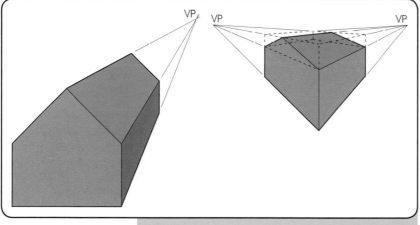

2.21 Parallel and angular perspective projection

Layout and production of drawings

Drawings can be produced by hand or on a computer using a CAD (computer-aided design) programme. The labelled drawings will also include figured dimensions, printed notes to explain exactly what is required and a title panel, which identifies and provides information about the drawing.

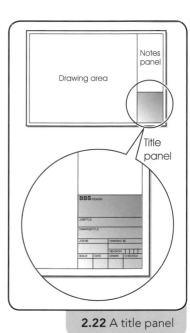

2.22 A title panel

PRINTING FOR TITLES SHOULD BE 8mm HIGH

3mm HIGH PRINTING SHOULD BE USED FOR NOTES AND ANY OTHER INFORMATION WHICH IS REQUIRED ON A DRAWING SHEET

FREEHAND PRINTING SHOULD BE BETWEEN TWO FAINT CONSTRUCTION LINES

TWO PARALLEL LINES 3mm APART

2.23 Hand printing on drawing sheets

DID YOU KNOW

The typical sizes for letters and numbers on drawings are between 5 and 8 mm for titles and between 1.5 and 4 mm for notes. As a guide, when hand printing on drawings you should first draw two faint parallel lines and then write between them using capital letters.

DID YOU KNOW

AO is
841 × 1189 mm;
A1 (594 × 841 mm) is
half A0;
A2 (420 × 594 mm) is
half A1;
A3 (297 × 420 mm) is
half A2;
A4 (210 × 297 mm) is
half A3.

Where sizes larger
than AO are
required, the A
is preceded by a
number, 2A being
twice the size of A0
etc.

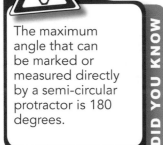

DID YOU KNOW

The maximum
angle that can
be marked or
measured directly
by a semi-circular
protractor is 180
degrees.

DID YOU KNOW

As an aid to
producing a 'clean'
drawing, set
squares, protractors
and rules should be
washed occasionally
in warm soapy
water and carefully
dried before reuse.

Paper sizes

Drawings are produced on a range of international paper sizes. 'A0' is the base size consisting of a rectangle having an area of one square metre and sides that are in the proportion of 1:√2. All the A series are of this proportion, enabling them to be doubled or halved in area and remain in the same proportion, which is useful for photographic reproduction.

Drawing equipment

A set of quality drawing equipment is required to produce accurate drawings:

○ **Drawing board**: an A2 sized one with either a sliding parallel rule or teesquare, used for drawing horizontal lines and provides a support when using set squares.

○ **Set squares**: two set squares, at least 150 mm long on the shortest sides, are required – a 45/45/90 degree one and a 60/30/90 degree one, which are used to draw vertical and inclined lines. Alternatively an adjustable square can be used, as it can be set to any angle up to 90 degrees.

○ **Protractor**: for setting out and measuring angles up to 180 degrees.

○ **Compasses and dividers**: used to draw circles and arcs. Dividers are used for transferring measurements and dividing lines.

○ **Scale rule**: containing the following scales: 1:5/1:50 1:10/1:100 1:20/1:200 1:250/1:2500.

○ **Pencils**: at least two sharp pencils are required – a HB for sketching, printing and to darken the outline of a finished drawing, and either a 2H or 3H for general drawing and geometry.

○ **Eraser**: required for alterations and corrections to pencil lines.

2.24 Drawing equipment

Sketches

These are rough outlines or first drafts of your ideas and thoughts before full working drawings are made. It is often much easier to produce a sketch of your intentions rather than to describe in words or produce a long list of instructions. Sketches can be produced either freehand (without the use of any equipment) or be more accurately produced using a ruler and set square to give basic guidelines. Methods of projection follow those used for drawing (i.e. orthographic or pictorial).

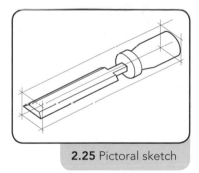

2.25 Pictoral sketch

Working drawings

These are scale drawings showing the plans, elevations, sections, details and locality of the proposed construction. These drawings can be divided into the following main types:

Location drawings

- ⬡ Block plans, to scales of 1:2500 or 1:1250, identify the proposed site in relation to the surrounding area.

- ⬡ Site plans, to scales of 1:500 or 1:200, give the position of the proposed building and the general layout of roads, services and drainage on the site.

> **◀◀◀ REMEMBER**
>
> Pictorial sketching is made easy if you imagine the object you wish to sketch with a three-dimensional box around it. Lightly draw the box first with a 2H pencil, and then draw in the object using a HB pencil.

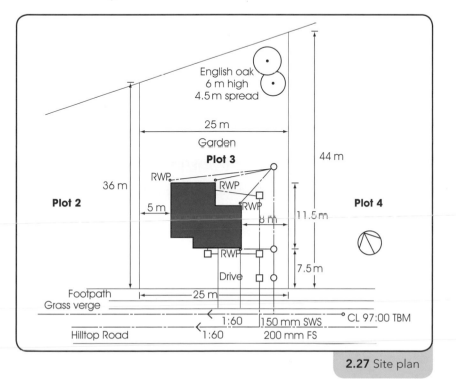

2.27 Site plan

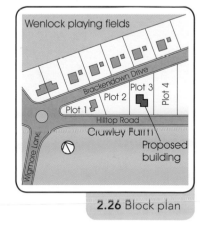

2.26 Block plan

General location plans, to scales of 1:200, 1:100 or 1:50, show the general position occupied by the various items within the building and identify the location of the principal elements and components.

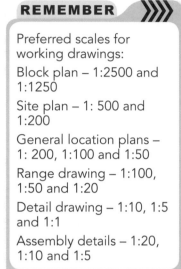
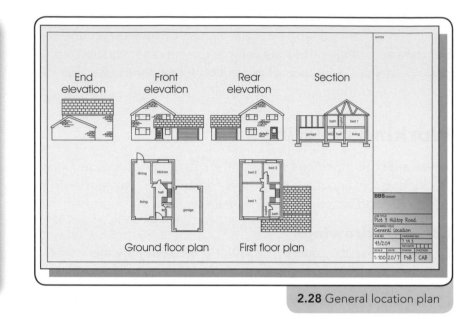

2.28 General location plan

Component drawings

Range drawings, to scales of 1:100, 1:50 or 1:20, show the basic sizes and reference system of a standard range of components.

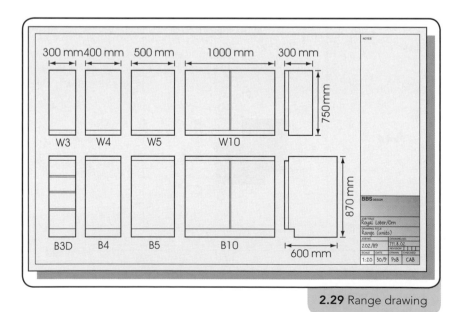

2.29 Range drawing

O Detail drawings, to scales of 1:10, 1:5 or 1:1, show all the information that is required in order to manufacture a particular component.

Assembly drawings

O Assembly details, to scales of 1:20, 1:10 or 1:5, show in detail the junctions in and between the various elements and components of a building.

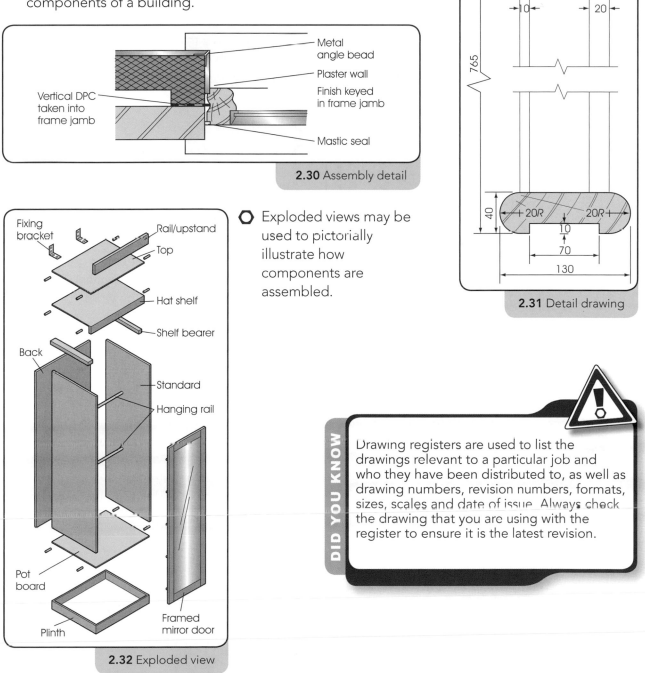

Metal angle bead

Plaster wall

Finish keyed in frame jamb

Vertical DPC taken into frame jamb

Mastic seal

2.30 Assembly detail

O Exploded views may be used to pictorially illustrate how components are assembled.

2.31 Detail drawing

Fixing bracket

Rail/upstand

Top

Hat shelf

Shelf bearer

Back

Standard

Hanging rail

Pot board

Framed mirror door

Plinth

2.32 Exploded view

DID YOU KNOW

Drawing registers are used to list the drawings relevant to a particular job and who they have been distributed to, as well as drawing numbers, revision numbers, formats, sizes, scales and date of issue. Always check the drawing that you are using with the register to ensure it is the latest revision.

Specification

BBS DESIGN

Specification of the works to be carried out and the materials to be used in the erection and completion of a new house and garage on plot 3, Hilltop Road, Brackendowns, Bedfordshire, for Mr W. Whiteman, to the satisfaction of the architect.

1.00   General conditions

1.01
1.02

1.03
1.04

2.00
2.01
2.02

2.03
2.04
2.05

2.06
2.07
2.08
2.09

10.00   Woodwork

10.01   Timber for carcassing work to be machine strength graded class C16

10.02   Timber for joinery shall be a species approved by the architect and specified as J2

10.03   Moisture content of all timber at time of fixing to be appropriate to the situation and conditions in which it is used. To this effect all timber and components will be protected from the weather prior to their use.

10.04

10.05

10.06

10.18   Construct the first floor using 50 mm × 195 mm sawn softwood joists at 400 mm centres supported on mild steel hangers.

Provide 75 mm × 195 mm trimmer and trimming around stairwell, securely tusk-tenoned together.

Provide and fix to joists 38 mm × 38 mm sawn softwood herring-bone strutting at 1.8 m maximum intervals.

Provide and fix galvanized restraint straps at 2 m maximum intervals to act as positive ties between the joists and walls.

10.19   Provide and secret fix around the trimmed stairwell opening a 25 mm Brazilian mahogany apron lining, tongued to a matching 25 mm 100 mm nosing.

10.20   Provide and lay to the whole of the first floor 19 mm × 100 mm prepared softwood tongued and grooved floor boarding, each board well cramped up and surface nailed with two 50 mm flooring brads to each joist. The nail heads to be well punched down.

2.33 Extracts from a typical specification

Except in the case of very small building works, the drawings cannot contain all of the information required by the builder. For this purpose, the architect will prepare a document called the specification to go with the working drawings. The specification is a precise description of all the essential information and job requirements that will affect the price of the work but which cannot be shown on the drawings. Typical items included in specifications are:

○ site description and/or address

○ availability of services such as water, electricity, gas, telephone

○ description of materials, quality, size, tolerance and finish

○ other requirements, such as site clearance, making good on completion, nominated suppliers and sub-contractors and who is authorised to approve the work.

○ restrictions such as limited access and working hours

Schedules

These are used to record repetitive design information about a range of similar components or fittings and are normally cross-referenced to the architect's drawings. The main areas where schedules are used include:

○ doors, frames, linings
○ windows
○ sanitary ware, drainage
○ finishes, floors, walls, ceilings
○ lintels
○ steel reinforcements.

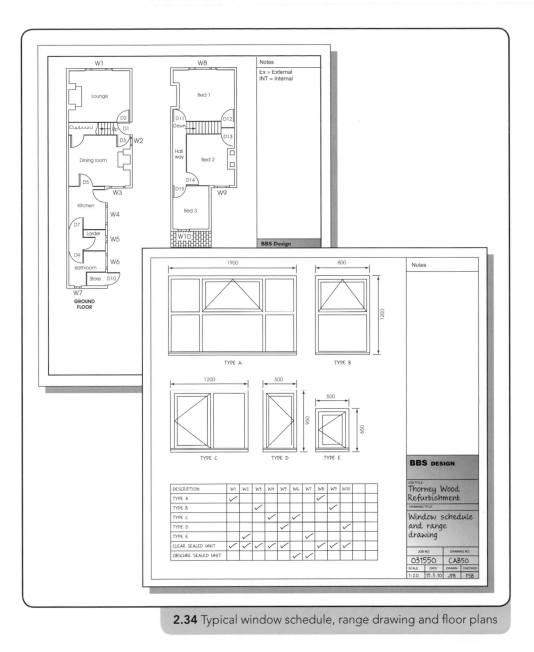

2.34 Typical window schedule, range drawing and floor plans

Bill of quantities

The bill of quantities (BOQ) is prepared by the client's quantity surveyor. This document gives a complete description and measure of the quantities of labour, material and other items required to carry out the work based on drawings, specification and schedules. Its use ensures that all estimators prepare their tender on the same information.

All BOQs will contain the following information:

Preliminaries	General particulars of the work, such as names of the parties involved, details of the works, description of the site and conditions of the contract
Preambles	Introductory clauses to each trade covering descriptions of the material and workmanship similar to those stated in the specifications
Measured quantities	Description and measurement of an item of work. The measurement is given in metres run, metres square, kilograms etc, or just in numbers as appropriate.
Provisional quantities	Where an item cannot be accurately measured, an approximate quantity to be allowed for is stated. Adjustments will be made when the full extent of the work is known.
Prime cost sum (PC sum).	An amount of money to be included in the tender for work services or materials provided by a nominated subcontractor, supplier or statutory body.
Provisional sum	A sum of money to be included in the tender for work that has not yet been finally detailed or a 'contingency sum' to cover the cost of any unforeseen work.

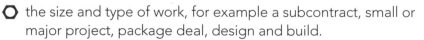

ITEM	DESCRIPTION	QUANTITY	UNIT	RATE £	AMOUNT £	
	Superstructure: Suspended upper floor					
A	Supply and fit the following C16 grade preservative treated softwood					
A1	50 × 195 mm joists	250	m	6.44	1610	00
A2	75 × 195 mm joists	60	m	8.58	514	80
A3	38 × 150 mm strutting	70	m	3.85	339	50
	Carried to collection:			£	2464	30

2.35 Extract from a typical bill of quantities

Conditions of contract

Most building work is carried out under a 'standard form of contract' such as one of the Joint Contractors Tribunal (JCT) forms of contract.

The standard form of contract used will depend on the following:

- the type of client, for example a local authority, public limited company or private individual.

- the size and type of work, for example a subcontract, small or major project, package deal, design and build.

- whether the contract documents include quantities or approximate quantities.

The contract should also include the rights and obligations of all parties and details of procedures for variations, interim payments, retention, liquidated and ascertained damages and the defects liability period.

Variation	A modification of the specification by the client or architect. The contractor must be issued with a written variation order or architect's instruction. Any cost adjustment as a result of the variation must be agreed between the quantity surveyor and the contractor.
Interim payment	A periodic payment made to the contractor by the client. It is based on the quantity surveyor's interim valuation of the work done and the materials purchased by the contractor. On agreeing the interim valuation the architect will issue an interim certificate authorising the client to make the payment.
Final account	The final payment the contractor will receive on completion. The architect will issue a certificate of practical completion when the building work is finished. The quantity surveyor and the contractor will then agree the final account, less the retention.
Practical completion	The time at which the building work has been completed to the client's/architect's satisfaction. A certificate of practical completion will be issued and the contractor will be entitled to the remainder of monies due, less any retention.
Main contractor's discount (MCD)	A sum of money that may be included in a subcontractor's quotation, often 2.5 per cent, to cover the main contractor's administration costs associated with a subcontract.
Retention	A sum of money that is retained by the client until the end of an agreed defects liability period.
Liquidated and ascertained damages	(LADs) often referred to as a **penalty clause**. A sum of money payable on a daily or weekly basis, agreed in advance in the contract, as being fair and reasonable payment for damages or loss of revenue to the client as a result in a delay of practical completion.
Defects liability period	A period, normally six months after practical completion, to allow any defects to become apparent. The contractor will be entitled to the retention after any defects have been rectified to the architect's satisfaction.

Work programmes

On obtaining a contract for a building project, a contractor will prepare a work programme or contract plan that shows the sequence of work activities.

Progress of work can be compared with the target times contained in the plan. If the target times are realistic, the plan can be a source of motivation for the site management who will make every effort to stick to the programme and catch up when required. There are a number of factors, some outside of the management's control, which could lead to a programme modification:

DID YOU KNOW

A contract plan shows the relationship between the different tasks and also indicates when and for how long resources such as materials, equipment and workforce are required.

○ Bad weather.

○ Labour shortages.

○ Labour disputes or strikes.

○ Late material deliveries.

○ Variations to contract.

○ Lack of specialist information.

○ Bad planning and bad site management, etc.

The contractor will normally make an addition of about 10 per cent to the target completion dates to allow for such factors.

Bar or Gantt charts

The most popular type of work programme is the bar or Gantt chart. The tasks are listed in a vertical column on the left-hand side of the sheet with a horizontal timescale along the top. A horizontal bar or block shows the target start and end times of the individual tasks. In addition to their use as overall contract management, bar charts can be used for short-term, weekly and monthly plans.

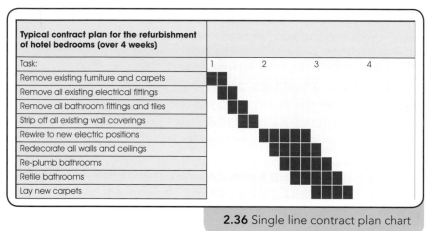

2.36 Single line contract plan chart

Other types of bar chart can be used to indicate actual progress on a contract:

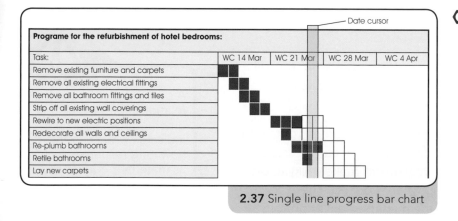

2.37 Single line progress bar chart

○ **Single line bar chart**: the same as the contract plan chart, but the block showing the planned activity is shown in outline and can be shaded as the actual work progresses. A sliding transparent date cursor is often laid over the chart to indicate the actual date. In Fig 2.37 the block showing the planned activity is shown in outline and can be shaded as the actual work progresses. A sliding transparent date cursor is often laid over the chart to indicate the actual date. The shading shows that both the rewiring and redecoration activities are behind the programme and the re-plumbing of the bathrooms is ahead of the programme.

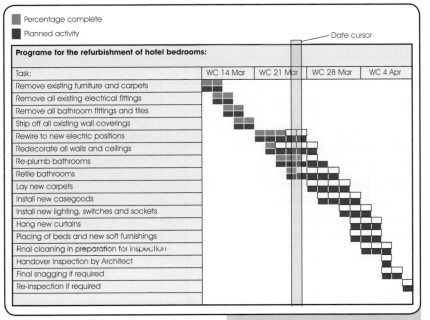

2.38 Two line progress bar chart

⬡ **Two line bar chart**: the planned activity box is divided into two; one shaded to show the planned activity and the other hatched to show the actual percentage of work completed.

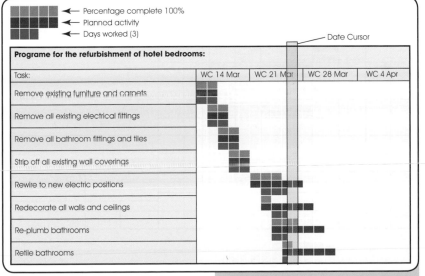

2.39 Three line progress bar chart

⬡ **Three line bar chart**: here the bar is divided into three, with the third line being used to indicate the actual days worked. The chart in Fig 2.39 shows that the rewiring and redecorating were both started a day late.

A typical bar/Gantt programme chart for the construction of a house is shown in Fig 2.40. This is a variation of the two line bar chart, in which the second bar is shaded in to show the work progress and the actual time taken for each task. Plant and labour requirements have also been included along the bottom of the sheet. The shading shows that two carpenters were on site in week 6 for the 1st fix and a JCB was being used in week 10 for the external finishing.

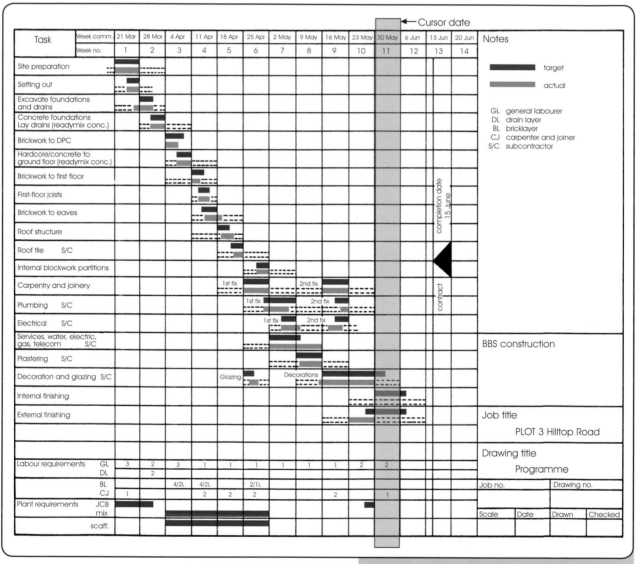

2.40 Bar chart for the construction of a house

Checking information for conformity

It is almost inevitable that the building information issued for a contract will be revised and updated. Therefore, it's essential that latest documents are used and all documents are checked for **conformity**.

Using documents that don't conform can lead to confusion, costly mistakes and delays. For example, the BOQ and first issues of a drawing indicate that solid oak T&G flooring is to be used to cover a suspended floor and the buyer orders this material for delivery to site to suit the work programme. However, in the meantime, the architect has issued a variation order and revised drawings that now change this to oak laminate boarding laid over chipboard T&G. At the very least, this would result in the additional cost of the revised material and delays by not having the correct material available when required. Even worse, if the error is not identified beforehand and the wrong flooring is laid, it would result in labour costs of putting the situation right, further delays and a loss of the client's confidence in the company.

KEY TERMS

Conformity: the following of a fixed standard. In a building context this means ensuring that all the information in related construction documents matches.

CHECK YOUR UNDERSTANDING

At levels 1 and 2:
- ⊘ Describe the type of information that is contained in a specification.
- ⊘ State the reason why drawings are normally produced to scale.
- ⊘ State what the following abbreviations stand for: DPC; DPM; BM; hwd; dwg; conc.
- ⊘ State the purpose of a schedule.
- ⊘ Produce sketches to show the symbols that are used on drawings to represent the following: brickwork; north point; prepared softwood; concrete; hardcore; top-hung casement window.

At level 2:
- ⊘ Name and describe three different types of building drawing.
- ⊘ Explain why it is important to check documents for conformity.
- ⊘ In addition to working drawings, name three other contract documents and state what information they contain.
- ⊘ List **three** factors that could have an effect on the duration of a contract programme.
- ⊘ Produce to a suitable scale an example of the three different types of building drawing you named and described in level 2 question 1 above.

ASSESSMENT CHECK

Now that you have completed this learning outcome you should now be able to:

At levels 1 and 2:

✅ state why documentation must be looked after and stored correctly

✅ identify the appropriate scale to be used with a range of drawings

✅ identify basic symbols and abbreviations used in working drawings

✅ select information from basic location drawings and specifications

✅ select information from basic work schedules in general use.

At level 2:

✅ state the types of information available, including drawings, programmes of work, procedures, hierarchical charts, mediation and disciplinary procedures, specifications, policies, mission statements, manufacturers' technical information, organisational documentation and training, and development records and documents (some of these information sources are considered in K3)

✅ interpret information from the above documents and check it for conformity

✅ use equipment to produce drawings and sketches, including scale rules, set squares, protractor and pencils.

K2 Determine quantities of materials and estimate quantities of resources

Calculations are used as a way of communicating daily information in the construction industry. Typical questions include the following:

○ How many do we need?

○ How long is it?

○ What is the area or volume?

○ How long will it take?

○ How much will it cost?

○ How much will I earn?

The answers to these require numerical calculations. Simple calculations may be carried out in your head. Other calculations can be written down and worked out, perhaps with a calculator. You may already be familiar with the main basic rules of numbers and numerical processes; however, these and other skills are briefly covered in this chapter to provide a source of reference and revision as required. Examples have been written out in full with the working out normally using a calculator.

When undertaking calculations, you will be using a number of resources including:

○ working drawings, diagrams, plans and schedules

○ material purchase orders, invoices, basic timesheets, schedules of labour rates, job sheets, site diaries, building suppliers' rates and price lists, and book or computer-based pricing systems used for both labour and materials

○ equipment such as rules and tapes, scale rules, calculators, computers and conversion tables.

Basic rules of numbers

The four basic rules of number calculations are **addition**, **subtraction**, **multiplication** and **division**.

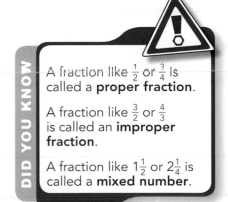

DID YOU KNOW

A fraction like $\frac{1}{2}$ or $\frac{3}{4}$ is called a **proper fraction**.

A fraction like $\frac{3}{2}$ or $\frac{4}{3}$ is called an **improper fraction**.

A fraction like $1\frac{1}{2}$ or $2\frac{1}{4}$ is called a **mixed number**.

2.41 $1\frac{1}{2}$ tins of paint is 1.5 tins in decimals

Addition is shown as a + (plus sign), which means 'add'.

Subtraction is shown as a − (minus sign), which means 'subtract'.

Multiplication is shown as a × (multiplication sign), which means 'multiply'.

Division is shown as a ÷ (division sign), which means 'divide'.

The result of addition, subtraction, multiplication or division is shown after a = (equals sign).

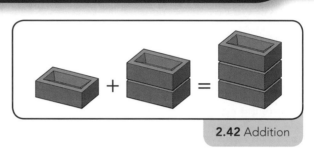

2.42 Addition

EXAMPLE $1\frac{2}{3}$

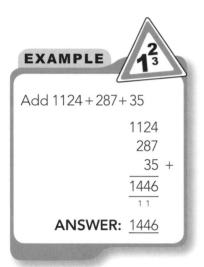

Add 1124 + 287 + 35

```
  1124
   287
    35 +
  ____
  1446
   1 1
```

ANSWER: 1446

EXAMPLE $1\frac{2}{3}$

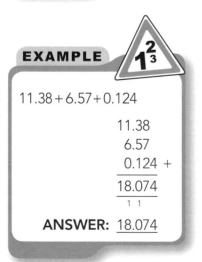

11.38 + 6.57 + 0.124

```
  11.38
   6.57
  0.124 +
  _____
 18.074
   1 1
```

ANSWER: 18.074

Addition

Adding involves putting, summing, adding and counting things together.

When adding, it is useful to make sure that the units are lined up underneath each other. The columns can then be easily added, starting from the right.

○ The right-hand column 4 + 7 + 5 = 16. As this is 1 ten and 6 units, the 6 is put in the units column and the 1 is carried forward to the tens column.

○ When adding the tens column, the 1 carried forward must be included: 2 + 8 + 3 + 1 = 14. As this is 1 hundred and 4 tens, put 4 in the tens column and carry the 1 forward to the hundreds.

○ Continue adding the remaining columns.

The final answer is called the **sum**. The sum of 1124, 287 and 35 is 1446.

Addition of decimals

Numbers containing decimal points must be written down with the points lined up underneath each other when preparing to add.

Subtraction

Subtraction involves taking things away.

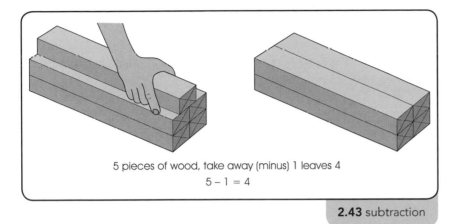

5 pieces of wood, take away (minus) 1 leaves 4

$5 - 1 = 4$

2.43 subtraction

Again, when subtracting, line up the units underneath each other and subtract the columns starting from the right.

⬡ When subtracting the units, we say in this example '8 from 4 will not go, so borrow 1 from the tens column', making 14 units and 8 tens.

⬡ When subtracting the next column, we must remember there is one less at the top.

Subtraction of decimals

Numbers containing decimal points are again written down with the points lined up underneath each other.

Multiplication

Multiplication is a quick way of adding groups of equal numbers:

$4 + 4 + 4 + 4 + 4 = 20$ is the same as $4 \times 5 = 20$

You do not have to count the number of tiles on the wall to tell that there are 20. There are five lots of four tiles.

When using the quick way, we say 'Four tiles multiplied by five lots equals 20 tiles' or simply 'Four by five equals 20'.

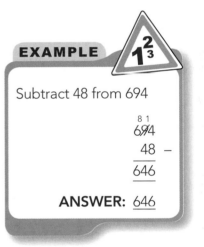

EXAMPLE

Subtract 48 from 694

$$\overset{8\ 1}{6\cancel{9}\cancel{4}}$$
$$48\ -$$
$$\overline{646}$$

ANSWER: 646

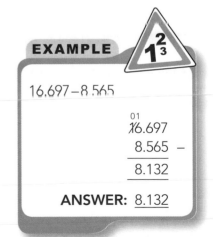

EXAMPLE

$16.697 - 8.565$

$$\overset{0\ 1}{1\cancel{6}.697}$$
$$8.565\ -$$
$$\overline{8.132}$$

ANSWER: 8.132

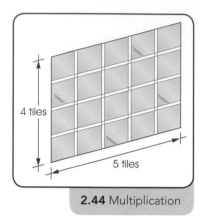

2.44 Multiplication

Hence:

$$4 \times 5 = 20$$

20 is called the **product** of 4 and 5. The product of any number up to 10 is shown in a **multiplication table**. In order to multiply, you must know your multiplication tables for products at least up to 10×10. The example shown in the multiplication table is for the product of 4×5.

To find 4×5, look at the intersection of row 4 and column 5. There you will find the product of 4 and 5, which is 20.

1	2	3	4	5	6	7	8	9	10
2	4	6	8	10	12	14	16	18	20
3	6	9	12	15	18	21	24	27	30
4	8	12	16	20	24	28	32	36	40
5	10	15	20	25	30	35	40	45	50
6	12	18	24	30	36	42	48	54	60
7	14	21	28	35	42	49	56	63	70
8	16	24	32	40	48	56	64	72	80
9	18	27	36	45	54	63	72	81	90
10	20	30	40	50	60	70	80	90	100

Multiplication table

2.45 Multiplication table

Multiplication of larger numbers

⬡ Start with the units. We say in this example '8 × 6 is 48'. (Use the multiplication table.)

⬡ Put the unit figure down (8) and carry the tens forward (4).

⬡ Then continue to multiply 5 × 8, which is 40 plus the carried 4 makes 44.

⬡ The product of 8 × 56 tiles is 448 tiles.

EXAMPLE $1\frac{2}{3}$

A larger wall is 8 tiles high and 56 tiles long. How many tiles?

Note:
8 × 56 means '8 lots of 56 make' or '8 by 56'

$$\begin{array}{r} 56 \\ 8 \times \\ \hline 448 \\ {\scriptstyle 4} \end{array}$$

ANSWER: 448 tiles

EXAMPLE $1\frac{2}{3}$

Multiply 146 × 92

$$\begin{array}{r} 146 \\ 92 \\ \hline {\scriptstyle 1}\,292 \times \\ {\scriptstyle 45}\\ 13140 \\ \hline {\scriptstyle 1}\,13432 \end{array}$$

ANSWER: 13432

⬡ In this example, first multiply 146 × 2, to give 292.

⬡ Then multiply 146 × 90. Do this by putting a zero down in the units and multiply 146 by 9.

⬡ 9 times 146 is 1314.

⬡ Add the two rows to get 13 432.

Multiplication of decimals

When multiplying, any decimal points can be ignored until the
two sets of numbers have been multiplied together.

EXAMPLE $1\frac{2}{3}$

11.6×4.5

Two places to the right of the decimal
point to start with.

Count 2 places to left for point in
answer.

$$
\begin{array}{r}
116 \\
45 \times \\
\hline
580 \\
4640 \\
\hline
5220 \\
\end{array}
$$

ANSWER: 52.20

The position of the decimal point can be located by the following
rule:

> the number of figures to the right of the decimal point in the
> answer will always equal the total number of figures to the right
> of the decimal point to start with.

Division

Division involves sharing or dividing things into equal parts. It is
the opposite of multiplication.

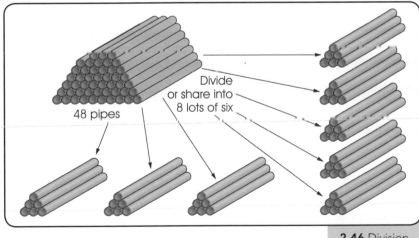

48 pipes

Divide
or share into
8 lots of six

2.46 Division

1	2	3	4	5	6	7	8	9	10
2	4	6	8	10	12	14	16	18	20
3	6	9	12	15	18	21	24	27	30
4	8	12	16	20	24	28	32	36	40
5	10	15	20	25	30	35	40	45	50
6	12	18	24	30	36	42	48	54	60
7	14	21	28	35	42	49	56	63	70
8	16	24	32	40	48	56	64	72	80
9	18	27	36	45	54	63	72	81	90
10	20	30	40	50	60	70	80	90	100

Multiplication table

2.47 Multiplication tables can be used backwards for division.

Division using tables

○ Use the multiplication table. Look for 48 in the 6th row.

○ Read up the column to get 8.

○ Hence 48 shares into 8 equal lots of 6.

○ We say '48 divided by (÷) 8 equals (=) 6'.

Division by calculation

Divide 384 by 6. This may be written down as $384 \div 6$.

The 6 is called the **divisor**, 384 is called the **dividend** and the answer is called the **quotient**.

Note how the calculation is laid out in the example. For division, we work from the left, not from the right, and the answer is written above, not below.

○ First we try to find how many times 6 goes into 3.

○ As 6 into 3 will not go, there is nothing to enter in the first position of the answer line.

○ Then we try 6 into 38 (from table) and the nearest number below 38 in the 6th row is 36.

○ Read up the column to get 6.

○ Put the 6 above the 8 in the second position of the answer line.

○ Subtract 36 from 38 to leave 2.

○ 'Bring down' the 4 to make 24.

○ Divide 24 by 6 (from table) equals 4. We say '6 into 24 goes 4 times'.

○ Put the 4 next to the 6 in the third position of the answer line.

This gives the answer 64.

Your division can be checked by multiplying back. This check proves the working out is correct. For example: $6 \times 64 = 384$.

DID YOU KNOW

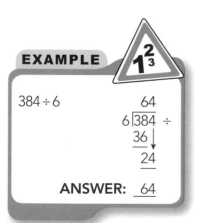

EXAMPLE $1\frac{2}{3}$

$384 \div 6$

$$\begin{array}{r} 64 \\ 6\overline{\smash{)}384} \div \\ \underline{36} \downarrow \\ 24 \\ \hline \end{array}$$

ANSWER: 64

Division with a remainder

When there is a remainder (number left over at the end of the division), the operation can be continued by inserting a decimal point and 'bringing down' zeros. As shown in the example:

○ '4 into 3 will not go.' (Nothing is entered in the first position of the answer line.)

○ '4 into 37 goes 9 remainder 1.' (9 is entered into the second position of the answer line.)

○ Insert decimal point next to 9 and bring down zero next to the remainder 1 making 10.

○ '4 into 10 goes 2 remainder 2.' (2 is entered into the answer line after the decimal point.)

○ Bring down another zero next to the remainder 2 making 20.

○ Now we say '4 into 20 goes 5 and nothing left over'.

The answer is = 9.25.

Division of decimal numbers

When dividing numbers with decimal points, first we need to make the divisor a whole number. We do this by moving its decimal point a number of places to the right until it is a whole number, but to compensate we must also move the decimal point in the dividend by the same number of places. (You may have to add zeros to do this.)

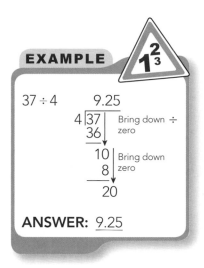

EXAMPLE $1\frac{2}{3}$

$37 \div 4$

	9.25
4 ⟌ 37	Bring down ÷ zero
36 ↓	
10	Bring down zero
8 ↓	
20	

ANSWER: 9.25

EXAMPLE $1\frac{2}{3}$

$164.6 \div 0.2$

$164.6 \div 0.2$
$1646 : 2$

Move both the decimal points until the division is a whole number.

	823
2 ⟌ 1646	÷
	823

ANSWER: 823

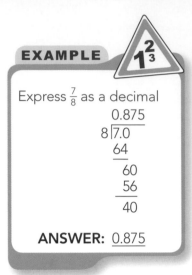

Express $\frac{7}{8}$ as a decimal

$$8\overline{)7.0} \quad 0.875$$

64
___
60
56
___
40

ANSWER: 0.875

Operating with fractions

Fractions are best converted into decimals before proceeding with addition, subtraction, multiplication or division operations. Conversion is done by dividing the bottom number into the top number.

Combined mathematical operations

You will need to understand the following combinations of mathematical statements:

- $12 - (6 + 4)$
- $3 \times (4 - 1)$ which can be written as $3(4 - 1)$
- $3 \times (12 \div 4)$ which can be written as $3(12 \div 4)$
- $(40 \div 2) + (4 \times 6)$

Rules for combined mathematical operations

You must work out the operation contained in the brackets ( ) first before proceeding with the remaining calculation. You must then do multiplication and division before addition and subtraction. A useful made-up word '**BODMAS**' can help you to remember the order in which calculations should be undertaken.

- So, $12 - (6 + 4)$ gives $12 - 10 = 2$
- $3(4 - 1)$ gives $3 \times 3 = 9$

KEY TERMS

BODMAS: Brackets, then the Order is Division, Multiplication, Addition and Subtraction

REMEMBER 》》》

Rough checks will be nearer to the correct answer if, when choosing approximate numbers, some are increased and some are decreased. In cases where the rough check and the correct answer are not of the same size, the calculation should be reworked to find the cause of the error.

$3(12 \div 3)$

$\qquad 3(12 \div 3)$

$= 3(4)$

$= 3 \times 4$

$= \underline{12}$

$40 \div 2 + (4 \times 6)$

$\qquad 40 \div 2 + (4 \times 6)$

$= 40 \div 2 + (24)$

$= 20 + 24$

$= \underline{44}$

Approximate answers

Common causes of incorrect answers to calculation problems are incomplete workings out and incorrectly placed decimal points. Rough checks of the expected size of an answer and the position of the decimal point would overcome this problem. These rough checks can be carried out quickly using approximate numbers:

⬡ $4.65 \times 2.05 \div 3.85$

⬡ For a rough check say $5 \times 2 \div 4 = 2.5$

⬡ The actual correct answer is 2.476

As the answers are of a similar size, this confirms that the answer is 2.476 and not 0.2476 or 24.76, etc.

Rounding to a number of decimal places

For most purposes, calculations that show three decimal figures are considered sufficiently accurate. These can therefore be rounded off to three decimal places. This, however, entails looking at the fourth decimal figure; if it is a five or above, add one to the third decimal figure. Where it is below five, we can ignore it.

EXAMPLE

33.012357 becomes 33.012

2.747642 becomes 2.748

Rounding to a number of significant figures

On occasions, a number may have far too many figures before and after the decimal place for practical purposes. This is overcome by expressing it to 2, 3 or 4 significant figures (S.F. or sig. fig.).

EXAMPLE

Express 68.936102 to 4 S.F.

ANSWER: 68.94

9.041

2.48 Decimal number expressed to 4 S.F.

Number	To 3S.F	To 2 S.F	To 1 S.F
6.308	6.31	6.3	6
5368	5370	5400	5000
0.051308	0.0513	0.051	0.05
0.1409	0.141	0.14	0.1

You should apply the same rule as for rounding numbers to a number of decimal places. If the next figure after the last S.F is 5 or more, then round up the last S.F. by 1. If it is less, then round down.

EXAMPLE

$1\frac{2}{3}$

Change 6500 m to km

6500
³²¹

Move point 3 places

ANSWER: 6.5 km

Change 0.55 m to mm

0.550
₁₂₃

ANSWER: 550 mm

ACTIVITY

Try changing 0.55 m to mm.

0.95 km   1.25 km

Long Eaton   Chilwell   Beaston

Long lengths in kilometres (km)

2.1 m

Intermediate lengths in metres (m)

75 mm

Small lengths in millimetres (mm)

2.49 Length

After rounding up to a number of significant figures, you must take care not to change the place value. For example, 4582 is 4600 to 2 S.F., so zeros are added to the end in order to maintain the place value.

However, 4.582 = 4.6 to 2 S.F., not 4.600, since trailing zeros are not added after the decimal point.

Units of measurement

The construction industry now almost totally uses the metric units of measurements and this is what you should use. Previously, the imperial units of measurement were used. You may still come across some of these occasionally, so knowledge of both is required. For most metric units we use there is a base unit, a multiple unit 1000 times larger and a sub-multiple unit 1000 times smaller.

The base unit of length is the metre (m).

Its multiple unit is the kilometre (km), which is 1000 times larger: 1 m × 1000 = 1 km

The sub-multiple unit of the metre is the millimetre (mm), which is 1000 times smaller: 1 m ÷ 1000 = 1 mm

Note that 1 mm × 1000 = 1 m and 1 km ÷ 1000 = 1 m

It is an easy process to convert from one unit to another in the metric system. The decimal point is moved three places to the left when changing to a larger unit of length and three places to the right when changing to a smaller unit.

So, to change 6500 m to km, move the point three places to the left to give 6.5 km.

Measuring length

Length is a measure of how long something is from end to end.

⬡ Long lengths, such as the distance between two places on a map, are measured in kilometres (km).

⬡ Intermediate lengths, such as the length of a piece of timber, are measured in metres (m).

⬡ Small lengths, such as a brick, the length of a screw and the width of a board are measured in millimetres (mm).

DID YOU KNOW

Although the metre and the millimetre are the main units of length used in the construction industry, sometimes centimetres (cm) are used as an intermediate measure of length.

Conversion into other metric units is as follows:

1 m = 100 cm
1 cm = 10 mm

To avoid confusion, measurements should always be given in metres or millimetres. For example, 55 cm should be converted and written as either 0.55 m or 550 mm.

Measuring perimeter

Perimeter is the distance around the outside of a shape. To find the perimeter of a shape, you have to know or measure the sides and add them together. The perimeter of the room shown in the floor plan (Fig 2.50) is 4 + 4 + 3 + 3 = 14 m.

Measuring area

Area is concerned with the extent or measure of a surface. The floor plan of the room in Fig 2.50 is 3 m wide and 4 m long. We say it has an area of 12 square metres (m²).

○ Two linear measurements multiplied together give the square area:

Area = width × length
= 3 × 4 = 12 m²

○ Square metres and square millimetres are used for the units of area.

○ These are written as m² or mm².

Measuring volume and capacity

Volume is concerned with the space taken up by a solid object. The room in Fig 2.51 is 4 m wide by 5 m long and 3 m high, so it has a volume of 60 cubic metres, written as 60 m³.

Volume = width × length × height
= 4 × 5 × 3
= 60 m³

Window

4 m length

3 m width

Door

2.50 Floor plan

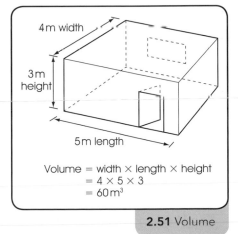

4 m width

3 m height

5 m length

Volume = width × length × height
= 4 × 5 × 3
= 60 m³

2.51 Volume

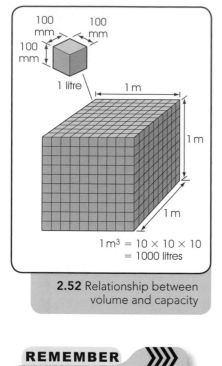

100 mm   100 mm
100 mm
1 litre   1 m
1 m
1 m
1 m

$1\,m^3 = 10 \times 10 \times 10$
$= 1000$ litres

2.52 Relationship between volume and capacity

⬡ Three linear measurements multiplied together give the volume.

⬡ Cubic metres and cubic millimetres are used for the units of volume.

⬡ These are written as m^3 or mm^3.

Capacity is concerned with the amount of space taken up by liquids or the amount of liquid that can fit into a given volume.

The litre is the unit of capacity. To avoid confusion with the number 1, 'litre' is best written in full or as 'L'.

⬡ The millilitre (ml) is the sub-multiple.

⬡ 1 litre = 1000 ml.

⬡ 1 ml = 0.001 L.

Capacity is linked to volume.

REMEMBER ⟫⟫

1 tonne = 1000 kg
1 kg = 1000 g
1 g = 1000 mg
1 mg = 0.001 g
1 g = 0.001 kg
1 kg = 0.001 tonne

EXAMPLE

$1\frac{2}{3}$

A carton $100 \times 100 \times 100$ mm encloses a volume of $0.1 \times 0.1 \times 0.1$ m $= 0.001\,m^3$.

This volume holds a litre of water.

It would, therefore, take 1000 of these cartons to fill $1\,m^3$.

Imperial to metric conversion

Comparisons between imperial and metric units of measurement can be made using the following information:

1 inch = 25.4 mm	1 litre = 0.22 gallons or 1.76 pints
12 inches = 1 foot = 0.3048 m or 304.8 mm	1 ml = 0.035 fluid oz
3 feet = 1 yard = 0.9144 m or 914.4 mm	1 ton = 2240 lb (pound)
1 m = 1.0936 yards or 3.281 feet	112 lb = 1 cwt (hundredweight)
1 yard² = 0.836 m²	14 lb = 1 st (stone)
1 m² = 1.196 yard² or 10.76 feet²	1 lb = 16 oz (ounces)
1 m³ = 1.31 yard³ or 35.335 feet³	1 tonne = 2205 lb
1 gallon = 8 pints	1 kg = 2.2 lb
1 pint = 20 fluid oz (ounces)	30 g = 1 oz

Measuring mass or weight

Mass is concerned with the weight of an object. The unit of mass is the kilogram (kg). Its multiple is the tonne (to avoid confusion with the imperial ton, no abbreviation is used). The sub-multiple unit is the gram (g). For very small objects, the sub-sub-multiple milligram (mg) is used.

Money

Pounds (£) and pence (p) are the UK monetary units:
£1 (pound) = 100 p (pence).

- ⬡ £6.50 = 6 pounds 50 pence and is often read as 'six pounds fifty'

- ⬡ £9.07 = 9 pounds 7 pence and is read as either '9 pounds 7' or '9 pounds 7 pence'.

It is important to remember the zeros, as they keep the place for the missing units and tens. Calculations with money can be simply undertaken using the previously covered rules of numbers.

EXAMPLE

Add £10.65 and £32.40

```
  10.65
  32.40 +
 ‾‾‾‾‾‾
  43.05
```

ANSWER: 43.05

DID YOU KNOW

Time and angular measurement are the only units in everyday use that are not based on multiples of 10.

EXAMPLE

You give a £10 note to pay for a £6.47 lock. What is the change?

£10 – £6.47

```
  10.00
   6.47 –
 ‾‾‾‾‾‾
   3.53
```

ANSWER: There is £3.53 change

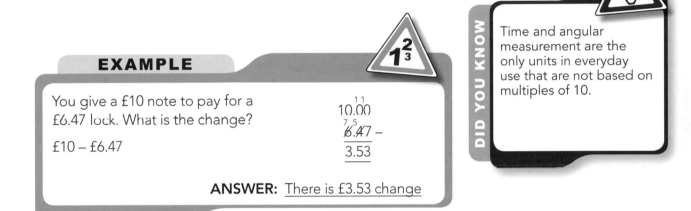

EXAMPLE

Four people are to get an equal share of £145 as a bonus. How much will each receive?

£145 ÷ 4

```
      36.25
   4)145
      12
     ‾‾‾
      25
      24
     ‾‾‾
      10
       8
     ‾‾‾
      20
```

ANSWER: Each will receive £36.25

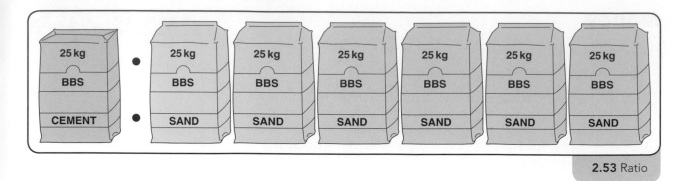

2.53 Ratio

Ratio and proportions

Ratios and proportions are ways of comparing or stating the relationship between two similar or related quantities. A bricklaying mortar mix may be described as 1:6 ('one to six'). This means the ratio or proportion of the mix is 1 part cement to 6 parts sand (or aggregate).

You could use bags, buckets or barrows as the unit of measure and, providing the proportions are kept the same, they will make a suitable mortar mix. All that changes is the volume of mortar produced.

To share a quantity in a given ratio:

⬡ add up the total number of parts or shares

⬡ work out what one part is worth

⬡ work out what the other parts are worth.

EXAMPLE

$1\frac{2}{3}$

If £72 is to be shared by two people in a ration of 5:3, what will each receive?

Number of shares = 5 + 3 = 8

One share = 72 ÷ 8 = £9

Five shares = 5 × 9 = £45

Three shares = 3 × 9 = £27

ANSWER: they will receive £45 and £27

EXAMPLE

A 1:3 ('one in three') pitched roof has a span of 3.6 m: what is its rise? This means for every 3 m span the roof will rise 1 m.

Rise = Span ÷ 3

$$\begin{array}{r} 1.2 \\ 3\overline{\smash{\big)}\,3.6} \end{array}$$

ANSWER: The rise is 1.2 m

Percentages

This is a standard way of representing a portion or part of a total quantity. Percentage (%) means 'per hundred' or 'per cent'.

In the diagram in the margin, four squares out of 80 have been filled in. What part or portion of the total do these four squares make? We can write this in four ways:

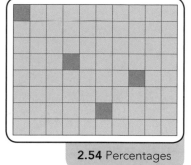

2.54 Percentages

○ **Proportion**: 4 in 80 of the squares have been filled in.

○ **Ratio**: 4/80 of the squares have been filled in.

○ **Percentage**: 5 per cent of the squares have been filled in.

○ **Decimal**: 0.05 of the squares have been filled in.

Converting to a percentage
If you need to convert a number to a percentage:

○ First divide the number by the total, i.e. $\frac{4}{80} = 0.05$

○ Then multiply by 100 to find the percentage, i.e. 0.05 × 100 = 5%

Converting from a percentage
If you need to convert a percentage to a number:

○ First divide the number by 100, i.e. 5% ÷ 100 = 0.05

○ Then multiply by the total quantity, i.e. 0.05 × 80 = 4

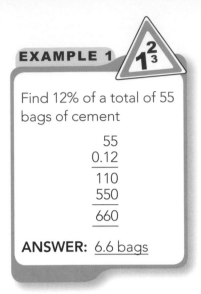

EXAMPLE 1

Find 12% of a total of 55 bags of cement

$$
\begin{array}{r}
55 \\
0.12 \\
\hline
110 \\
550 \\
\hline
660 \\
\end{array}
$$

ANSWER: 6.6 bags

Using percentages

There are three circumstances where percentages are used:

1   Where a straightforward percentage of a number is required: turn the percentage into decimal and multiply the total by it (see example 1).

2   Where a number plus a certain percentage (increase) is required: turn the percentage into decimal, place a one in front of it to include the original quantity and multiply by it (see example 2).

EXAMPLE 2

Find 55 plus 12%

55 + 12% = 55 + 6.6 (see above example) = 61.6 bags.

Alternatively, multiply 55 by 1.12:

$$
\begin{array}{r}
55 \\
1.12 \\
\hline
110 \\
550 \\
5500 \\
\hline
6160 \\
\end{array}
$$

ANSWER: 61.6 bags

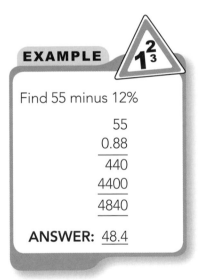

EXAMPLE

Find 55 minus 12%

$$
\begin{array}{r}
55 \\
0.88 \\
\hline
440 \\
4400 \\
\hline
4840 \\
\end{array}
$$

ANSWER: 48.4

3   Where a number minus a certain percentage (decrease) is required: take away percentage from 100, convert to decimal and then multiply by it.

Powers and roots of numbers

Powers

A simple way of writing repeated multiplications of the same number is:

⬡ $10 \times 10 = 100$ or 10^2

⬡ $10 \times 10 \times 10 = 1000$ or 10^3

⬡ $10 \times 10 \times 10 \times 10 = 10\,000$ or 10^4

The small raised number is called the power or index. Numbers raised to the power 2 are usually called square numbers. We say 10^2 is '10 squared', and 10^3 is '10 cubed' but we say 10^4 is '10 to the power 4'.

Roots

It is sometimes necessary to find a particular root of a number. Finding a root of a number is the opposite process of finding the power of a number. So the square root is a number multiplied by itself:

The square of 5 is 5^2 or $5 \times 5 = 25$.

Therefore the square root of 25 is 5.

The common way of writing this is to use the square root sign $\sqrt{\ }$. For example $\sqrt{25} = 5$.

Calculating roots

Roots of a number can be found using a calculator with a $\sqrt{\ }$ function key.

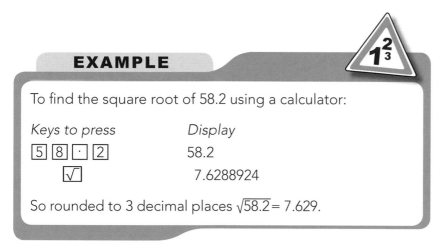

EXAMPLE

To find the square root of 58.2 using a calculator:

Keys to press	Display
5 8 · 2	58.2
√	7.6288924

So rounded to 3 decimal places $\sqrt{58.2} = 7.629$.

Formulae

Formulae are normally stated in algebraic terms. Algebra uses letters and symbols instead of numbers to simplify statements and allow general rules and relationships to be worked out.

Transposition of formulae

When solving a problem, sometimes formulae have to be rearranged to change the subject of the formulae before the calculation is carried out. Basically anything can be moved from one side of the equals sign to the other by changing its symbol.

This means that on crossing the equals sign:

- Plus changes to minus
- Multiplication changes to division
- Powers change to roots.

This is also true vice versa.

Alternatively, we can cross-multiply. This means that on crossing the equals sign anything on the top line moves to the bottom line, and conversely anything on the bottom line moves to the top line.

Triangles

Area

The area of a triangle can be found by using the formula:

Area = Base × Height ÷ 2.

If we say:

- Area = A
- Base = B
- Height = H

Then: $A = B \times H \div 2$. Using algebra, we can abbreviate by missing out the multiplication sign (×) and expressing a division in its fractional form.

$$A = \frac{BH}{2} \text{ means the same as}$$

$$A = B \times H \div 2$$

Height

If the area and base of a triangle are known but we wanted to find out its height, the formula could be transposed to make the height the subject.

$$\text{Area} = \text{Base} \times \text{Height} \div 2$$

$$A = \frac{BH}{2}$$

$$\text{Then } \frac{A}{B} = \frac{H}{2}$$

EXAMPLE

Find the area of a triangle having a base of 2.5 m and a height of 4.8 m

$$\text{Area} = \text{Base} \times \text{height} \div 2$$

$$A = \frac{B \times H}{2}$$

$$= \frac{2.5 \times 4.8}{2}$$

$$= \frac{12}{2}$$

$$= 6$$

ANSWER: Area = 6 m²

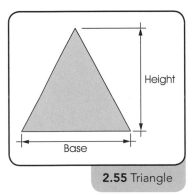

2.55 Triangle

EXAMPLE

Find the height of a triangle having an area of 4.5 m and a base of 1.5 m

$$\text{Area} = \frac{\text{Base} \times \text{height}}{2}$$

$$A = \frac{BH}{2}$$

$$\frac{2A}{B} = H$$

$$\frac{2 \times 4.5}{1.5} = H$$

$$6 = H$$

ANSWER: Height = 6 m

(B moves from above to below on crossing the = sign)

And $\dfrac{2A}{B} = H$

(2 moves from below to above on crossing the = sign)

Therefore, Height = 2 × Area ÷ Base

Rectangles

Perimeter

The perimeter of a rectangle can be found by using the formulae:

Perimeter = 2 × (Length + Breadth)

This can be abbreviated to: P = 2(L + B).

Plus and minus (+ and –) signs cannot be abbreviated and must always be shown in the formulae. To obtain the correct answer, L must be added to B before multiplying by 2.

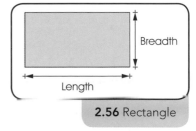

2.56 Rectangle

Circles

Perimeter and diameter

The formula for the perimeter or circumference of a circle is:

Circumference = π × Diameter

Which can be abbreviated to C = π × D

REMEMBER

For the correct order of working you must use the 'BODMAS' rule (see page 128).

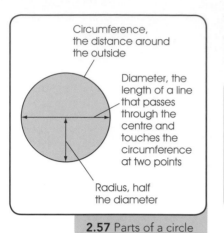

Circumference, the distance around the outside

Diameter, the length of a line that passes through the centre and touches the circumference at two points

Radius, half the diameter

2.57 Parts of a circle

The symbol π (spoken as pi) is used to represent the number of times that the diameter will divide into the circumference. It is the same for any circle and is taken to be 3.142.

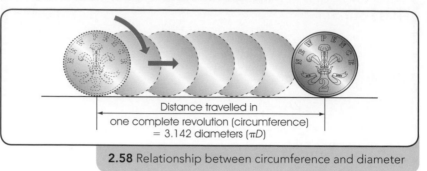

Distance travelled in
one complete revolution (circumference)
= 3.142 diameters (πD)

2.58 Relationship between circumference and diameter

Suppose we were given the circumference and asked to find the diameter.

Since $C = \pi \times D$, then $C \div \pi = D$ (π is moved across = and changes from $\times$ to $\div$). Hence:

$$\text{Diameter} = \text{Circumference} \div \pi$$

EXAMPLE

For the diameter of a circle having a circumference of 7.855 m

$$\text{Circumference} = \pi \times \text{Diameter}$$
$$C = \pi \times D$$
$$C \div \pi = D$$
$$= 7.855 \div 3.142$$
$$= 2.5$$

ANSWER: Diameter = 2.5 m

Calculating perimeters and areas

Values of common shapes can be found by using the following formulae:

⬡ The **perimeter** of a figure is the distance or length around its boundary, linear measurement, usually given in metres run (m).

⬡ The **area** of a figure is the extent of its surface, square measurement, usually given in square metres (m^2).

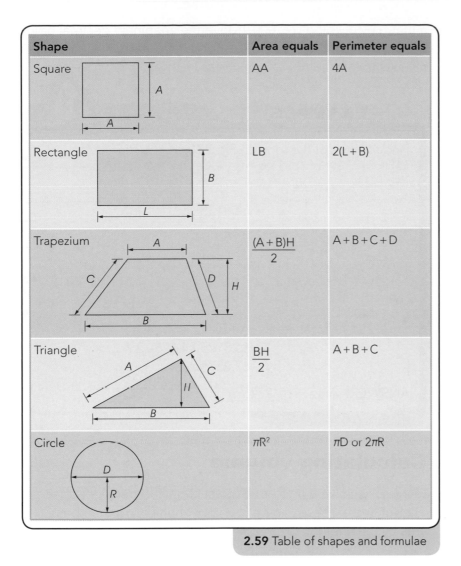

Shape		Area equals	Perimeter equals
Square		AA	4A
Rectangle		LB	2(L + B)
Trapezium		$\dfrac{(A + B)H}{2}$	A + B + C + D
Triangle		$\dfrac{BH}{2}$	A + B + C
Circle		πR^2	πD or $2\pi R$

2.59 Table of shapes and formulae

Complex areas

Complex areas can be calculated by breaking them into a number of recognisable areas and solving each one in turn, for example the area of the room shown in Fig 2.60 is equal to area A plus area B minus area C.

Converting to the same units

We can only multiply where there are the same units of measurement. Where metres and millimetres are contained in the same problem, first convert the millimetres into a decimal part of

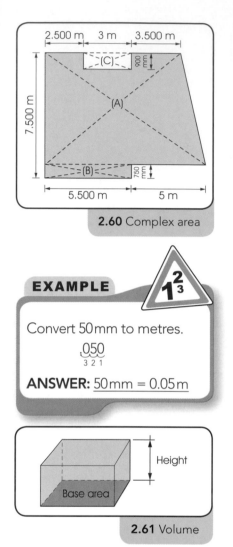

2.60 Complex area

a metre by dividing by 1000. (Move the imaginary decimal point behind the number three places forward.) Alternatively, convert all units to millimetres.

EXAMPLE 1^2_3

Find the area of the room in Fig 2.60.

$$\text{Area A} = \left(\frac{9+10.5}{2}\right) \times 6.75$$
$$= 65.8125\,\text{m}^2$$

$$\text{Area B} = 0.75 \times 5.5$$
$$= 4.125\,\text{m}^2$$

$$\text{Area C} = 0.9 \times 3$$
$$= 2.7\,\text{m}^2$$

$$\text{Total area} \quad \text{A} + \text{B} - \text{C}$$
$$65.8125 + 4.125 - 2.7$$
$$67.2375\,\text{m}^2$$

ANSWER: Area = <u>67.2375 m²</u>

EXAMPLE 1^2_3

Convert 50 mm to metres.

.050
3 2 1

ANSWER: <u>50 mm = 0.05 m</u>

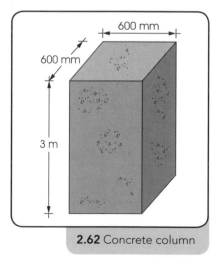

2.61 Volume

Calculating volume

Many solids have a uniform cross-section and parallel edges. The volume of these can be found by multiplying their base area by their height:

Volume = Base area × Height

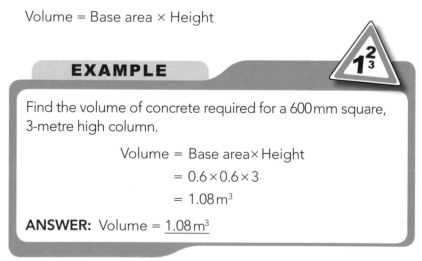

2.62 Concrete column

EXAMPLE 1^2_3

Find the volume of concrete required for a 600 mm square, 3-metre high column.

$$\text{Volume} = \text{Base area} \times \text{Height}$$
$$= 0.6 \times 0.6 \times 3$$
$$= 1.08\,\text{m}^3$$

ANSWER: Volume = <u>1.08 m³</u>

EXAMPLE

Find the volume of a cylinder having a radius of 0.6 m and a height of 2.4 m.

Volume = Base area × Height

$$= \pi r^2 \times H$$

$$= 3.142 \times 0.6 \times 0.6 \times 2.4$$

$$= 2.714688$$

ANSWER: Volume = $\underline{2.715\,m^3}$ (rounded to 3 decimal places)

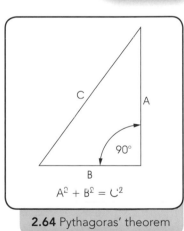

2.63 Cylinder

Pythagoras' theorem

The lengths of the sides in a right-angled triangle can be found using Pythagoras' theorem. According to this theorem, in any right-angled triangle the square of the length of the longest side is equal to the sum of the squares of the other two sides.

If we know the lengths of two sides of a right-angled triangle, we can use Pythagoras' theorem to find the length of the third side. In fact, this theorem forms the basis of pitched roof calculations.

EXAMPLE

Calculate the length of the common rafter shown in Fig 2.65.

A = Rise 2.1 m
B = Run 2.8 m
C = Common rafter

$$= A^2 + B^2 = C^2$$

$$= 2.1^2 + 2.8^2 = C^2$$

$$= 4.41 + 7.84 = 12.25$$

Therefore:
$$C = \sqrt{12.25} = 3.5\,m$$

ANSWER: The common rafter is 3.5 m long

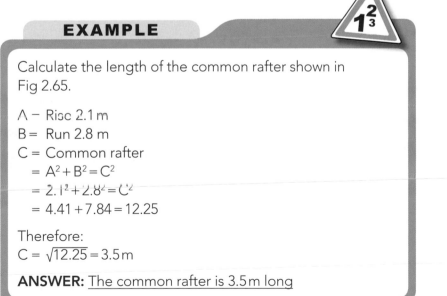

$$A^2 + B^2 = C^2$$

2.64 Pythagoras' theorem

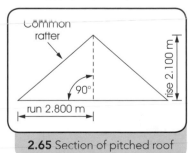

2.65 Section of pitched roof

Measuring materials

Timber

Where timber is sold by the cubic metre, you may be required to calculate the metres run of a particular cross-section that can be obtained from it.

To calculate the metres run of a section that can be obtained from a cubic metre, divide the cross-sectional area of a cubic metre (in square millimetres) by the cross-sectional area of the section required.

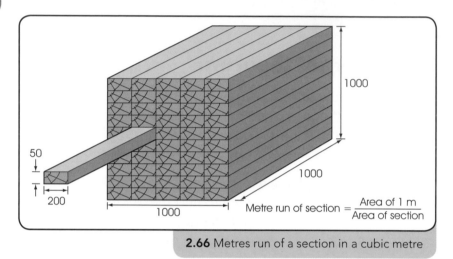

$$\text{Metre run of section} = \frac{\text{Area of 1 m}}{\text{Area of section}}$$

2.66 Metres run of a section in a cubic metre

Flooring

In order to determine the amount of floor covering materials required for an area, multiply its width by its length.

Floorboards

To calculate the metres run of floorboards required to cover a floor area of say 4.65 m², if the floorboards have a covering width of 137 mm:

Metres run required = Area ÷ Width of board

$$= 4.65 \div 0.137$$

$$= 33.94\,\text{m}$$

say, 34 m run

It is standard practice to order an additional amount of flooring to allow for cutting and wastage. This is often between 10 and 15 per cent.

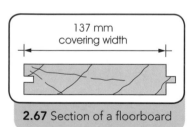

137 mm
covering width

2.67 Section of a floorboard

If 34-metre run of floor boarding is required to cover an area, calculate the amount to be ordered including an additional 12 per cent for cutting and wastage.

$$\text{Amount to be ordered} = 34 \times 1.12$$
$$= 38.08, \text{ say } 38\,\text{m run}$$

In order to determine the number of sheets of plywood, chipboard or plasterboard required to cover a floor or ceiling either:

- divide area of room by area of sheet, or

- divide width of room by width of sheet and divide length of room by length of sheet. Convert these numbers to the nearest whole or half and multiply them together.

To calculate the number of $600 \times 2400\,\text{mm}$ chipboard sheets required to cover a floor area of $2.05 \times 3.6\,\text{m}$:

EXAMPLE

$1\tfrac{2}{3}$

2.68 Area of floor

Number of sheets required	= Area of room ÷ Area of sheet
Area of room	= 2.05 m × 3.6 m
	= 7.38 m²
Area of sheet	= 0.6 m × 2.4 m
	= 1.44 m²
Number of sheets	= 7.38 × 1.44
	= 5.125, say 6 sheets

Alternatively:

Number of sheet widths in room width	= 2.05 ÷ 0.6
	= 3.417, say 3.5
Number of sheet lengths in room length	= 3.6 ÷ 2.4
	= 1.5
Total number of sheets	= 3.5 × 1.5
	= 5.25, say 6 sheets

Joists

To determine the number of joists required and their centres for a particular area, the following procedure can be used:

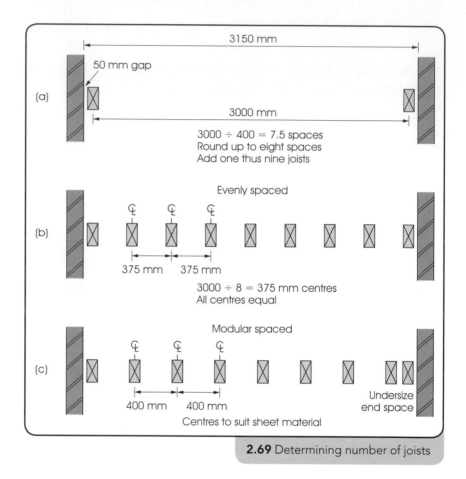

2.69 Determining number of joists

⬡ Measure the distance between adjacent walls, say 3150 mm.

⬡ The first and last joist would be positioned 50 mm away from the walls. The centres of 50 mm breadth joists would be 75 mm away from the wall. The total distance between end joists centres would be 3000 mm. (See Fig 2.69 (a).)

⬡ Divide the distance between end joist centres by the specified joist spacing, say 400 mm. This gives the number of spaces between joists. Where a whole number is not achieved, round up to the nearest whole number above. There will always be one more joist than the numbers of spaces, so add another one to this figure to determine the number of joists. (See Fig 2.69 (b).)

◯ Where T&G boarding is used as a floor covering, the joist centres may be spaced out evenly (i.e. divide the distance between end joist centres by the number of spaces).

◯ Where sheet material is used as a joist covering to form a floor, ceiling or roof surface, the joist centres are normally maintained at 400 mm or 600 mm module spacing to coincide with sheet sizes. This would leave an undersized spacing between the last two joists. (See Fig 2.69 (c).)

Stud partitions

To determine the number of studs required for a particular partition, the following procedure can be used:

◯ Measure the distance between the adjacent walls of the room or area, which the partition is to divide, say 3400 mm (see Fig 2.70).

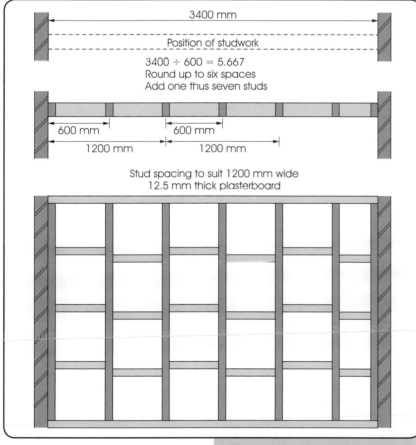

3400 mm

Position of studwork

3400 ÷ 600 = 5.667
Round up to six spaces
Add one thus seven studs

600 mm

600 mm

1200 mm

1200 mm

Stud spacing to suit 1200 mm wide
12.5 mm thick plasterboard

2.70 Determining number of studs

○ Divide the distance between the walls by the specified spacing, say 600 mm. This gives the number of spaces between the studs. Use the whole number above. There will always be one more stud than the number of spaces, so add one to this figure to determine the number of studs. Stud centres must be maintained to suit sheet material sizes leaving an undersized space between the last two studs.

○ The lengths of head and sole plates are simply the distance between the two walls.

○ Each line of noggins will require a length of timber equal to the distance between the walls.

The total length of timber required for a partition can be determined by using the following method:

○ Seven studs at 2.4 mm: $7 \times 2.4 = 16.8$ m

○ Head and sole plates at 3.4 m: $2 \times 3.4 = 6.8$ m

○ Three lines of noggins at 3.4 m: $3 \times 3.4 = 10.2$ m

○ Total metres run required: $16.8 + 6.8 + 10.2 = 33.8$ m, say 34 m.

○ Again, it is normal to allow for cutting, thus add say 10 per cent: $34 \times 1.1 = 37.4$ m, say 38 m.

Rafters

The number of rafters required for a pitched roof can be determined using the same method as used for floor joists. For

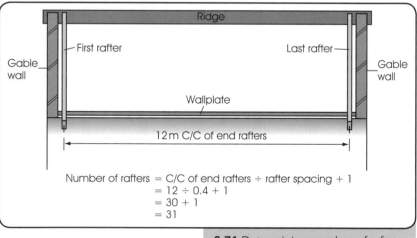

Number of rafters = C/C of end rafters ÷ rafter spacing + 1
= 12 ÷ 0.4 + 1
= 30 + 1
= 31

2.71 Determining number of rafters

example, divide the distance between the end rafter centres by the rafter spacing. Round up and add one. Remember to double the number of rafters to allow for both sides of the roof.

If the distance between end rafter centres is 12m and spacing is 400mm:

Number of rafters:

= Distance between end rafter centres ÷ Rafter spacing + 1

= 12 ÷ 0.4 + 1

= 30 + 1

= 31 rafters

Therefore, total number of rafters required for both sides of the roof is 62.

Where overhanging verges are required, additional rafters must be allowed at each end to form gable ladders, which provide a fixing for the bargeboard and soffit.

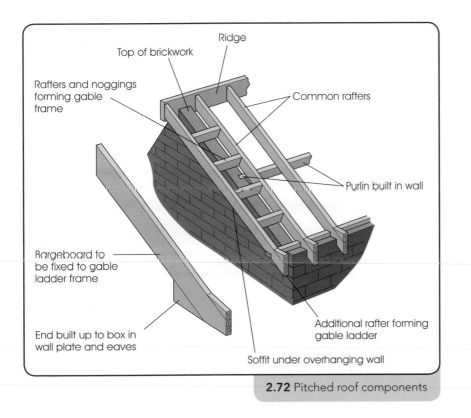

2.72 Pitched roof components

To determine the length of rafters, Pythagoras' theorem of right-angled triangles can be used. An allowance must be added to this length for the eaves overhang and the cutting. Say 0.5 m and 10 per cent.

Total length of rafter = 3.905 + 0.5 + 10%

$$= 4.405 \times 1.1$$

$$= 4.845\,m$$

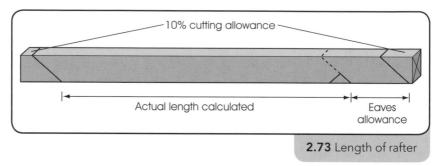

2.73 Length of rafter

EXAMPLE $1\frac{2}{3}$

Calculate the length of the common rafter shown.

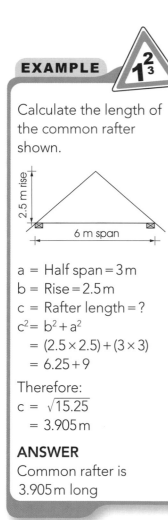

a = Half span = 3 m
b = Rise = 2.5 m
c = Rafter length = ?
$c^2 = b^2 + a^2$
   $= (2.5 \times 2.5) + (3 \times 3)$
   $= 6.25 + 9$

Therefore:
$c = \sqrt{15.25}$
  $= 3.905\,m$

ANSWER
Common rafter is 3.905 m long

Fascia, barge and soffits

Calculating the lengths of material required for fascia boards, bargeboards and soffits is often a simple matter of measuring, allowing a certain amount extra for jointing, and adding lengths together to determine total metres run. A hipped-end roof requires two 4.4-metre lengths and two 7.2-metre lengths of ex 25 × 150 mm PAR softwood for its fascia boards.

Metres run required = (4.4 × 2) + (7.2 × 2)

$$= 8.8 + 14.4$$

$$= 23.2\,m$$

Again, it is standard practice to allow a certain amount extra for cutting and jointing, say 10 per cent.

Total metres run required = 23.2 × 1.1

$$= 25.52\,m$$

The length of timber for bargeboards may require calculation using Pythagoras' theorem for right-angled triangles.

Sheet material

Where sheet material is used for fascias and soffits, the amount that can be cut from a full sheet often needs calculating. This entails dividing the width of the sheet by the width of the fascia or soffit, and then using the resulting whole number to multiply by the sheet's length, to give the total metres run.

EXAMPLE

$1\frac{2}{3}$

Determine the total metres run of 150 mm wide soffit board that may be cut from a 1220 mm × 2440 mm sheet.

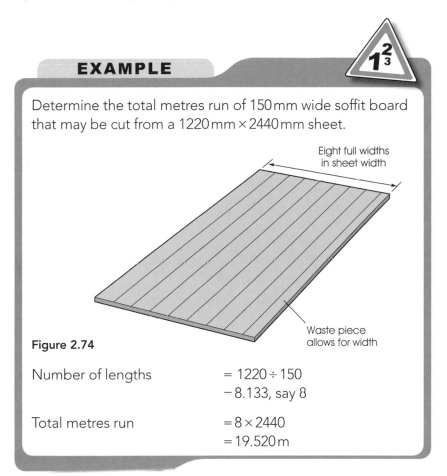

Eight full widths in sheet width

Waste piece allows for width

Figure 2.74

Number of lengths	= 1220 ÷ 150
	− 8.133, say 8
Total metres run	= 8 × 2440
	= 19.520 m

Trim

Determining the amount of trim required for any particular task is a fairly simple process, if the following procedures are used.

Architraves

The jambs or legs in most situations can be taken to be 2100 mm long. The head can be taken to be 1000 mm. These lengths assume a standard full-size door and include an allowance for mitring the ends. Thus, the length of architrave required for one face of a door lining/frame is 5200 mm or 5.2 m.

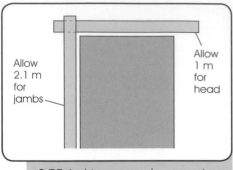

2.75 Architrave to a door opening

Multiply this figure by the number of architrave sets to be fixed. This will determine the total metres run required, say eight sets, both sides of four doors:

$$5.2 \times 8 = 41.6\,\text{m}$$

Skirting, dado and picture rails

Horizontal trim can be estimated from the perimeter. This is found by adding up the lengths of the walls in the area. The widths of any doorways and other openings are taken away to give the actual metres run required.

EXAMPLE

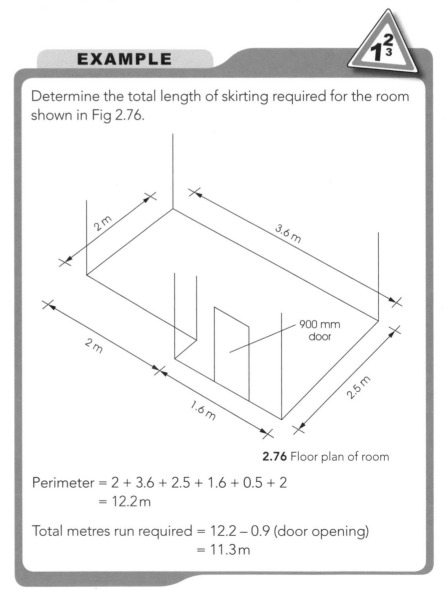

Determine the total length of skirting required for the room shown in Fig 2.76.

2.76 Floor plan of room

Perimeter = 2 + 3.6 + 2.5 + 1.6 + 0.5 + 2
         = 12.2 m

Total metres run required = 12.2 − 0.9 (door opening)
                 = 11.3 m

Allowing 10 per cent for cutting and jointing the total metres run required is:

= 11.3 × 1.13

= 12.43, say 13 m

Brickwork and mortar

There are 60 bricks per m² in half brick thick walls and 120 bricks per m² in one brick thick walls. An additional percentage of 5 per cent is normally allowed for cutting and damaged bricks.

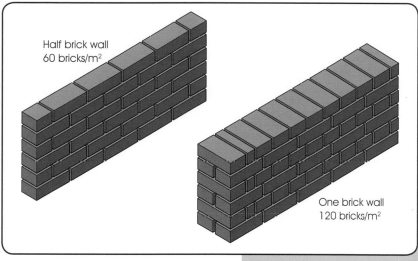

Half brick wall 60 bricks/m²

One brick wall 120 bricks/m²

2.77 Half and one brick walls

Approximately, 1 kg of mortar is required to lay one brick. This figure can be used for small areas of new brickwork and making good. A 25 kg bag of mortar mix is sufficient to lay up to 25 bricks, depending on the thickness of joints. One 25 kg bag of cement and six 25 kg bags of sand are sufficient to lay up to 175 bricks using a 1:6 cement–sand ratio.

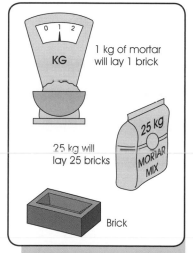

1 kg of mortar will lay 1 brick

25 kg will lay 25 bricks

Brick

2.78 Relationship between number of bricks and mortar

For larger areas of brickwork, the amount of mortar can be assessed as 0.03 m³ per square metre of brickwork or 0.5 m³ per 1000 bricks for half brick walls. Just over double the amount per square metre if required for one brick walls, 0.07 m³, or 0.58 m³ per 1000 bricks. An additional percentage of 10 per cent is normally allowed for wastage.

Where brickwork returns around corners, as in a building, the wall's centre line length is used to calculate the area.

Calculate the number of bricks and amount of mortar required for a half brick wall 3m high and 5m long, allow 5% extra for cutting and 10% for mortar.

Area of wall	= Height × Length
	= 3 × 5
	= 15 m²

Number of bricks required	= Area × Number of bricks per m²
	= 15 × 60
	= 900 bricks

| 5% allowance | = 900 × 1.05 |
| | = 945 bricks |

Amount of mortar	= Area × Mortar/m²
	= 15 × 0.03
	= 0.45 m²

| 10% allowance | = 0.45 × 1.1 |
| | = 0.495 m³, say 0.5 m³ |

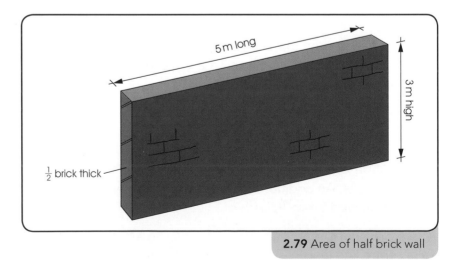

5m long

3m high

½ brick thick

2.79 Area of half brick wall

EXAMPLE

Calculate the number of bricks and the amount of mortar required to form a half brick wall 2.4 m high and 6 m long, containing a 2.1 × 0.9 m door opening and a 0.6 × 2.2 m window opening.

Area of brickwork	= Total area – Area of door and window
Total area	= 2.4 × 6
	= 144 m²
Area of door	= 2.1 × 0.9
	= 1.89 m²
Area of window	= 0.6 × 2.2
	= 1.32 m²

Therefore:

Area of brickwork	= 14.4 – 1.89 – 1.32
	= 11.19 m²
Number of bricks	= Area × Number of bricks/m²
	= 11.19 × 60
	= 671.4, say 672
5% allowance	= 672 × 1.05
	=705.6, say 706
Amount of mortar	= Area × Mortar/m²
	= 11.19 × 0.03
	= 0.336 m³
10% allowance	= 0.336 × 1.1
	= 0.369 m³

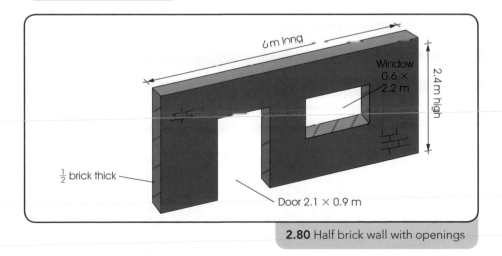

2.80 Half brick wall with openings

Blockwork and mortar

There are approximately ten 450 × 215 mm blocks per square metre. An additional allowance of 5 per cent may be added for cutting and damaged blocks. Each m² of 100 mm thick blocks can be assessed as requiring m³ of mortar. An allowance of 10 per cent is normally added for wastage.

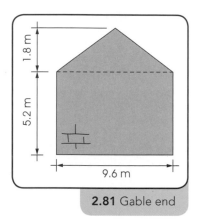

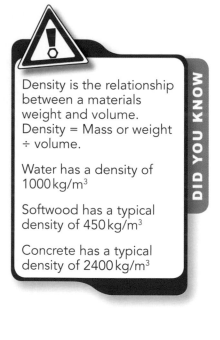

2.81 Gable end

Density is the relationship between a materials weight and volume. Density = Mass or weight ÷ volume.

Water has a density of 1000 kg/m³

Softwood has a typical density of 450 kg/m³

Concrete has a typical density of 2400 kg/m³

DID YOU KNOW

ACTIVITY

Calculate the number of 450 × 215 mm blocks and mortar required for the inner leaf of the gable end (Fig 2.81). Allow 5 per cent extra on the blocks and 10 per cent extra on the mortar.

EXAMPLE

Area of blockwork	= Triangular area + Rectangular area
Area of triangle	= Base × Height + 2
	= 9.6 × 1.8 ÷ 2
	= 8.64 m²
Area of rectangle	= Length × Height
	= 9.6 × 5.2
	= 49.92 m²
Total area	= 8.6 ÷ 49.92
	= 58.56 m²
Number of blocks	= Area × Number of blocks per m²
	= 58.56 × 10
	= 584.6 blocks
5% allowance	= 585.6 × 1.05
	= 614.8, say 615 blocks
Amount of mortar	= Area × Mortar per m²
	= 58.56 × 0.01
	= 0.685 m³
10% allowance	= 0.586 × 1.1
	= 0.644 m³

Blockwork walls with returns and openings are calculated in the same ways as those in brickwork using the centre line length when working out the area.

Dry materials

Mortar

The density of mortar is typically $2000\,kg/m^3$. Different mixes are specified for different situations.

A 1:6 mix contains 7 parts:

○ 1 part cement

○ 6 parts sand (fine aggregate).

A 1:1:8 mix contains 10 parts:

○ 1 part cement

○ 1 part lime

○ 8 parts sand.

To determine dry materials for a given quantity of mortar, multiply volume by density for total mass and divide by number of parts. This gives the amount of cement; multiply cement by required number of parts to give other quantities.

$1\frac{2}{3}$

EXAMPLE

For $0.5\,m^3$ of 1:6 mortar:

Mass of mortar	$= 0.5 \times 2000 = 1000\,kg$
Number of parts in mix	$= 7$
Amount of cement	$= 1000 \div 7$ $= 142.857\,kg$, say $6 \times 25\,kg$ bags
Amount of sand	$= 142.857 \times 6$ $= 857.142\,kg$, say almost 1 tonne or $35 \times 25\,kg$ bags

Mixed on-site concrete

It is necessary to determine the amount of cement, fine and coarse aggregates for ordering. The density of compacted concrete is typically 2400 kg/m³.

A mix of 1:3:6 contains 10 parts:

○ 1 part cement

○ 3 parts fine aggregate

○ 6 parts coarse aggregate.

To determine dry materials for a given quantity of concrete, multiply volume by density, which gives total mass, and then divide by the number of parts. This gives the amount of cement; multiply cement by 3 to give fine aggregate and then multiply cement by 6 to give coarse aggregate.

EXAMPLE

$1\frac{2}{3}$

For 2.5 m³ of 1:3:6 concrete:

| Mass of concrete | = 2.5 × 2400 |
| | = 6000 kg |

| Number of part | = 10 |

| Amount of cement | = 6000 ÷ 10 |
| | = 600 kg or 24 × 25 kg bags |

| Amount of fine aggregate | = 600 × 3 |
| | = 1800 kg, say almost two 1 tonne bags or 72 × 25 kg bags |

| Amount of coarse aggregate | = 600 × 6 |
| | = 3600 kg, say almost four 1 tonne bags or 144 × 25 kg bags |

Tiles and paving slabs

For a particular area, tiles and slabs can be calculated using the following method:

○ Determine the total area to be covered in m².

○ Determine the total area of a tile or slab in m².

○ Divide the area to be covered by the area of the tile or slab.

○ Add percentage for cutting and waste (typically 5–10 per cent).

To determine the number of 150 mm square tiles required for a kitchen floor see the example in the margin.

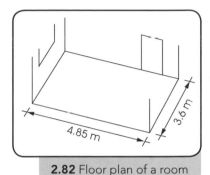

2.82 Floor plan of a room

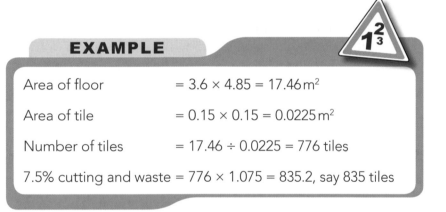

EXAMPLE $1\frac{2}{3}$

Area of floor	$= 3.6 \times 4.85 = 17.46\,m^2$
Area of tile	$= 0.15 \times 0.15 = 0.0225\,m^2$
Number of tiles	$= 17.46 \div 0.0225 = 776$ tiles

7.5% cutting and waste $= 776 \times 1.075 = 835.2$, say 835 tiles

Paint

The paint required for a particular area can be calculated using the following method:

○ Determine the total area to be covered in m² (excluding any openings).

○ Divide the total area by the recommended covering capacity (coverage) of the paint to be used. This will give the number of litres required for one coat.

○ Multiply litres for one coat by number of coats, to give total litres required.

Determine the amount of paint required to paint the wall of a factory with two coats of emulsion. See the example on page 160.

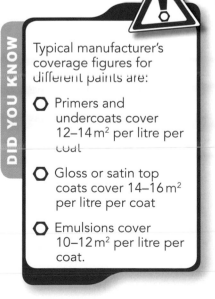

DID YOU KNOW

Typical manufacturer's coverage figures for different paints are:

○ Primers and undercoats cover 12–14 m² per litre per coat

○ Gloss or satin top coats cover 14–16 m² per litre per coat

○ Emulsions cover 10–12 m² per litre per coat.

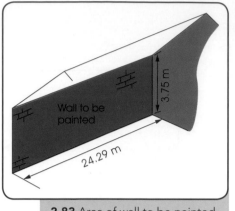

2.83 Area of wall to be painted

Area of wall = 24.29 × 3.75 = 91.0875 m²

Amount of paint for 1 coat = 91.0875 ÷ 10 (coverage per m²) = 9.10875 litres

Total amount of paint = 9.10875 × 2 (coats) = 18.2175 litres, say 20 litres or 4 × 5-litre tins.

Wallpaper

Most rolled wallpapers are made to a standard width of 530 mm and have a roll length of about 10 m. The wallpaper required for a particular area can be calculated using the following method:

⬡ Measure the length of the wall or perimeter of the room to be covered including door and windows and divide by the roll width to determine the number of strips required.

⬡ For plain paper without a repeating pattern, divide the length of the roll by the height of the room to determine the number of strips in a roll (where patterned paper with a drop repeat is being used the length of the repeat must be added to the room height, when determining the number of strips in a roll).

EXAMPLE

Determine the number of rolls of plain wallpaper required for the entire room shown in Fig 2.84.

Perimeter of room
= 3.9 + 4.97 + 2.7 + 2.47 + 1.2 + 2.5 = 17.74 m

Number of strips
= 17.74 ÷ 0.53 = 33.472 say 35 strips in total

Number of strips in roll
= 10 ÷ 2.35 = 4.255 say 4 strips per roll

Number of rolls required
= 35 ÷ 4 = 8.75 say 9 rolls

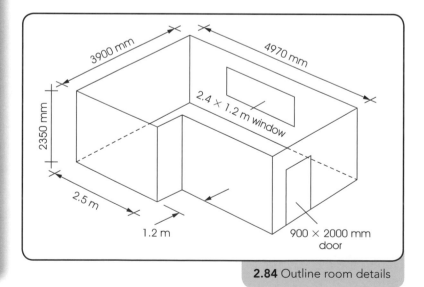

2.84 Outline room details

⬡ Divide the number of strips required for the whole area by the number of strips in a roll to determine the number of rolls required.

Alternatively, you can look up the number of rolls required using a typical wallpaper supplier's table. However, in general, you will get four strips per roll for ceiling heights up to 2.45 m using a plain paper, but this will reduce to three strips or even two strips, when using a repeating drop pattern or for higher ceilings.

Costing materials

Material costs can be carried out once the required quantities of material have been calculated. It is a simple matter of finding out prices and multiplying these by the number of items required, plus the addition of **VAT** if applicable.

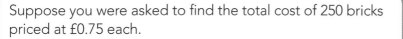

EXAMPLE

Suppose you were asked to find the total cost of 250 bricks priced at £0.75 each.

Total price = Price per brick × Number of bricks

= £0.75 × 250

= £187.50

If VAT is applicable, an additional 20 per cent needs to be added.

Thus, total price including VAT = £187.50 × 1.2 = £225.00

Costing labour

Labour costs for undertaking a particular task are based on the estimated amount of time required to complete the task, multiplied by the hourly charge out rate.

EXAMPLE

Suppose a carpenter is allowed 1.25 hrs to hang a door and the charge out rate is £30 an hour: the cost of hanging the door would
= 1.25 × 30 = £37.50.

Therefore, the cost of hanging 10 doors would
= £37.50 × 10 = £375.

DID YOU KNOW

Over estimating a contract will put the bid too high and may result in the company not getting the work. Under estimating will put the bid too low and involve financial loss to the company if the contract is won.

Estimating, quoting and tendering

Estimate, quotation, and tender are three words that are often thought to have the same meaning. Although they are linked, their meanings are very different.

○ An **estimate** is an educated or best guess as to what a job may cost. It should be a realistic evaluation of what the client can expect to be charged, but it's not binding.

○ A **quotation** is a fixed price for a fixed amount ('quota') of work carried out to a fixed specification. Adjustments to the final price can only be made if the client authorises additional work or deviates from the specification.

○ A **tender** is a formal bid document that is prepared by or for the client, which gives details of the work required to enable contractors to provide an estimate or quotation.

The tender process

○ **Tendering** is the competitive process. A contractor uses the information contained in the contract documents (drawings, schedules, specification and BOQ) prepared by the client team, to arrive at a price to carry out the specified works.

○ **Estimating** is the process where an estimator or estimating team using the contract documents, determine or calculate the costs of the material, labour, overheads, preliminaries and profit to be included in the tender bid.

○ **Material costs** are determined by calculating the amount required (including an amount for cutting and wastage) and applying the purchasing price. Materials are normally specified by the client or their architect, with the contractor being free to choose a supplier based on availability and cost. However, the client may demand a particular supplier (client nominated) in the contract documents, which the contractor must use.

○ **Labour costs** are determined from the estimated length of time required to complete each process and then applying an hourly rate. If using directly employed labour, the estimator may use standard company times, records of past performance, or estimating systems to determine length of time. The actual hourly rates applied to these times will depend on the company's charge out rates. Alternatively, companies may choose to use sub-contractors for part or all of the work, in which case the estimator will ask them to give a fixed price for undertaking each process. Again, the client may demand a particular sub-contractor for certain works in the contract documents.

- **Overheads** are the costs added to the material and labour rates to cover the cost of running the company, such as: staff salaries; head office costs, including rates; and plant machinery and consumable costs. These are often added as a fixed percentage of the costs of material and labour.

- **Preliminaries** are the costs associated with the setting up and running of a particular contract, such as temporary roadways, hoardings, welfare facilities, specialist equipment, site security and health and safety provision.

- **Adjudication** is the final stage in the tender process before a bid is submitted to the client. This is where the estimating team meets with the commercial team to review the estimate of labour and materials and agree the level of overheads and profit to be added. During this process, they will assess the potential financial implications and risks to the company in undertaking the contract and adjust rates accordingly.

Careful estimating is required at all stages of the tender process. It is essential that nothing has been over measured or overlooked, that all calculations are accurate and that the profit margin relates to the company and market conditions.

CHECK YOUR UNDERSTANDING

At levels 1 and 2:

⊘ Convert the following dimensions into metres:

1264 mm   920 mm   21 950 mm   68 mm

⊘ A rectangle has a length of 6.39 m and a breadth of 2.15 m:

a What is the area?   **b** What is the perimeter?

⊘ What is the area of a circle that has a diameter of 4.5 m?

⊘ The longest side in a right-angled triangle measures 5 m; one of the other sides is 3 m. What is the length of the remaining side?

⊘ How many metres run of floor boarding is required to cover a floor area of 12.825 m², if the floorboards have a covering width of 95 mm?

At level 2:

⊘ A concrete mix is expressed as 1:3:6, being the proportion of cement, fine aggregate and course aggregate. How much of each is required for 2.4 m³?

⊘ The Fig 2.85 shows the estimated costs for a building job, as a percentage of the total cost £8762.50. What is the estimated cost of the brickwork?

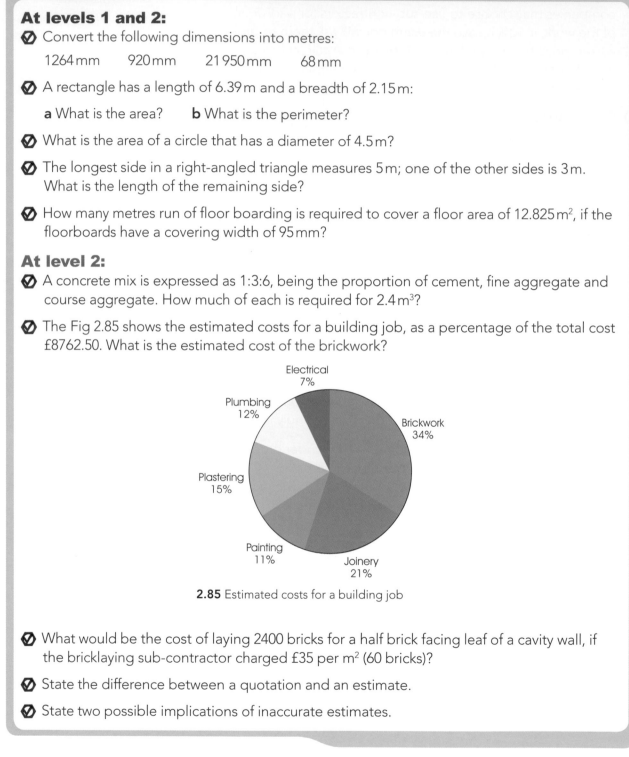

2.85 Estimated costs for a building job

⊘ What would be the cost of laying 2400 bricks for a half brick facing leaf of a cavity wall, if the bricklaying sub-contractor charged £35 per m² (60 bricks)?

⊘ State the difference between a quotation and an estimate.

⊘ State two possible implications of inaccurate estimates.

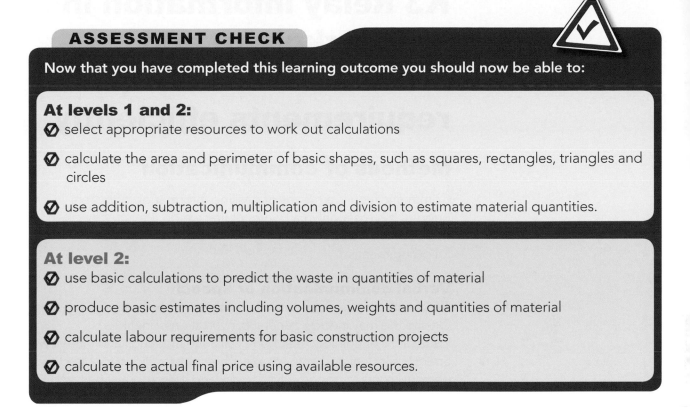

ASSESSMENT CHECK

Now that you have completed this learning outcome you should now be able to:

At levels 1 and 2:

- select appropriate resources to work out calculations

- calculate the area and perimeter of basic shapes, such as squares, rectangles, triangles and circles

- use addition, subtraction, multiplication and division to estimate material quantities.

At level 2:

- use basic calculations to predict the waste in quantities of material

- produce basic estimates including volumes, weights and quantities of material

- calculate labour requirements for basic construction projects

- calculate the actual final price using available resources.

K3 Relay information in the workplace and communicate workplace requirements efficiently

Methods of communication

Communication is a means of passing information between people. It is essential in all walks of life; we do it every day often without thinking about it, using one or a combination of the following means:

Verbal communication or speech

The most common form of communication is speaking and listening. On-site this may include general conversations; briefings, instructions or training; telephone calls; site meetings and interviews. Speech is instant and enables a quick response; allows for direct personal contact; opportunities to ask and answer questions; and seek clarification. However, there can be disadvantages:

- Disputes can arise at a later stage, as there are no written records that can be referred to.

- There may not always be enough time to think clearly or interpret what has been said and respond accordingly.

- Speech may not be the most effective method of communication where large numbers of people are involved.

- Often, it can be harder for an individual to voice a comment or criticism.

- Speech can often be misunderstood due to a poor grasp of the English language, regional accents or the use of slang language. Instructions might be passed on inconsistently or forgotten altogether.

Body language

This is the unspoken communication between people. A person's posture, facial expressions, eye contact and hand gestures can say more about them than their actual speech. However, body language is often misinterpreted.

ACTIVITY

Think of all the different types of communication you use in a day. Which do you find the most effective and why?

LINK

For more information on body language, see page 189 of this chapter.

Written or printed information

This may include writing or reading the following: orders; reports; forms; letters, memos; e-mails; notices; minutes of meetings; specifications; descriptions and BOQs. Written and printed information has a number of advantages over other methods of communication:

- O Can be used to provide confirmation of earlier verbal communications.

- O Complicated ideas and details can often be more easily understood.

- O Can be used to provide evidence of actions taken or tasks completed.

- O Can be referred to at a later stage in the event of a dispute or query.

- O Is evidence that a communication has taken place, can be re-read if not understood the first time and can be passed on to others consistently.

REMEMBER

Poor language skills and handwriting can cause confusion and misunderstandings.

Visual and graphic information

On-site this may include the interpretation or production of plans; drawings; details; sketches; tables; graphs; photographs; video; and architectural models. Visual communication is considered effective:

- O Complicated ideas and details are often easier to understand visually

- O Visual information clearly shows the whole process, details, methods and techniques.

- O Illustrations and visual aids help to reinforce spoken or written information.

- O Aids understanding for those with reading or language difficulties.

Electronic communications

This includes e-mails, text messages, faxes and the internet. This method combines the instant nature of verbal communication with the evidence trail of written communication.

REMEMBER >>>>

Site rules normally include all of the company's general policies and procedures. These should be explained to you when you are first employed. However, there may be variations or additional site rules that are specific to a particular site or workplace, such as hours of work, meal times and welfare arrangements.

Company policies, procedures and site rules

Companies have a range of policies, procedures and site rules that all employees are required to observe.

A policy states a programme of actions or a set of principles on which they are based. For example: a 'safety policy' will set out the company's approach to health and safety matters; likewise an 'environmental policy' will set out the company's approach with regards to protecting the environment.

Procedures lay out the correct method of doing something. For example, 'emergency procedures' will set out the actions, roles and responsibilities of individuals in an emergency situation; and a 'procurement procedure' will set out who is authorised to buy materials and equipment, etc. and which forms have to be completed.

Examples of other policies, procedures and statements
Mediation policy
Mediation is a way of resolving disputes or conflicts. An independent, impartial person (mediator) helps the individuals or groups reach a solution that's acceptable to all concerned. The mediator will talk to both sides either together or separately – they do not make judgments, decisions or decide outcomes.
Training and development records
Most employers have a training policy that sets out how it intends to equip its employees with the necessary skills and knowledge. This can include inductions, toolbox talks, in-house training, specialist training in the use of tools, equipment and materials, as well as formal qualifications. A record of training undertaken by employees should be kept by the employer.
Disciplinary procedures
A disciplinary or warning can be given for breach of an organisation's policies and procedures or for unsatisfactory conduct. Warnings can be either verbal or in writing and can lead to termination of employment. Many companies operate a 'three strike' system, where a verbal warning is given in the first instance, followed by a written warning. Failure to heed the written warning may lead to dismissal. Serious breaches such as theft, falsification of records, acts of violence or actions which put people in danger can result in instant dismissal.
Performance review procedures
A performance review or appraisal, is an evaluation of an employee's job performance. Normally this happens in an annual face-to-face meeting between the employee and their line manager or supervisor, as part of a personnel development programme. Recent successes and failures, personal strengths and weaknesses, disciplinary warnings and suitability for promotion or further training will be considered.
Mission statements
A mission statement defines a company's reason for existence and what it aims to do.

Positive and negative communication

Receiving positive communication can boost motivation and create a sense of achievement. Negative communication can damage confidence and reduce motivation.

LINK

For more information on site rules, see Inductions and toolbox talks on page 18 of Chapter 1.

When communicating, always try to sound **positive**. **Be clear**, so what's being communicated is understood. **Get to the point** without wandering off the subject or including unnecessary information. **Be personal**; the person you are communicating with should know that you are willing to take their concerns into account. **Listen** or take into account the other person's point of view; effective communication is a two-way process. **Think** before you speak or write to avoid misunderstandings or saying something you might later regret.

On occasions, it may be necessary to expose and tackle problem situations in order to resolve them. Highlight the positive to maintain people's desire to achieve and assist and do not sound negative. For example, instead of saying 'You made a right mess of this job', consider 'On this occasion, your work fell below your normal high standards'.

The building team

The construction of a building is a complex process that requires a team of professionals working and communicating with each other. As a group they are known as the building team and are a combination of the following parties:

Client	The person(s) who has a need for building work (e.g. the construction of a new house, office block or factory, or extension, repairs and alterations to existing buildings). The client is the most important member of the building team. The client is responsible for commissioning and financing the work.
Architect	Acts as the client's agent. Their role is to interpret the client's requirements, translate them, along with other specialist designers, into a building form and generally supervise all aspects of the work until it is completed.
Quantity surveyor	Acts as the client's economic consultant or accountant. They advise during the design stage as to how the work will fit into the client's budget and measure the quantity of labour and materials necessary to complete the project from drawings and other information. They measure and prepare valuations of the work carried out to date to enable interim payments to be made to the building contractor and, at the end, they prepare the final account for presentation to the client. They advise the architect on the cost of any additional work or variations.
Consulting (specialist) engineer	Part of the design team who assists the architect in the design of the building within their specialist fields (e.g. civil engineers, structural engineers and service engineers).
Clerk of works	Appointed by the architect or client to act as their on-site representative. The clerk of works (COW) is an 'inspector of works' and, as such, ensures that the contractor carries out the work in accordance with the drawings and other contract documents.
Local authority	Responsible for ensuring that proposed building works conform to the requirements of relevant planning and building legislation. They employ planning officers and building control officers to approve and inspect building work. In some areas, building control officers are known as building inspectors or district surveyors (DS).
Health and safety inspector	Ensures that the government legislation concerning health and safety is fully implemented by the building contractor.
Principal building contractor	Enters into a contract with the client to carry out agreed works. Each contractor has their own method and procedures for tendering and carrying out building work which, in turn, together with the size of the contract, will determine the personnel required.
Sub-contractor	The building contractor may call upon a specialist firm to carry out a specific part of the building work. For this, they will enter into a sub-contract, hence the term sub-contractor.
Supplier	Building materials, equipment and plant are supplied by a wide range of merchants, manufacturers and hirers.

DID YOU KNOW

Sub-contractors appointed by a contractor may also be known as domestic sub-contractors. The client or architect often names or nominates a specific sub-contractor in the contract documents for specialist construction or installation work. These must be used for the work and are known as nominated sub-contractors. Likewise, the client or architect will often nominate specific suppliers who must be used and are, therefore, called nominated suppliers.

The recognised pattern by which the building team operates and communicates can be illustrated in a 'hierarchical chart'. This shows the level of authority and reporting lines in a construction project. The client, who has the most authority, is positioned at the top, with the chart continuing on to members with less authority towards the bottom of the chart.

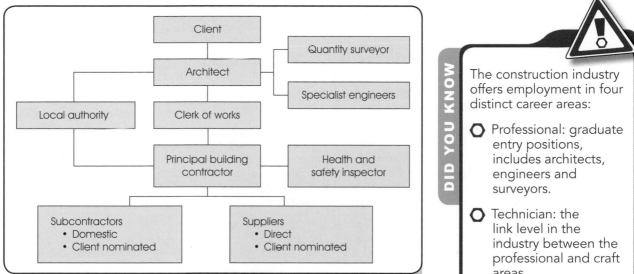

2.86 The hierarchy of the building team

2.87 Members of the building team

The construction industry offers employment in four distinct career areas:

- Professional: graduate entry positions, includes architects, engineers and surveyors.

- Technician: the link level in the industry between the professional and craft areas.

- Building craft: the skilled operatives who undertake the physical skilled tasks of constructing a building.

- Building operative: general building operatives and specialist building operatives.

The building contractors' team

Estimator	Estimates the cost for carrying out a building contract. They break down each item contained in the BOQ into parts (labour, materials and plant) and apply a rate to each, representing the amount it will cost the contractor to complete the item. A percentage for overheads (head/site office costs, site management/administration salaries) and profit is included.
Buyer	Purchases materials. They obtain quotations, negotiate the best possible terms, order materials and ensure that they arrive on-site at the required time, in the required quantity and quality.
Building contractor's quantity surveyor	Measures and evaluates the building work carried out each month, including the work of sub-contractors. An interim valuation is prepared on the basis of these measurements and passed on to the client for payment. They are also responsible for preparing interim costings to see whether the contract is within budget. Finally, they will prepare and agree the final accounts on completion of the contract.
Planning engineer	Responsible for the pre-contract planning of the building project. They plan the work in the most efficient way in terms of labour, materials, plant and equipment. Within their specialist field of work, planning engineers are often supported by a work study engineer (to examine various building operations to increase productivity) and a bonus surveyor (to operate an incentive scheme, which is also aimed at increasing productivity by awarding operatives additional money for work completed over a basic target).
Plant manager	Responsible for all items of mechanical plant (machines and power tools) used by the building contractor. At the request of the contracts manager/site agent, they will supply from stock, purchase or hire the most suitable plant item to carry out a specific task. They maintain plant items and train the operatives who use them.
Safety officer	Responsible for health and safety. They advise on all health and safety matters, carry out safety inspections and risk assessments, keep safety records, investigate accidents and arrange staff safety inductions and training.
Contracts manager	The supervisor/coordinator of the site's management team across a number of contracts. The contracts manager has an overall responsibility for planning, management and building operations. They will liaise between the head office staff and the site agents on the contracts for which they are responsible.
Site agent/site manager/project manager	The building contractor's resident on-site representative and leader of the site workforce. They are directly responsible to the contracts manager for day-to-day planning, management and building operations.
General foreman	Works under the site agent and is responsible for coordinating the work of the craft foreman, ganger and sub-contractors. They will also advise the site agent on constructional problems, liaise with the clerk of works and may also be responsible for the day-to-day employing and dismissing of operatives. On smaller contracts that may not require a site agent, the general foreman will have total responsibility for the site.
Site engineer	Sometimes called the site surveyor, they work alongside the general foreman. Responsible for ensuring that the building is the correct size and in the right place. They will set out and check the line, level and vertical (plumb) of the building during its construction.
Craft foreman	Works under the general foreman to organise and supervise the work of a specific craft (e.g. foreman bricklayer and foreman carpenter).
Ganger	Works under the general foreman but is responsible for the organisation and supervision of the general building operatives.

Charge hand/working foreman	On large contracts, employing a large number of craft operatives in each craft (normally bricklayers and carpenters), charge hands are often appointed to assist the craft foreman and supervise a sub-section of the work, as well as carry out the skilled physical work of their craft.
Operatives	The people who carry out the actual physical building work. Operatives can be divided into two main groups: craft and building operatives.
Craft operatives	The skilled craftsmen who perform specialist tasks with a range of materials; such as the bricklayer, carpenter, electrician, painter, plasterer and plumber.
Building operatives	These are further broken down into general building operatives, who mix concrete, lay drains, off-load material and assist craft operatives; and specialist building operatives; such as the ceiling fixer, glazier, plant mechanic and scaffolder.
Site clerk	Responsible for all site administrative duties and the control of materials on-site. They will record the arrival and departure of all site personnel, prepare wage sheets for head office, record the delivery and transfer of plant items, record and check delivery of materials and note their ultimate distribution (assisted by a storekeeper).

Workplace communication

Effective communication is essential between all members of the building team to ensure that the project operates smoothly, runs on time and finishes within budget.

Organisational documentation and paperwork

Timesheet: a weekly record of hours worked and a description of the job or jobs carried out. Timesheets are used by the employer to determine wages and spend, as well as assessing the accuracy of target programmes, providing information for future estimates and forming the basis for claiming daywork payments.

2.88 Timesheet

DID YOU KNOW

A daywork sheet is not the same as a timesheet. Take care not to confuse the two.

Daywork sheet: daywork is work carried out without an estimate. This may range from emergency or repair work carried out by a jobbing builder to work that was unplanned at the start of a major contract, such as repairs, replacements, demolition, extra ground work and late alterations.

BBS CONSTRUCTION
DAYWORK SHEET

Sheet no. _201/05_

Job title _EAST WOOD LANE_

Week commencing _14 MAR 11_

Registered office

BRETT HOUSE
1 HAGELY ROAD
BIRMINGHAM
B11 N4

Description of work

GENERAL SNAGGING TO PLOT 2. INC. NEW FRONT DOOR FITTED AS A RESULT OF VANDALISM

Labour	Name	Craft	Hours	Gross rate	Total	
201/05	J. BROWN	C & J	2.5	£20	£50	00
			Total labour		£50	00

Materials	Quantity	Rate	% Addition	Total	
NEW DOOR	1	£75	20	£90	00
		Total materials		£90	00

Plant	Hours	Rate	% Addition	Total	
		Total plant		00	00

Note Gross labour rates include a percentage for overheads and profit as set out in the contract conditions

Sub total	£140	00
VAT (where applicable) N/A %	–	–
Total claim	£140	00

Site manager/foreman _BB Brett_

Architect _____

2.89 Daywork sheet

Variation order: an instruction given by the architect to the builder concerning any changes made to the original contract, including additions, omissions and alterations.

Variation Order

Project: ALFA HOUSE REFURBISHMENTS

Location: NOTTINGHAM

Client: CREASTA HOTELS GROUP

Project No: 14/035

C A B
ARCHITECTS

CAB ARCHITECTS LTD
BRETT HOUSE
BEASTON
NOTTINGHAM
NG10 2XF
TEL: 0115 9000010
FAX: 0115 9000011
EMAIL: CAB@ARCH.COM

From: JAMES BLUNT To: DAVID SMURTHWAITE

Position: PROJECT DESIGNER Position: M.D. HOTELS

Additions:

PROVIDE ADJUSTABLE SHELVING TO BACK BAR FITTING AS DETAILED ON DRAWING NO. 14/0356 REV B.

Omissions:

DELETE FIXED SHELVING TO BACK BAR FITTING DETAILED ON DRAWING NO. 14/0356 REV A.

Variation Order No.: CHG/VO/004

Approved by: CABLEX

Date: 15 MARCH 2011

2.90 Variation order

Confirmation notice: written confirmation of verbal instructions from the architect for daywork or variation instructions before any work is carried out. This avoids misunderstanding and prevents disputes over payment at a later date.

BBS CONSTRUCTION
CONFIRMATION NOTICE

No. 106/05   Date 14 MAR 11
Job title EAST WOOD LANE
From PETER BRETT
To A J ARCHITECTURAL

Registered office
BRETT HOUSE
1 HAGELY ROAD
BIRMINGHAM
B11 N4

I confirm that today I have been issued with *verbal/written instructions from   A. J. POWELL
Position ARCHITECT
to carry out the following *daywork/variation to the contract

Additions

SUPPLY AND INSTALL NEW FRONT DOOR TO PLOT 2
(VANDALISM DAMAGE)

Omissions

N/A.

Please issue your official *confirmation/variation order

Copies to head office

Signed P B Brett
Position PROJECT MANAGER

*Delete as appropriate

2.91 Confirmation notice

Daily report/site diary: helps to supply information to head office and provides a source for future reference. This is useful should a problem or dispute occur from spoken instructions, site visitors, late deliveries, late starts or bad weather conditions. Its purpose is to record facts; therefore, it should be brief and to the point. Many contractors use a duplicate book for the combined daily report and site diary. After completion, the top copy is sent to head office; the carbon copy is kept on-site.

BBS CONSTRUCTION
DAILY REPORT/SITE DIARY

No. 24/1005   Date 28 MAR 11

Job title   PROJECT MANAGER

Registered office
BRETT HOUSE
1 HAGELY ROAD
BIRMINGHAM
B11 N4

Labour force on site		Labour force required	
Our employ	Subcontract	Our employ	Subcontract
6	22	6	24 2 EXTRA JOINERS REQUESTED

Materials		Information	
Received (state delivery no.)	Required by (state requisition no.)	Received	Required by
N/A	POD 24/205	N/A	N/A

Plant		Information	
Received (state delivery no.)	Required by (state requisition no.)	Received	Required by CASE GOODS LAYOUT 30 OCT 10
N/A	PRD 32/205	N/A	

Telephone calls	Site visitors
To	J. BIRD HAVELOCK P. M. PRE-START MEETING
From	

Accidents	Stoppages
NONE	NONE

Weather conditions	Temperature
WET AND OVERCAST ALL DAY	a.m. 6°C p.m. 9°C

Brief report of progress and other items of importance
GOOD PROGRESS IN LINE WITH BAR CHART
HAVELOCK'S CONFIRMED THAT CASEGOODS TO LEVEL 1 WILL BE
UNDERTAKEN ON 1 MAY.

Site manager/foreman   BS Brett
Note: Send top copy daily to head office and retain carbon copy as an on-site record.

2.92 Daily report/site diary

Orders/requisitions: the majority of building materials are obtained through the firm's buyer, who at the estimating stage would have got quotes from the various suppliers in order to compare prices, qualities and discounts. It is the buyer's responsibility to order and arrange phased deliveries of the required materials to match the progress of the contract programme. Each job is issued with a duplicate order/requisition for obtaining assorted items from the firm's central stores or, in the case of a smaller builder, direct from the supplier. Items of plant are requisitioned from the plant manager or plant hirers using a similar order/requisition.

BBS CONSTRUCTION
ORDER/REQUISITION

Registered office
BRETT HOUSE
1 HAGELY ROAD
BIRMINGHAM
B11 N4

No. POD 14/205

Date 14 MAR 2011

To M. L. MEYERS   From TIM BRETT

Address MEYERS YARD   Site address THE JOINERY WORKS
HEARTLANDS   LONG EATON
BIRMINGHAM   NOTTINGHAM

Please supply or order for delivery to the above site the following:

Description	Quantity	Rate		Date required by
18 MM MDF 2440 x 1220	100	12	40	28/3/11

Site manager/foreman PB BJett

Note: Please advise site within 24 hours of request if order cannot be fulfilled by the date requested

2.93 Order/requisition

Delivery notes: the foreman signs the driver's delivery note. A careful check should be made to ensure all the materials are there and undamaged. Any missing or damaged goods must be clearly indicated on the delivery note and followed up by a letter to the supplier. Many suppliers send out an advice note prior to delivery, which states details of the materials and the expected delivery date. This enables the site management to make provision for its unloading and storage. Some material suppliers use a paperless system when making deliveries. Details of the delivery are stored on an electronic hand-held notebook, which the receiver of the goods will sign for on a digital screen.

BBS SUPPLIES
DELIVERY NOTE

No. __8914__

Date __22 MARCH 2011__

Registered office
BRETT HOUSE
1 HAGELY ROAD
BIRMINGHAM
B11 N4

Delivered to

__T. JOYCEE__
__25 DAWNCRAFT WAY__
__STENSON DERBY D. 70__

Invoice to

__FELLOWS, MORTON PLC__
__JOSHER STREET__
__BIRMINGHAM B21__

Please receive in good condition the undermentioned goods

SAWN, TREATED SOFTWOOD
50 OFF   25 x 50 x 3600
50 OFF   50 x 50 x 4.800

KILN SEASONED HARDWOOD
25 OFF   25 x 150 x 2400 (REBATED WINDOW SILLS)

(SHRINK-WRAPPED IN PLASTIC)

Received by ____

Remarks   ONLY 48 LENGTHS OF 50 x 50 RECEIVED

Note: Claims for shortages and damage will not be considered unless recorded on the sheet

2.94 Delivery

Delivery record: a complete record of all the materials received on-site. This should be filled in and sent to head office along with the delivery notes on a weekly basis. This record is used to check deliveries before paying suppliers' invoices and also when determining the interim valuation.

T. Joycee Construction
DELIVERIES RECORD

Week no. __P3 WK3__   Date __MARCH 14__

Job title __STENSON FIELDS__

Registered office

RIDGE HOUSE
NORTON ROAD
CHELTENHAM
GL59 1DB

Delivery note no.	Date	Supplier	Description of delivery	For office use only	
				Rate	Value
241	14/3/11	G. BLOGGS	SANITARY WARE		
1535	14/3/11	I. BLUNDER	READY–MIX CONCRETE		
				Total	

Site manager/foreman _____
Note: Send weekly to head office with delivery notes

2.95 Delivery record

Memorandum (memos): printed forms on which internal communications can be carried out. It is normally a brief note about the requirements of a particular job or details of an incoming enquiry while a person was unavailable. Internal memos and messages written between site staff should be friendly, brief and factual.

BBS CONSTRUCTION   **MEMO**

From   PETER BRETT   To   DAVE SUTTON

Subject   NOGGIN DETAILS   Date   15.3.11

Message

DAVE.
HAVELOCK ARE SENDING ME THE NOGGIN DETAILS TODAY. I'LL BRING THEM TO THE MEETING TOMORROW. PETER

2.96 Memo

Letters: provide a permanent record of communication between organisations and individuals. They can be handwritten, but most formal business letters are created on a computer. The language should be simple and to the point. The tone should be polite and business-like, even if it is a letter of complaint. Letters must be clearly constructed, with each new point contained in a separate paragraph for easy understanding.

○ Write your address in full, complete with the postcode.

○ Include the recipient's details. This is the title of the person (plus name if known) and the name and address of the organisation you are writing to in full. This should be the same as appears on the envelope.

○ Write the date in full (for example, 30 January 2011).

○ For greetings, use 'Dear Sir/Madam' if you are unsure of the name and gender of the person you are writing to, otherwise 'Dear Sir' or 'Dear Madam' as applicable. Use the person's name if you know it.

○ For endings, use 'Yours sincerely' if you have used the person's name in the greeting, otherwise use 'Yours faithfully'.

○ Sign below the ending. Your name should also be printed below the signature for clarity, with your status if appropriate.

40 St. James Road
Great Barr
Birmingham
BB4 5EL

15 March 2011

Your address

Inside address of who letter is going to

The Personnel Manager
BBS Supplies
Brett House
1 Hagley Road
Birmingham
B11 N4

Dear Sir — **Greeting**

Thank you for your letter of 11th March 2011, inviting me for interview for the position of Trainee Store Person.

I look forward to meeting you on Friday 25th March 2011 at 10.30 a.m.

Yours faithfully — **Ending**

C. White — **Signature**

C. White

2.97 Typical letter

Telecommunications

Facsimile transmission or FAX: a method of sending information, both text and pictures, by a telecommunications link. Most fax transmissions are via the normal telephone network. Fax machines can send and receive handwritten notes, drawings, diagrams, photographs or printed text from one fax machine to another, anywhere in the world. Often used as a fast means of sending letters, which can then be followed up with a postal copy.

BBS Joinery Services
Brett House
1 Hagley Road
Birmingham
B11 N4

Fax

To:	David Clarke	Fax:	0121 0543360
From:	Ivor Gunne	Date:	15/11/11
Re:	Standard Window Details	Pages:	2 including this one
CC:			

☑Urgent ☐For Review ☐Please Comment ☐Please reply ☐Please recycle

David

Please find attached details of our standard range of casement windows as requested.

We are also able to purpose manufacture to your requirements, should the standard range not be suitable.

Trust this information is sufficient for your purposes, however do not hesitate to contact me should you have any further queiries.

Regards

Ivor Gunne

Ivor Gunne

Production manager

Window type		Frame dimensions width x height
	V	634 x 921 634 x 1073 634 x 1226 634 x 1378
	V	921 x 921 921 x 1073 921 x 1226
	V	1221 x 1073 1221 x 1226
	CV AS CV OPP	1221 x 1073 1221 x 1226
	C AS C OPP	634 x 1073
	CD AS CD OPP	1221 x 1073
	CVC	1808 x 1073 1808 x 1226

Side hung

Fanlight opening

Notes:
V = Ventlight **C** = Casement **OPP** = Opposite hand
D = Fixed light **AS** = Hand as shown

2.98 Example of a fax

E-mail: It is advisable to print out important e-mails and file them for others to refer to. Electronic copies should be stored and backed up for contractual purposes.

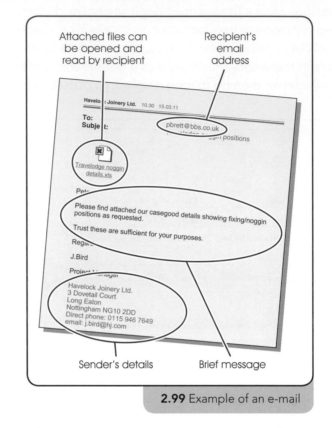

Attached files can be opened and read by recipient

Recipient's email address

Havelock Joinery Ltd.   10.30 15.03.11

To:
Subject:

pbrett@bbs.co.uk

positions

Travelodge noggin
details.xls

Pet

Please find attached our casegood details showing fixing/noggin positions as requested.

Trust these are sufficient for your purposes.

Regar

J.Bird

Project

Havelock Joinery Ltd.
3 Dovetail Court
Long Eaton
Nottingham NG10 2DD
Direct phone: 0115 946 7649
email: j.bird@hj.com

Sender's details

Brief message

2.99 Example of an e-mail

Two-way radio: many large sites use a two-way radio system to enable workers to remain in direct communication with the site office, while roaming the site.

Internet: information can be stored and shared instantly via the internet. 'Virtual' electronic rooms can be used to file project documents, such as the latest drawings, specifications, correspondence and digital photographs of work in progress.

Telephone: telephones play an important communication role both within an organisation and to customers and suppliers. It is useful to keep a record of incoming and outgoing calls in the form of a log. Telephone manner is very important. The tone, volume and pace of your voice are important as you cannot be seen. Speak clearly and loud enough to be heard without shouting; sound cheerful and speak at a speed which allows the recipient to take down any message, key words or phrases.

If you make the call, you are more likely to be in control of the conversation. Make notes before you begin. Have times, dates and other necessary information ready, including words you find difficult to spell 'from your head'. The call may take the following form:

⬡ 'Good morning' or 'Good afternoon'.

⬡ 'This is [your name] from [organisation] speaking.'

⬡ Give the name of the person you wish to speak to, if a specific individual is required.

⬡ State the reason for your call.

⬡ Keep the call brief but polite.

⬡ Thank the recipient, even if the call did not produce the results required.

If you are receiving a call, it may take the following form:

⬡ 'Good morning' or 'Good afternoon'.

⬡ State your name and the name of your organisation.

⬡ Ask 'How can I help you?'

Telephone Message
Date 15 MARCH Time 09:45
Message for SID
Message from (Name) JUDY
(Address) STENSON FIELDS
CONTRACT DERBY
(Telephone) 07814 445 733
Message CAN YOU BRING TWO 5 LITRE CANS OF
BLUE GLOSS PAINT WHEN YOU ATTEND THE
SITE MEETING TOMORROW

Message taken by JOE

2.100 Example of a telephone message

Taking messages

If the call is not for you and the person required is unavailable, take a message. It is important that you understand what someone is saying to you on the telephone, and you may need to make notes of the conversation. Make sure that the message contains all the necessary details including:

⬡ the date and time of the message

⬡ the name of the person who the message is intended for (recipient or receiver)

- the content or subject of the message

- the name and contact details of the person who sent the message

- your name (as the person taking the message)

Lack of details could lead to problems later. Do not guess how to spell names and other details; ask the caller to spell them for you.

2.101 Various posters, notices and signs

Posters, notices and signs

Safety signs are often displayed at the site entrance to inform the general public as well as authorised personnel entering the site of potential dangers and site safety requirements. They may also be displayed around the site as appropriate. Statutory notices, such as an insurance certificate, are normally displayed in the site manager's office. Safety posters and site 'dos' and 'don'ts' are often displayed in the site canteen or other communal area.

Site meetings

Regular meetings are an effective means of communication between members of the building team. They can be held to provide or update information and to discuss problems and make decisions.

- A 'kick-off' meeting should involve the client team, design team and the construction team. It provides the opportunity for those involved to get to know each other, agree methods of communication and points of contact.

- Monthly progress meetings are held to discuss progress made to date, problems or issues that have arisen since the last meeting and to make any amendments to drawings, specifications or other contract documents.

- Weekly domestic meetings between the project manager, site foreman and sub-contractors are held to discuss and resolve general site issues, including progress of work, reasons for delay, site safety and security issues.

- Informal meetings may be called at short notice to discuss and resolve any urgent problems arising during the project that cannot wait until the next programmed meeting.

- Performance reviews are annual one-to-one meetings between an employee and a line manager. These are used to discuss an employee's successes and failures, strengths and weaknesses, and their suitability for promotion or further training, etc.

A successful site meeting needs to be well structured and should be led by a chairperson who is also responsible for setting the date, time and place of the meeting, writing and sending the **agenda** and ensuring **minutes** are taken.

> **KEY TERMS**
>
> **Agenda:** a document listing the main topics and order of discussion. This is sent out before the meeting to allow people to prepare.
>
> **Minutes:** a document that lists the issues to be resolved arising from a meeting and actions for individuals.

Details of meeting	**MEETING AGENDA** **BBS** CONSTRUCTION
	Meeting title:
Names of people attending the meeting	Date: Time:
Names of people invited but could not attend the meeting	Location:
	Attendees:
Review of action points from previous meeting	Apologies:
	Matters arising:
List of topics for discussion	Topics: 1. 2. 3. 4. 5. 6.
List of issues to be resolved, by whom and by when	
An opportunity to raise and discuss issues not on the agenda	Actions
	Any other business
Agree date of next meeting at end to ensure all are available	Date of next meeting:

2.102 Site meeting agenda

Manufacturer's technical information

In addition to safety data sheets, manufacturers also produce technical information, which is distributed via catalogues, brochures, data sheets and user instructions. These are often available in a printed form or can be downloaded from the internet.

Communication with work colleagues

In order for companies to function effectively, colleagues need to establish and maintain good working relationships within their organisational structure. This can be achieved by cooperation. Communication between the various sections and individual workers is important. However, a good team spirit is also important, where people are motivated, appreciated and allowed to work on their own initiative under supervision for the good of the company as a whole.

Communication between trades

Good communication between trades is essential to the smooth operation of a site. What is being done, by whom and when needs to be clear to all. Poor communication between trades can lead to costly mistakes, delays, work stoppages and abortive work.

Communication with customers

Customers should always be treated with respect as they are paying for the work. Be polite, even to difficult customers. Listen carefully to their wishes and pass anything you cannot deal with on to a higher authority in the company.

Body language

Your body language can say more about you than your speech. You can use body language when trying to make a good impression, as well as reading someone else's to get an impression of whether or not they mean what they are saying.

2.103 Posture

Posture

⬡ Turning your body towards someone shows you are paying attention, more so if you lean forwards towards them at the same time.

⬡ Turning away or leaning back shows a lack of interest or a level of reserve.

⬡ Keeping your head down or hunching your shoulders indicates that you feel insignificant and do not want to draw attention to yourself.

⬡ Sitting with legs crossed can indicate boredom, whereas legs slightly apart shows you are open and relaxed.

⬡ Folding your arms across your chest indicates defensiveness, while arms open, especially with palms uppermost, shows you are honest and accepting.

2.104 Facial expression

Facial expressions

⬡ A relaxed brow shows that you are comfortable with the situation, while a tense or wrinkled brow indicates confusion, tension or fear.

⬡ A smile or a relaxed face helps you to appear open, confident and friendly, while not smiling or a tensed face can make you appear disapproving or disinterested.

2.105 Eye contact

Eye contact

⬡ Direct eye contact indicates that you are interested, confident and calm. However, maintaining eye contact for a long time, along with a tense face can indicate aggression.

⬡ Limited or no eye contact can indicate that you are disinterested, uncomfortable or distracted.

○ Your gaze can show that you are alert and interested. When walking into a room, look around to give the impression that you care about where you are; keeping your eyes averted makes you appear nervous and less approachable; look up and direct your gaze around the room or at the group you are with from time to time to maintain contact.

○ Making the eyes look larger, combined with an open mouth or smile, shows happiness. However, when combined with a tense brow or frown, it can indicate that you are unhappily surprised.

Hand gestures

○ Moving your hands apart with palms uppermost makes you appear more open and honest; moving your hands together can draw emphasis to what you are saying.

○ Pointing a finger can be used for emphasis, but pointing or poking a finger at someone also indicates anger.

○ Rubbing hands together shows anticipation; wringing or clenching hands shows tension; clenching the hand to make a fist shows aggression.

○ Tapping or drumming fingers indicates impatience; lightly pressing the fingertips of both hands together is seen as authoritative.

○ Fidgeting with hands or objects can indicate boredom, fear or difficulty in coping with a situation.

○ Avoid too many hand gestures, as this can make you appear uncontrolled or nervous.

The need for clear communications

Clear and effective communication at all times is vital to promote efficient working relations between all members of the team. This is especially the case when circumstances could have a wider impact on the company as a whole, sub-contractors and those working around you. The following examples should be noted:

Alterations to drawings	Drawings are used by estimators, buyers, work programmers as well as the construction team. Changes to drawings are normally communicated by the issue of a revised drawing register; this will list the latest revision number. When a revised drawing is issued, the person responsible should ensure that all old copies are taken out of circulation and that the relevant people are issued with the revised up-to-date copies. Failure to do so can be very costly!
Variations to contract documents	Remember that the contract documents include: – working drawings – specification – schedules bill of quantities – conditions of contract. These determine the where, what, how, when, and for how much of a building project. Any changes should be communicated in the case of drawings by the issue of a revised drawing register, or by the issue of a variation order for other documents. Changes must be advised as soon as possible throughout the business to all relevant people. Again, failure to do so can be very costly!
Risk assessments	Remember that risk assessment is the process of identifying the hazards involved in the workplace, assessing the likelihood of any harm arising and deciding on adequate precautionary control measures. The results of these assessments have a direct impact on the safety of all people in and around the workplace and should be communicated to all. Failure to do so can result in accidents, ill health, fatalities and prosecution.
Work restrictions	Work restrictions are rules that must be observed in certain circumstances. They may be laid out in the contract documents, such as hours of working or delivery restrictions, or they may be set out in the site rules, such as the need to notify the site manager before certain works are undertaken. Failure to communicate work restrictions can lead to a breach of contract terms and, as site work restrictions are normally put in place for safety reasons, could place everyone in danger.

CHECK YOUR UNDERSTANDING

At levels 1 and 2:

✔ Describe **four** different means of communication.

✔ In hierarchical order, name **five** members of the building team.

✔ Describe **two** benefits of positive communication.

✔ Explain the purpose of a variation order.

✔ State the circumstances in which you would use 'Yours faithfully' or 'Yours sincerely' at the end of a letter.

At level 2:

✔ Explain why clear and effective communication is vital in the workplace at all times.

✔ What is the role of an estimator?

✔ Explain why the client is generally considered to be the most important member of the building team.

✔ State the difference between nominated sub-contractors and domestic sub-contractors.

✔ Describe **two** advantages and **two** disadvantages of one written form of communication.

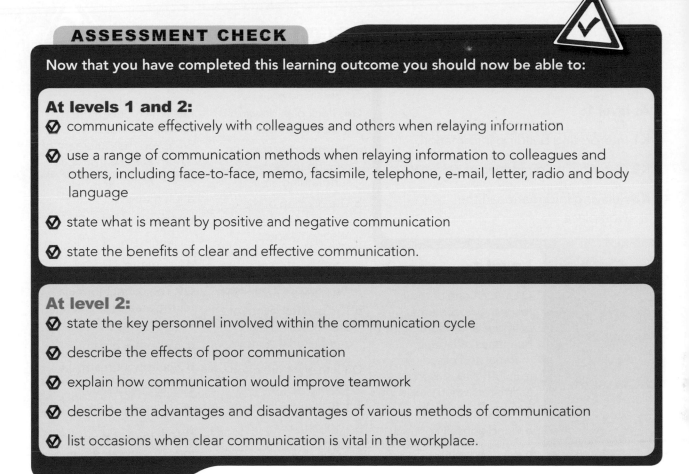

ASSESSMENT CHECK

Now that you have completed this learning outcome you should now be able to:

At levels 1 and 2:
- communicate effectively with colleagues and others when relaying information

- use a range of communication methods when relaying information to colleagues and others, including face-to-face, memo, facsimile, telephone, e-mail, letter, radio and body language

- state what is meant by positive and negative communication

- state the benefits of clear and effective communication.

At level 2:
- state the key personnel involved within the communication cycle

- describe the effects of poor communication

- explain how communication would improve teamwork

- describe the advantages and disadvantages of various methods of communication

- list occasions when clear communication is vital in the workplace.

REVISION QUIZ

From this chapter you should have a good understanding of:

At level 1:

K1 Interpreting building information

K2 Determining quantities of materials

K3 Relaying information in the workplace

Level 1

Q1 Which one of the following documents provides a measure of the quantities of labour, material and other items required and is used by estimators when preparing a tender?

a Conditions of contract

b Bill of quantities

c Specification

d Schedule

Q2 Symbols are used on building drawings to:

a Represent different material and components

b Indicate the company who designed the building

c Brighten up a drawing

d Avoid the use of long words

Q3 What would 15 mm on a drawing to a scale of 1:50 stand for?

a 75 mm

b 150 mm

c 750 mm

d 7500 mm

Q4 Block plan drawings are used to show:

a The proposed site in relation to the surrounding area

b The position of the proposed building in relation to roads, services and drainage

c The general layout of the proposed building

d The general layout of site accommodation and material storage

Q5 Site plans are often drawn using a scale of:

a 1:10

b 1:100

c 1:200

d 1:1250

Q6 Detail drawings are used to show:

a The basic sizes and range of standard components

b The information required to manufacture a component

c The general site layout

d The joints between various building elements

Q7 The word 'building' may be abbreviated on a drawing to:

a bdg

b bldg

c blg

d bg

Q8 Which one of the following is not a preferred measurement of length in the construction industry?

a Kilometre

b Metre

c Centimetre

d Millimetre

Q9 The correct formula for the area of a rectangle is:

a 2(length + breath)

b 2(length × breath)

c Length + breath

d Length × breath

Q10 If the length of a room measures 3500 mm and the area is 17.5 m, what is its width?

a 61.25 m

b 5 m

c 0.5 m

d 6.125 m

REVISION QUIZ

Level 2

Q1 Which of the following is not an advantage of written communication?

a Can provide confirmation of earlier verbal communications

b Poor language skills and poor handwriting can cause confusion and misunderstandings

c Complicated ideas and details can often be more easily understood

d Provides evidence of actions taken or tasks completed

Q2 The purpose of a programme of work is to:

a Show the hierarchy of the building team

b Indicate when materials have to be ordered by

c Show the order in which site operations are to be undertaken

d Indicate the lines of communication

Q3 The person appointed to resolve disputes or conflicts between individual people or groups who can't agree is called a:

a Communicator

b Conciliator

c Mediator

d Judge

Q4 Which one of the following is not normally kept on-site as a reference source during building work?

a Architects' working drawings

b Conditions of contact

c Schedules

d Specifications

Q5 A sum of money included in a BOQ for work or services to be provided by a nominated sub-contractor is known as a:

a Preamble

b Retention

c Provisional sum

d Prime cost sum

Q6 Which one of the following statements is false?

a An agenda is a document that lists the issues to be resolved arising from a meeting and actions for individuals

b A variation order is an instruction given by the architect to the builder concerning any changes made to the original contract

c The internet is a huge collection of computers around the world, which are all linked together

d The plant manager is responsible for all items such as machines and power tools used by the building contractor

Q7 The person who would normally produce a BOQ is the:

a Estimator

b Engineer

c Architect

d Project manager

Q8 The contract document that contains written descriptions of the material quality and standards of workmanship for a particular job is the:

a Schedule

b Specification

c BOQ

d Contract conditions

Q9 Details of all windows and associated ironmongery required for a particular job would be shown on a:

a Schedule

b Specification

c Variation order

d Confirmation order

Q10 The most common form of communication between operatives working on the same site is via:

a Text

b Voice mail

c Spoken word

d Body language

From this chapter you should have gained a good understanding of:

At level 2:

K1 Interpreting and producing building information

K2 Estimating quantities of resources

K3 Communicating workplace requirements efficiently

Building methods and construction technology

All buildings are constructed using similar basic principles and contain common elements. Whatever the type of building, they will all have a suitable foundation, walls, floors and a roof. The aim of this chapter at level 1 is to provide an overview of a range of traditional and modern methods used in the construction of buildings. This is extended at level 2 to include the principles of internal work and the delivery and storage of building materials.

This chapter covers the following learning outcomes for Unit 1003K level 1:

K1 Foundations, walls and floor construction

K2 Construction of internal and external masonry

K3 Roof construction

This chapter also covers the following learning outcomes for Unit 2003K level 2:

K1 Principles of building methods and construction technology

K2 Principles of internal building work

K3 Delivery and storage of building materials

K1 in this chapter is intended to cover all three learning outcomes at level 1 and the first learning outcome at level 2.

This chapter also supports the learning outcomes of the NVQ Diploma unit QCF 03 Moving and handling resources.

K1 Principles of building methods and construction technology

Purpose of buildings and structures

Buildings and structures are normally constructed for a specific purpose. This determines their shape, style, quality and overall cost. A building encloses space and creates an internal environment. The actual structure of a building is called the external envelope. This protects the internal environment from the outside elements, known as the external environment and provides security, privacy and warmth to the occupants.

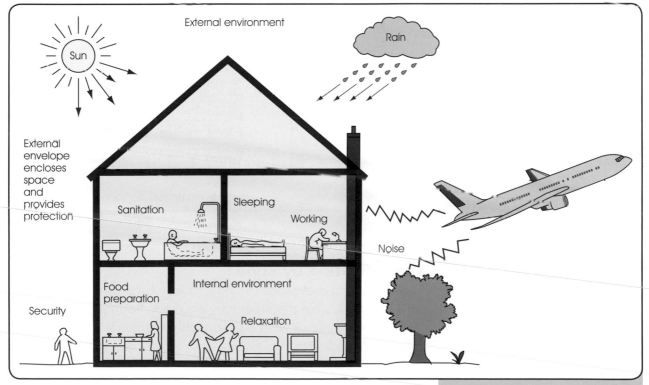

3.1 Internal/external environment

KEY TERMS

Residential: houses and flats, etc. that are called dwellings.

Commercial: shops and offices, etc.

Industrial: factories, workshops, mills and warehouses, etc.

Facilities for transport: roads, bridges, railways, harbours and airports, etc.

Types of buildings and structures

Today's ever-demanding society requires many different types of buildings and structures, such as **residential**, **commercial**, **industrial** and **facilities for transport**.

Together, these buildings and structures are known as the built environment, while individually they are known as elements of the built environment.

Classification by height

All buildings may be classified into three main categories according to their height or the number of floors (storeys) they contain:

⬡ Low-rise buildings (one to three storeys).

⬡ Medium-rise buildings (four to seven storeys).

⬡ High-rise buildings (above seven storeys).

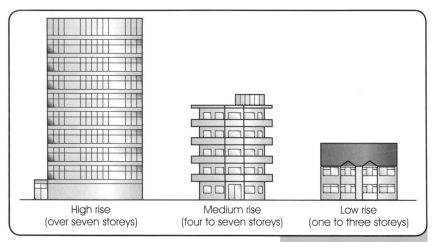

High rise (over seven storeys) Medium rise (four to seven storeys) Low rise (one to three storeys)

3.2 Height of buildings

Classification by style

These building categories can be further sub-divided according to how they look, what materials they are made from, what historical period they fit into or what buildings they are connected to. A detached building stands alone. A semi-detached building is joined to a building on one side. It shares a dividing wall or party wall. A terraced house is in a row of three or more buildings, and the inner ones share a party wall on each side.

3.3 Detached, semi-detached and terraced buildings

Structural form

There are many different structural forms which allow the best possible use of new materials and developing techniques. The majority of buildings are constructed as solid structures, framed structures, panel structures or structures using a combination of these, in addition to surface structures which are used much less.

Solid structures

These are also known as mass wall structures. Walls are constructed of brickwork, blockwork or concrete. They form a stable box-like structure, but are normally limited to low-rise, short-span buildings.

Framed structures

These consist of an interconnected framework of members having a supporting function. Either external cladding or infill walls are used to provide the protecting external envelope. Frames made from steel,

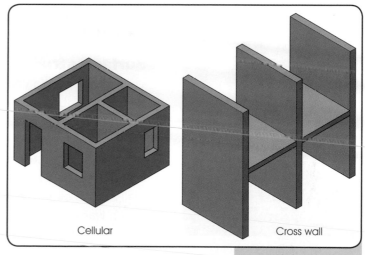

Cellular

Cross wall

3.4 Solid structures

concrete or timbers are often pre-made in a factory as separate units, which are simply and speedily erected on-site. Framed construction is suitable for a wide range of buildings and civil engineering structures from low to high rise.

3.6 Panel structure – 'The Gherkin'

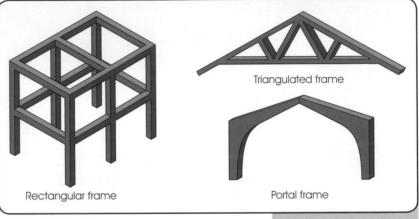

Rectangular frame

Triangulated frame

Portal frame

3.5 Framed structures

Panel structures

These consist of a system of structural or cladding panels, manufactured off-site in a strictly controlled environment and then transported for on-site installation. Typical examples include **pre-cast concrete** floor, wall and roof panels; timber-based structural insulated panels known as SIPs; formed long-span steel-insulated panels; and structural glazing. In addition, insulated timber and steel panels are used to provide the external cladding for framed structures.

Surface structures

These consist of a very thin material that has been curved or folded to obtain strength or, alternatively, stretched over supporting members or medium. Typical examples include concrete or timber shells, steel vaults and air-supported structures. Surface structures are often used for large, clear-span buildings with a minimum of internal supporting structure. One well-known example of a surface structure is 'The O^2' in London, which was previously called the Millennium Dome. This consists of twelve 100 m-high steel towers with a stretched fabric spanning between them and enclosing the space to create a marquee or tent-like structure.

DID YOU KNOW

Although they are classified as separate parts, the substructure and the superstructure are designed to operate together as one structural unit.

3.7 Surface structure – 'The O$_2$'

Structural parts

All buildings and structures consist of two main parts: the **substructure** below ground; and the **superstructure** above ground.

3.8 Substructure and superstructure

KEY TERMS

Substructure: comprises of structure below ground up to and including the ground floor. Its purpose is to receive the loads from the main building superstructure and its contents and transfer them safely down to a suitable load-bearing layer of ground.

Superstructure: comprises all of the structure above the substructure, both internally and externally. It encloses and divides space, and transfers loads safely on to the substructure.

Structural members and loading

The two main types of load that a structure is subjected to are:

O **dead loads**: the weight of the building materials used in the construction, service installations and any permanent built-in fixtures and fitments

DID YOU KNOW

The parts of a structure that carry or transfer any dead or imposed load are called load bearing. Parts that do not or are not intended to carry or transfer loads are called non-load bearing.

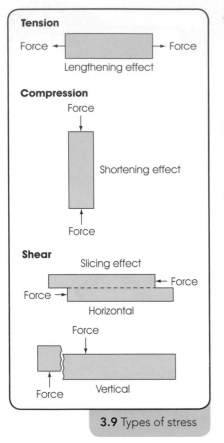

3.9 Types of stress

Stress: when a body is subjected to a force.

Struts: bracing members that are mainly in compression.

Ties: bracing members that are mainly in tension.

imposed or superimposed loads: the weight of any movable load, such as the occupants of a building, their furniture and other belongings. Also included are any environmental forces exerted on the structure from the external environment, such as the wind, rain and snow.

Stress

The load-bearing parts of a structure are said to be in a state of **stress**. There are three types of stress:

- **Compressive** causes squeezing, pushing and crushing; it has a shortening effect.

- **Tensile** tends to pull or stretch a material; it has a lengthening effect.

- **Shear** occurs when one part of a member tends to slip or slide over another part; it has a slicing effect.

There are three main types of load-bearing structural members:

- Horizontal members carry and transfer a load back to its own point of support. They include beams, joists, lintels, floor or roof slabs. When a load is applied to a horizontal member, bending will occur, resulting in a combination of tensile, compressive and shear stresses. This bending causes compression in the top of the member, tension in the bottom and shear near its supports and along its centre line. Bending causes the member to sag or deflect. (For safe design purposes, deflection is normally limited to a maximum of 3 mm in every 1 m span.) In addition, slender members, which are fairly deep in comparison with their width, are likely to buckle unless restrained (for example, strutting to floor joists).

- Vertical members transfer the loading of the horizontal members down on to the substructure. They include walls, columns, stanchions and piers. Vertical members are in compression when loaded. Buckling tends to occur in vertical members if they are excessively loaded or are too slender.

- Bracing members are used mainly to triangulate rectangular frameworks in order to stiffen them. They can be divided into two types: **struts** and **ties**.

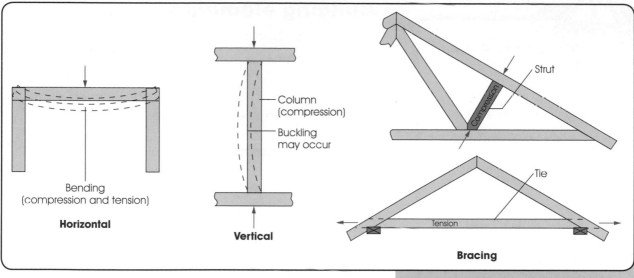

An example of dead and imposed loads in a typical low-rise structure and how they are transferred down through the structural members to the subsoil is illustrated in Fig 3.11.

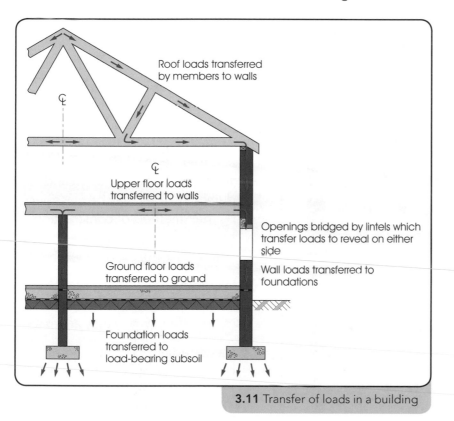

3.11 Transfer of loads in a building

Foundations: part of a structure that transfers loads safely onto the supporting ground.

Walls: vertical enclosing and dividing elements of a building.

Floors: horizontal ground and upper levels in a building, which provide a walking surface.

Roofs: uppermost part of a building that spans the walls and protects the building and contents.

Stairs: series of steps that divide a vertical space into smaller rises so that they can be walked up and provide floor to floor access.

Building elements

Building elements are the constructional parts of the substructure and superstructure. Each element is made up from one or more components. For example, a brick wall uses bricks and mortar as components. Building elements are classified into three main groups:

Primary elements

These are named because of the importance of their supporting, enclosing and protection functions. In addition, they have the mainly internal role of dividing space and providing floor-to-floor access.

Secondary elements

These are the non-essential elements of a structure, mainly completing openings in primary elements and within the building in general.

○ **Frames and linings**: provide a finishing surround to wall openings and also a means of fitting doors and windows.

○ **Doors**: allow access and may have other functional requirements, including weather protection, fire resistance, sound and thermal insulation, security, privacy, ease of operation and durability. They may be classified by their method of construction, method of operation and materials used.

○ **Windows**: normally classified by their method of opening and the material from which they are made.

○ **Balustrades**: consist of the handrail and infilling that guards the open edge of a stair, landing or floor.

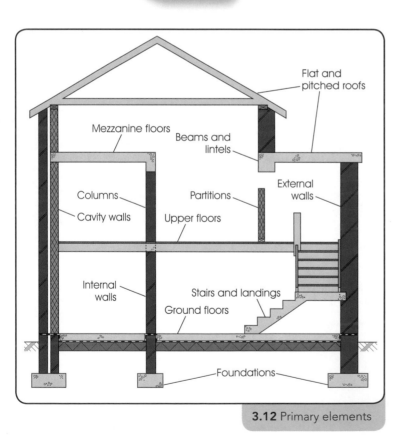

3.12 Primary elements

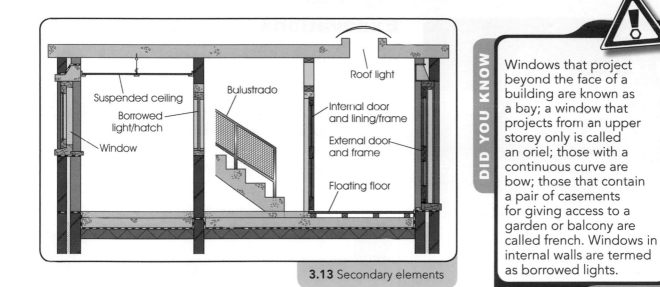

3.13 Secondary elements

DID YOU KNOW

Windows that project beyond the face of a building are known as a bay; a window that projects from an upper storey only is called an oriel; those with a continuous curve are bow; those that contain a pair of casements for giving access to a garden or balcony are called french. Windows in internal walls are termed as borrowed lights.

Finishing elements

A finish is the final surface of an element. This can be a self-finish as with face brickwork, fair-faced blockwork and concrete, or an applied finish such as plaster or plasterboard, wallpaper and paint. Also included in this category are **internal trims**, **external flashings** and **cladding**.

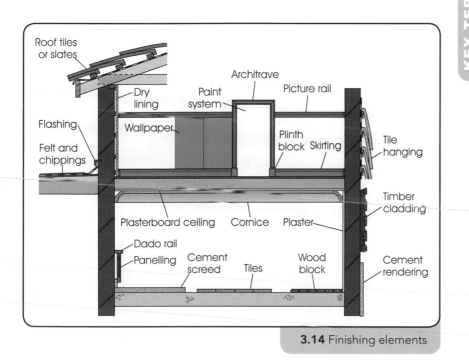

3.14 Finishing elements

KEY TERMS

Internal trims: skirting, architraves and coving or cornices, which mask the joint between touching elements.

External flashings: weatherproof joints between elements.

Cladding: cement rendering and tile hanging, which are all used to either weatherproof or give a decorative finish to external walls.

3.15 Digger excavator

KEY TERMS

Oversite excavation: removal of topsoil and vegetable matter prior to starting building work. Depth is typically between 150 and 300mm. The excavated topsoil can be used later for landscaping. If it is not required later, additional labour and transport costs may be offset by selling the soil.

Reduced level excavation: carried out after oversite excavation on undulating ground. It consists of cutting and filling operations to produce a level surface, called the formation level.

Trench excavations: long, narrow holes in the ground made to accommodate strip foundations or underground services. Deep trenches may be battered or timbered to prevent the sides from caving in.

Pit excavations: deep rectangular holes in the ground, normally for column base pad foundations. Larger holes may be required for basements etc. Sides may be battered or timbered, depending on depth.

Excavations

When undertaking building works the first stage is excavation. This is the removal of earth that is in the way, to clear or level the site and form pits or trenches in the ground. Most excavations are carried out mechanically using a digger excavator. The front shovel is used to strip topsoil and reduce level, whilst the back actor is used to dig trenches and isolated holes.

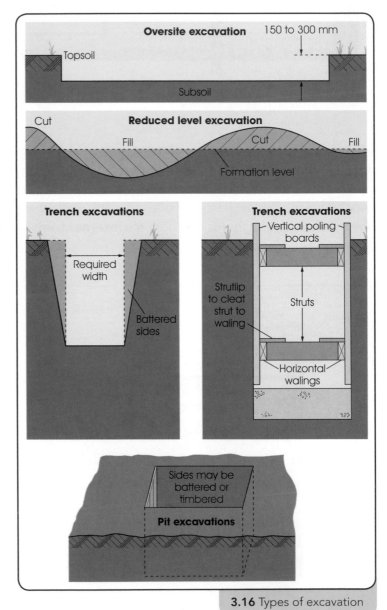

3.16 Types of excavation

Site setting-out requirements and procedures

The setting out of a building can be divided into two distinct operations: establishing the position of the building and setting up profiles; and establishing a datum peg and transferring required levels to various positions.

LINK

For more information on block plan drawings, see page 109 of Chapter 2.

Pegs, string lines and profile boards

The setting out of a building is done from the building line. This is a line on a plot of land, set back from the front boundary and beyond which no building is allowed to project. It will be shown on a block plan drawing and will have been determined by the local authority. Pegs and string lines are used to indicate the building line and the outer wall faces of the building.

From the setting out lines, profile boards are established clear of the intended foundation trench runs at each corner of the building. Four nails or saw cuts are driven or cut into the top of each profile board to indicate the edges of the foundation trench and the edges of the walls. String lines can be strained between the nails on the profiles to indicate the exact positions for the excavators and bricklayers. During excavation these lines will be removed and, therefore, the position of the trench should be marked by sprinkling sand or spray painting on the ground directly under the lines to indicate the sides of the trenches.

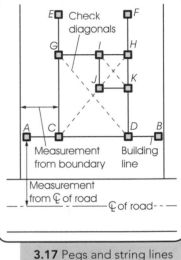

3.17 Pegs and string lines used to establish the position of a building

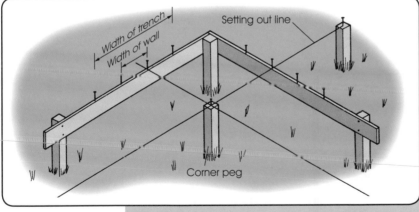

3.18 Transferring setting out lines to profile boards

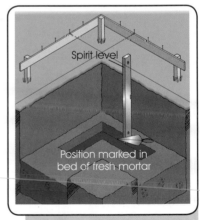

3.19 Marking wall positions

Once the foundations have been excavated and concreted, one line is re-strained around the nails on the profile boards to indicate the face of the brickwork. From this line, the position of the brickwork can be marked on the foundation concrete.

Bench marks and datum levels

These are identified points from which all other positions on-site or in a building are either taken or are related. For example, the relative levels for excavations, roads, paths, drains, brick courses, finished floors and other internal components.

- **A bench mark or Ordnance Survey mark** is a level or mark related to the Ordnance Datum (OD), which is the mean sea level at Newlyn in Cornwall, England. From this datum, the Ordnance Survey has established Ordnance bench marks (OBMs) throughout the country. They are normally lines cut into the vertical faces of stone or brick permanent structures. However, bolt-and-pivot bench marks are also to be found. A chiselled broad arrowhead points to the mark, bolt or pivot.

- **Temporary bench marks (TBMs) or datum pegs** are marks transferred from the nearest OBM to the building site, from which all on-site levels are taken. TBMs are normally steel or timber pegs driven into the ground to a convenient level value and set in concrete. They may be enclosed by a low fence for protection.

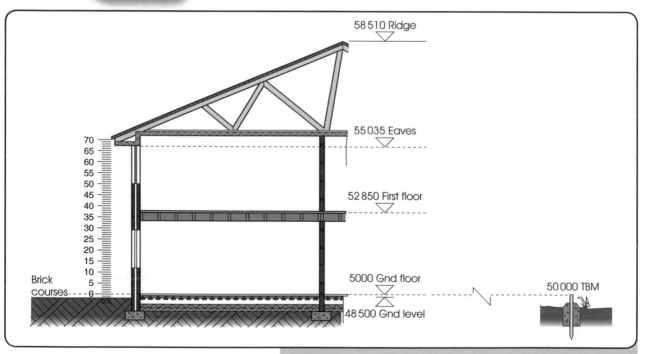

3.20 Relationship between TBM and the levels of the building

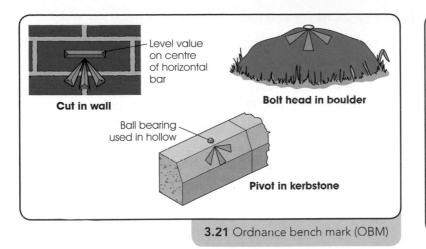

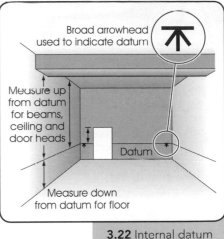

3.21 Ordnance bench mark (OBM)

3.22 Internal datum

⬡ **Datum marks or lines** are temporary positions established on a site or in a room or area, from which other points nearby, are measured. A broad arrowhead should be used to indicate the datum level.

Foundations

Foundations are the part of the substructure that transfers the loads of the superstructure safely down on to a suitable load-bearing layer of ground. The width of a foundation is determined by the total load of the structure exerted per square metre on the foundation, and the safe load-bearing capacity of the ground or subsoil. Wide foundations are used for either heavy loads or weak ground and narrow foundations for light loads or high-bearing capacity subsoils.

The load exerted on foundations is spread to the ground at an angle of 45 degrees. Shear failure leading to building subsidence (sinking) will occur if the thickness of the concrete is less than the projection from the wall/column face to the edge of the foundation. Alternatively, steel reinforcement may be included to enable the load to spread across the full width of the foundation.

Foundations are taken below ground level into the subsoil to protect the structure from damage resulting from ground movement. The actual depth below ground level is dependent on a number of factors: load-bearing capacity of the subsoil; need to protect against ground movement; tree roots; and so on. In most circumstances, a depth of 1 m to the bottom of the foundation is considered to be the minimum.

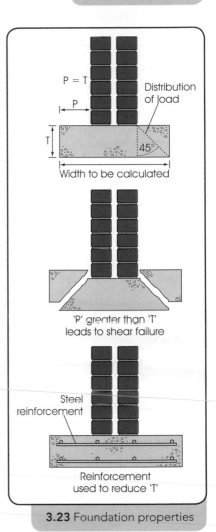

3.23 Foundation properties

KEY TERMS

Greenfield: undeveloped land that has never been built on. The term should not be confused with 'greenbelt', which refers to land around urban areas left permanently open or largely undeveloped to restrict further expansion.

Brownfield: previously developed land that is now vacant or derelict, and also land currently in use with a potential for redevelopment.

Contaminated: land (often brownfield) that contains concentrations of hazardous waste or pollution that requires cleaning up before building work can start.

Natural water table: the underground depth or level at which point the ground is totally saturated with water.

DID YOU KNOW

The presence of mine workings and wells increases the risk of subsidence and landslip.

Different types of subsoil have different bearing capacity:

○ Rock is normally able to bear high loads, but may contain faults that can collapse under load, causing settlement.

○ Granular subsoils (e.g. compacted sands and gravels) are able to bear medium to high loads. However, sand can be affected by flooding, and loose sand is unstable and requires containing.

○ Cohesive subsoils (e.g. firm/stiff clays, sandy clays, soft silt, soft clay) are capable of supporting medium to low loads.

○ Organic soils (e.g. peat and topsoil) have a low load bearing capacity as they contain a high proportion of organic material, as well as air and water and are normally unsuitable for building on unless piles are used.

Ground movement is caused mainly by the shrinkage and expansion of the ground near the surface due to wet and dry conditions.

○ Rock and compact granular subsoil suffers little movement, but clay is at high risk as moisture changes cause it to shrink in the summer and swell in the winter.

○ Frost causes ground movement through frost heave (when water in the ground expands on freezing). This is limited to about 600 mm below ground level.

○ Tree roots can cause shrinkage owing to the quantity of water they extract from it. The roots of a tree can extend in all directions, greater than its height.

Site investigation

A site investigation is normally carried out during the initial design stage to determine the most suitable type of foundation to use. The surveyor undertaking the site investigation will typically consider the following points in their report to the structural engineer:

○ Is it a **greenfield** or **brownfield** site?

○ Is the land **contaminated**? Samples may need to be taken for laboratory analysis.

○ What is the type of soil? Trail holes may be dug or bored samples taken for laboratory analysis.

○ What is the **natural water table**? Again, trail holes may be dug to establish this or a search of local or British Geological Survey records made.

○ Is **radon** gas present or is the site subject to **subsidence** and **landslip**? A search of local or British Geological Survey records will reveal if the site is in an 'at-risk' area; further site tests may also be required.

○ Are mine workings or wells present? Again, a search of local or British Geological Survey records may be required.

Foundation types

There are four common types of foundations:

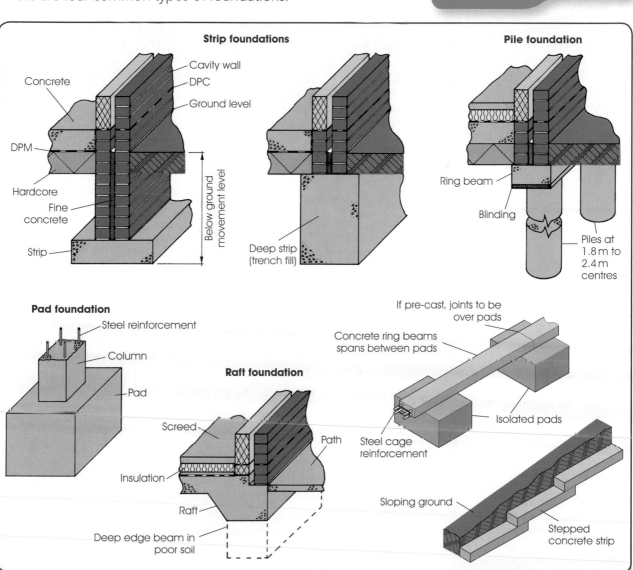

3.24 Foundation types

Type of Foundations	Use and Methods
Strip	Narrow and often used for dwellings and low-rise solid structures. "Stepped" in sloping ground reduces excavation. "Deep" saves bricklaying well below ground but needs more concrete.
Raft	Float on surface where subsoil is poor quality and unstable. Concrete slab covers footprint of building and thickened edge beam round edges takes additional wall loading.
Pad	Normally for steel or concrete framed structures. Pads at column positions transfer structural loads into subsoil. Can also be used with a perimeter ring beam to provide bearing surface for walls.
Pile	Used for low-rise structures on poor and unstable subsoil. Building loads are transferred deep into the subsoil, reducing excavation needed if deep strip foundations were used. Series of holes bored around perimeter of building at between 1.8 and 2.4m centres and up to 4m deep and filled with concrete. These are then spanned by concrete ring beams to bear loads of the walls.

DID YOU KNOW

Concrete rapidly increases in strength during this initial curing process (setting). It will have obtained 85 per cent of its strength after 28 days, and will continue to gain the remaining 15 per cent of its strength during the rest of its life.

KEY TERMS

In-situ cast concrete: concrete that is poured in its liquid form directly into position on-site. It can be mixed either on-site or be supplied to site in a ready-mixed form.

Pre-cast concrete: concrete that is poured in to a mould and allowed to cure before being moved to its location.

Materials used in foundations

The main material used to form foundations is **in-situ cast concrete**, which is a mixture of cement, fine and coarse aggregates and water. On mixing, the fine aggregate fills the voids in the coarse aggregate; the cement mixes with the water and coats the surfaces of the aggregate, bonding them together. The concrete then sets by a chemical reaction between the cement and the water. Concrete may also be reinforced with steel and require formwork for support.

Cement is the binder or adhesive in a concrete mix that holds the aggregates together. It is manufactured from chalk or limestone and clay, which are ground into a powder, mixed together and fired in a kiln causing a chemical reaction. On leaving the kiln, the resulting material is ground to a fine powder. Hence, a popular site term for cement is 'dust'.

Aggregates are the filler materials used in concrete and consist of fine aggregate (sand) and coarse aggregate (gravel and crushed rock).

Water allows the cement to set and makes the mix workable. It should be free from any impurities that could affect the concrete's strength. As a general rule, it should be of a **potable** quality.

Reinforcement in the form of steel bars or mesh may be required in certain situations to provide sufficient strength and prevent the concrete from cracking, which could even result in structural failure. Concrete is very strong when being compressed (squashed), but much weaker when in tension (stretched or bent). Thus, to prevent concrete being pulled apart when used in wide strip foundations, ring beams and piles (may be in tension), reinforcement will be specified.

Formwork, also called shuttering, is the temporary structure that is designed to shape and support wet concrete until it cures enough to support itself. Strip, pad and pile foundations do not normally require any formwork, as the concrete is normally cast against and supported by the trench, pit or bored hole sides. Raft foundation and edge beams may require formwork around the edges to contain the concrete.

Concrete mixes

Concrete mixes can be specified by either weight or volume. A typical mix for non-reinforced strip foundations and ground floor slabs might be specified as 1:3:6, meaning one part cement, three parts fine aggregate and six parts coarse aggregate. Reinforced concrete normally has a higher percentage of cement compared to the aggregate and may be specified as 1:2:4 mixes.

Walls

The walls of a building may be classed as either load-bearing or non-load bearing. In addition, external walls have an enclosing role and internal walls a dividing one. Thus, load-bearing walls carry out a dual role of supporting and enclosing or dividing. Internal walls, both load and non-load bearing, are normally called partitions. Openings in load-bearing walls for windows and doors are bridged by either arches or lintels, which support the weight of the wall above. External walls may be divided into three main groups according to their method of construction: solid; cavity and framed.

LINK

Fine aggregate (sand) has grains that are smaller than 5mm. Coarse aggregates (gravel and crushed rock) has grains which are 5mm or larger. See page 232 for further detail on aggregates.

KEY TERMS

Potable: liquid that is suitable for drinking because it's clean and uncontaminated.

DID YOU KNOW

The amount of water used in a concrete mix should be kept to the minimum required to make it workable. The more water in a mix, the weaker the concrete will be.

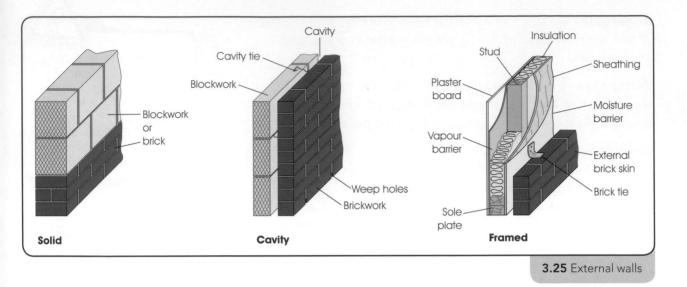

3.25 External walls

Solid walls

These are made from bricks, blocks or concrete. When used externally, very thick walls are required (450 mm or over) in order to provide enough thermal insulation and prevent internal dampness through rain absorption. However, due to the high costs involved, this method is now rarely used.

The modern alternative is to use thinner external solid walls (normally lightweight insulating blocks) and apply an impervious (waterproof) surface finish to the outside, such as cement rendering, tile hanging or cladding in timber, metal and plastics. The surface can even be made to resemble brick or stonework by bonding thin brick slips or stone panels on to the plain solid wall surface. Internally, they can be plastered or dry lined with plasterboard.

Cavity walls

These consist of an inner and outer wall (also known as leaves) separated by a void, known as a cavity. The cavity prevents the transfer of moisture from the outside to the inside and also improves the wall's thermal-insulation properties. Solid blockwork may be used up to ground level with a cavity wall above that or, alternatively, the cavity can go down to the foundation. In this case, the cavity should be filled up to ground level with a fine concrete to resist ground pressures. Cavity walls are commonly used for low to medium-rise buildings.

The standard form of the wall is a brick outer leaf and an insulating block inner leaf. Any moisture that penetrates into the cavity is allowed to disperse at ground level through 'weep holes' left in vertical joints. Industrial and commercial buildings are often constructed using a cavity wall for the lower part with insulated steel panels fixed to the structural steel frame above.

When first built, the cavity was left as an air void. However, modern standards require the cavity to be partially or fully filled with an insulating material (mineral wool, glassfibre, polyurethane foam or polystyrene) in order to reduce sound and heat transfer through the wall. Where insulation batts are used to partially fill a cavity, these should be clipped back to the inner leaf as the work progresses.

Framed walls

These are normally of timber construction, although steel frames are also in use. They are made up in units called panels and may be either load or non-load bearing for external or internal use. The panels consist of vertical members called studs and horizontal members, the top and bottom of which are called the head and sole plates, while any intermediates are called noggins. Sheathing is fixed to one or both sides of the panel for strength. Thermal and sound-insulating properties are achieved by filling the spaces between the members with mineral wool, glassfibre or similar. Suitable vapour and moisture barriers are included to keep the timber and insulation dry.

Bonding of solid and cavity walls

The strength of brickwork and blockwork is dependent on its **bonding**. Bonding spreads any load evenly throughout the wall.

The actual overlap or bonding pattern will vary depending on the type of wall and the decorative effect required:

⬡ Solid walls are normally built in either **English** or **Flemish bond**.

⬡ Cavity walls are built in **stretcher bond**. To ensure sufficient strength, the inner and outer leaves are tied together across the cavity at intervals with cavity ties.

DID YOU KNOW

Today most timber-frame house construction uses the type of framed wall panel described as the load-bearing internal leaf of the cavity wall. A non-load-bearing brick or blockwork outer weathering leaf is then used, which is tied back to the timber frame for support.

KEY TERMS

Bonding: the overlapping of vertical joints in brickwork and blockwork.

English bond: consists of alternate rows (courses) of bricks laid lengthways along the wall (stretchers) and bricks laid width-ways across the wall (headers).

Flemish bond: consists of alternate stretchers and headers in the same course. In both, the quarter lap is formed by placing a queen closer (brick reduced in width) next to the quoin (corner brick).

Stretcher bond: where all bricks show their stretcher faces, although adjacent courses overlap by half a brick.

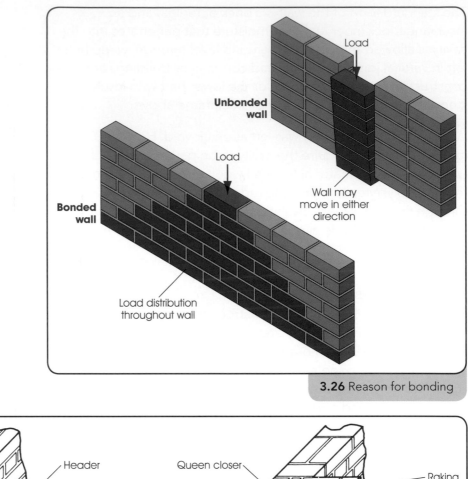

3.26 Reason for bonding

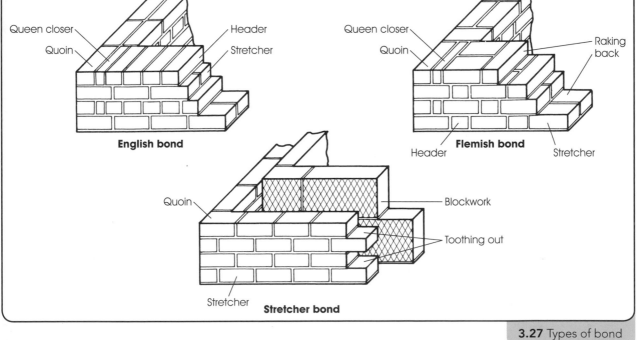

3.27 Types of bond

Jointing of walls

Brickwork and blockwork walls are joined using mortar. Mortar is a mixture of sand and cement and/or lime that forms an adhesive. Sufficient potable water is added so that the mix has the consistency of soft butter, which is firm enough not to collapse when heaped, but easily compressed with a shovel.

Horizontal mortar joints are known as bed joints and vertical ones as perpends or perps. The face of these joints may be finished in a variety of profiles, which are intended to improve the weathering resistance and appearance of the work. The most common joint profiles are:

Flush: created using a timber or plastic block to compact and smooth the surface mortar, suitable for internal brickwork or sheltered external locations.

Tooled: concave 'bucket handle' finish created by working along the drying mortar with a special jointing tool, a piece of 15 mm copper pipe or a metal bucket handle (hence the name). Suitable for external work.

Recessed: created by brushing out the drying mortar with a stiff-bristle hand brush. Working the joint with a piece of timber with a protruding countersunk screw will give a more consistent depth. Suitable for internal work only as water gathers easily.

Weathered or stuck jointed: created by drawing the blade of a small pointing trowel backwards along the joint. The trowel should be tilted slightly inwards at the top with its top edge in contact with the underside of the bricks above the joint. Creates a downward sloping joint that easily sheds rainwater.

These are often formed as the completed brickwork is laid and is called 'jointing or 'striking'. Alternatively, the joints may be recessed during the build ready to receive the later addition of mortar in which the joint profile is formed and is known as 'pointing'.

Gauging mortar mixes

Gauging is the measuring of materials used in a mortar to achieve the required strength and specification. Mortar mixes can be specified by either weight or volume.

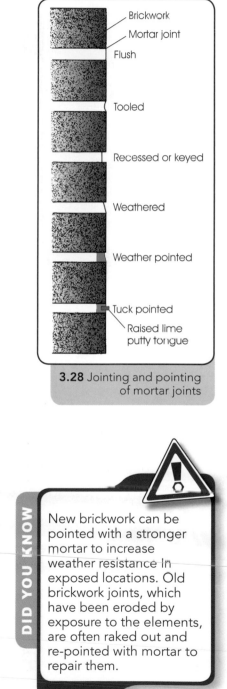

Brickwork
Mortar joint
Flush
Tooled
Recessed or keyed
Weathered
Weather pointed
Tuck pointed
Raised lime putty tongue

3.28 Jointing and pointing of mortar joints

DID YOU KNOW

New brickwork can be pointed with a stronger mortar to increase weather resistance In exposed locations. Old brickwork joints, which have been eroded by exposure to the elements, are often raked out and re-pointed with mortar to repair them.

○ **Gauging by weight** is the most accurate method, but is normally restricted to large sites using either batch weighing mixers, where the weight of the sand and cement is recorded as it is shovelled into the hopper; or dry-silo mortar systems that are filled with the correctly proportioned materials in a dry state.

○ **Gauging by volume** is the most common method used for small quantities of mortar. This can be done using a 10 litre builder's bucket or a gauge box. The use of a shovel to gauge by volume is not to be recommended as each 'shovel full' can vary considerably.

Mixing mortar

Once the materials have been gauged, the mortar can be mixed. Small quantities of mortar are often mixed by hand; larger quantities of mortar are mixed in a mechanical mixer that is powered by petrol, diesel or electricity. It's more common practice to have ready-mixed mortars delivered to the site. This is deposited from the mixing lorry into specially provided plastic tubs and is ready to use immediately. The mortar is normally retarded using a chemical retarding agent; so that it can be used over a period of 48 hours. Tubs should be kept covered to prevent water evaporation and early setting.

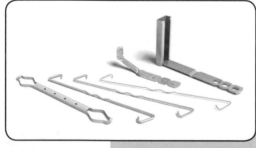

3.29 Types of wall tie

Wall ties

Wall ties are used in cavity walls to tie the inner and outer leaves together. Without wall ties, the two leaves would bulge or bow under load. Ties are made from a number of materials including stainless steel, galvanised steel and plastic and in a range of patterns including fishtail, butterfly and double triangular. Each tie will include a design feature such as a twist or bend in the centre that prevents moisture passing between the two leaves of the wall. Wall ties are simply bedded into the mortar joint at set distances as the wall is being built.

Lintels

Openings in walls for doors and windows are spanned by steel or concrete lintels. These bridge the opening and transfer loads to the reveal on either side. Concrete lintels will contain steel reinforcement towards their bottom edge, to resist tensile forces.

When being carried, it is most important that lintels are moved the right way up, as they will be used, otherwise they may simply fold in two. Where the steel bars or wires cannot be seen on the end, the top edge is often marked with a 'T' or 'TOP' for identification.

Damp-proof courses (DPCs)

DPCs are built into the horizontal course of brick and blockwork walls, positioned at least 150 mm above the exterior ground level. This is to prevent dampness rising up from the ground through the wall and penetrating into the building. In the past, slate and lead were used as DPCs. Today DPCs are commonly made from polythene sheet, which is available in rolls of various widths to suit the wall size.

Internal walls

Internal walls are constructed either as solid or framed walls.

Solid internal walls

Partitions consist of bonded blocks or bricks bedded in cement mortar.

⬡ Block partitions in industrial and other heavily trafficked buildings may be left unplastered (called fair faced) to provide a hardwearing finish. Extra care must be taken with the joints as these will be exposed. Paint grade blocks are available for use in fair-faced partitions where a painted finish is required.

DID YOU KNOW

Damp-proof membranes (DPMs) are used under the concrete in ground floors to waterproof them against ground moisture.

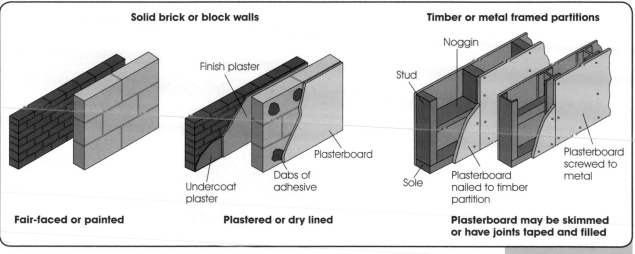

Solid brick or block walls

Finish plaster

Plasterboard

Undercoat plaster

Dabs of adhesive

Fair-faced or painted

Plastered or dry lined

Timber or metal framed partitions

Noggin

Stud

Sole

Plasterboard nailed to timber partition

Plasterboard screwed to metal

Plasterboard may be skimmed or have joints taped and filled

3.30 Internal walls

⬡ In other locations, block partitions are more often finished using a two-coat plaster system, or have plasterboard bonded to the surface called dry lining.

⬡ 'Dot and dab' is the term given to bonding plasterboard to a wall surface. It involves applying dots of plasterboard adhesive to the wall surface or the back of the plasterboard and pushing the board directly on to the wall.

⬡ Brick walls may also be built using either facing bricks to provide a decorative feature or common bricks that can be painted, plastered or dry lined.

Framed internal walls

Partitions are commonly known as stud partitions or stud partitioning. These are walls built using timber or metal studs fixed between sole and head plates, often incorporating noggins for stiffening and fixing. Plasterboard is mainly used as the covering material fixed by nailing to timber partitions or with self-tapping screws to metal ones. Boards can be dry finished where the joints are filled and taped or wet finished using a skim coat of plaster.

Floors

The main function of a floor is to provide a level surface and insulation and to carry and transfer any loads imposed upon them. Ground floors must also prevent moisture penetration and weed growth.

Ground floors

There are two main types of ground floor construction: solid and suspended. A solid ground floor is in direct contact with the ground and a suspended floor spans from wall to wall.

DID YOU KNOW

An advantage of using plasterboard as a lining for internal wall surfaces is that it means there is less need for using wet trades and the associated drying out times.

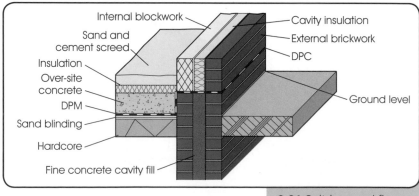

Internal blockwork
Cavity insulation
Sand and cement screed
External brickwork
Insulation
DPC
Over-site concrete
DPM
Ground level
Sand blinding
Hardcore
Fine concrete cavity fill

3.31 Solid ground floors

Solid ground floors	These are built up from a number of layers: – Well-compacted hardcore provides a suitable base. – A thin layer of sand or weak concrete is often used to fill voids or level out the rough edges of the hardcore in order to reduce grout loss or the risk of puncturing the DPM. – A DPM is placed between the hardcore and concrete slab to prevent ground moisture rising through the floor. A DPM is a plastic material, usually polythene or PVC, that comes in a roll. Any joints between rolls should be well lapped and sealed with a self-adhesive tape to ensure the joints don't open up when the concrete is poured. It is essential that the DPM is lapped into the walls' DPC in order to prevent any possibility of ground moisture by-passing the DPM. – A concrete floor slab, also known as the over-site concrete since it covers the whole site of the building. The over-site is not built into the walls but acts as an independent raft transferring its imposed loading directly to the ground and not the foundations. – For industrial use, such as factories, warehouses, garages, and so on, the over-site concrete may be power floated or grinded to form the actual floor finish. – In other buildings, it is normal to lay a cement and sand screed. This screed levels the slab, takes out any irregularities and provides a smooth surface to receive the final floor finish (e.g. carpet, lino, tilesetc.) – Alternatively, a floating timber floor can be laid over the concrete subfloor to provide the final finish. – Insulation is included in solid floors to provide the required thermal standards. This can be positioned either between the over-site and the screed('cold slab' construction), or under the over-site ('warm slab' construction).
Suspended ground floors	Timber joists and floor boarding are rarely used today. The modern method is to use pre-cast concrete beams, in-filled with concrete blocks, known as beam and block floors.
Timber ground floors	In common with solid ground floors, these require the hardcore and over-site concrete layers. – The dwarf or sleeper walls, which support the timber floor construction, are built on top of the over-site at about 1.8 m centres using honeycomb bond (a bond that leaves half-brick voids in the wall to allow air circulation). – Airbricks must also be included in the outside walls at ground level to enable through ventilation in the under-floor space. This prevents the moisture content of the timber rising too high. Dry-rot fungi will almost inevitably attack timber in poorly ventilated areas with moisture content above 20 per cent. – Floor boards or sheets are supported by joists that bear on wall plates that, in turn, spread the load evenly along the sleeper walls. – A DPC is placed between the wall plate and sleeper walls to prevent the rise of ground moisture into the timberwork. – Insulation supported on bearers or meshing should be placed between the joists to prevent the cool ventilated under-floor space drawing the warm air from the room.
Beam and block ground floors	These consist of pre-cast concrete beams and an infill of lightweight concrete infill slabs or blocks. – The ends of the inverted 'tee' section beams are supported on either the inner skin of the cavity wall or by separate sleeper walls. – Intermediate sleeper walls may also be required, to provide mid-span support or to enable beams to be joined in length. – The beams should be evenly spaced to receive the concrete infill blocks. – Infill blocks are laid edge to edge and are supported on the beam's protruding bottom edge. – After laying, any gaps between the blocks and beams can be filled by brushing in a sand and cement grout. – Insulation is placed over the beams and blocks to provide the required thermal standards. – The actual finished floor surface can be formed using either sand and cement screed or a timber floating floor.
Floating ground floors	These provide a timber floor construction over concrete floors. They consist of bearers, which are laid unfixed on a layer of resilient insulating material. When the floor boarding or sheeting is fixed to the bearers, the whole floor floats on the insulation and is held down by its own weight and the skirting around the perimeter of the room. In addition to providing enhanced thermal insulation, floating floors also provide increased levels of impact sound insulation as there are breaks in the construction.

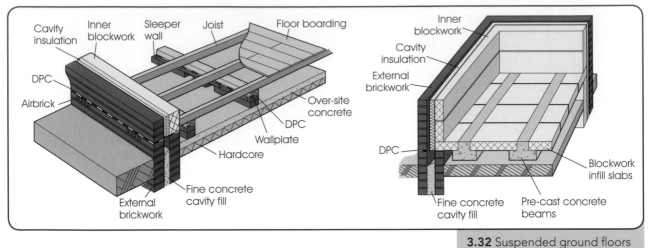

3.32 Suspended ground floors

Upper floors

These are also known as suspended floors. Timber construction is mainly used for house construction and concrete for other works.

Timber suspended upper floors	These consist of a number of bridging joists supported at either end by load-bearing walls.
	– The joists are covered on their topside by floor boarding or sheeting to provide the floor surface and on their underside with plasterboard to form the ceiling.
	– The end of the joists can either be supported by building them into the internal leaf of the cavity wall or, alternatively, metal joist hangers may be used; these have a flange that locates in the joint of the wall.
	– Where openings in the floor are required for stairs, chimney breasts, and so on, the joists must be framed or trimmed around the opening. A number of bridging joists are cut short so that they do not protrude into the opening. These are called trimmed joists.
	– Trimmer and trimming joists, which are thicker than the bridging, are framed around the opening to provide support for the ends of the trimmed joists.
	– In order to prevent joists longer than 2 m buckling when under load, they must be strutted at their centre. This has the effect of stiffening the whole floor.
	– Galvanised restraint straps, also known as lateral restraint straps, are used at intervals in modern lightweight structures to provide a positive joint between walls and joisted areas. These tie the structural elements together for strength, to ensure wall stability in windy conditions.
	– Insulation may be added between the joists to prevent heat loss, particularly where the floor separates a heated room from an unheated room or space below. This also provides increased levels of sound insulation.
Concrete suspended upper floors	These are supported on the walls or structural framework. They may be formed using either reinforced in-situ cast concrete or some form of pre-cast concrete units.
	– In both cases, the top surface will require screeding to receive the floor finish or a timber floating floor. The bottom surface will need plastering or another form of finishing to provide the ceiling surface.
	– In situ-cast concrete floors will require the erection of formwork to cast and support the wet concrete.
	– In general, concrete floors are more sound resistant to airborne noise and have better fire-resistant properties than timber floors.

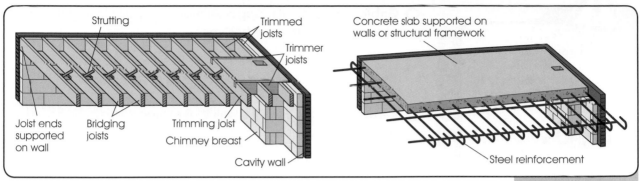

3.33 Upper floors

Roof structures

The roof is the part of the external envelope that spans the building at high level and has structural, weathering and insulation functions. Roof structures provide lateral (sideways) restraint and stability to the walls of a building by linking them together using galvanised metal restraint straps and tie down straps. Roofs are classified according to the slope of the roof surface, which is known as the pitch, and also by their shape.

Roof elements

○ **Abutment**: the intersection where a lean-to or flat roof meets the main wall structure.

> **DID YOU KNOW**
>
> Timber used for joists should be machined to a regular size to provide a flat, level surface for the floor boarding and the ceiling.

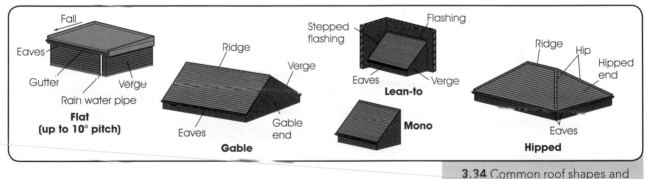

3.34 Common roof shapes and elements

○ **Eaves**: the lower edge of a roof overhanging the walls and where rainwater is discharged into a gutter and then into a drain via a rainwater pipe (RWP). May be finished with a timber or plastic fascia board and soffit.

○ **Flashing**: the pieces of sheet metal, normally lead or zinc, attached around the joints and angles of a roof to protect against rainwater penetration.

DID YOU KNOW

Thermal insulation is required in flat roofs. This can be put either in the roof space between the joists or above the roof space on top of the decking:

- Insulation in the roof space, known as cold roof construction, has thermal insulation and a vapour check at ceiling level. The roof space itself is cold and must be vented to the outside air to prevent interstitial condensation.

- Insulation above the roof space, known as warm roof construction, has its thermal insulation and vapour barrier placed over the roof decking. The roof space is kept warmer than the outside air temperature and does not require ventilation.

- **Gable**: the triangular upper section of a wall closing the end of a building with a pitched roof.

- **Hip**: the line between the ridge and eaves of a pitched roof, where the two sloping surfaces meet at an external angle.

- **Parapet**: the section of a wall that projects above and finishes some way beyond the roof surface.

- **Ridge**: the horizontal line where two sloping roof surfaces meet at their highest point or apex.

- **Valley**: the line between the ridge and eaves of a pitched roof, where the two sloping surfaces meet at an internal angle.

- **Verge**: the edge of a pitched roof at the gable or the sloping edge (non-drained) of a flat roof. May be finished with a timber or plastic bargeboard and soffit.

Flat roofs

Timber flat roofs are similar in construction to that of upper floors. They consist of joists that span between the walls; their means of support, tying in with lateral restraint straps, stiffening with the use of strutting and the decking are all similar to those of upper floors.

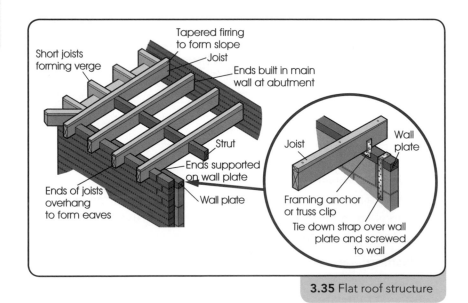

3.35 Flat roof structure

○ Although the surface of the roof is flat, it is not horizontal. It should have a slope or fall on its top surface of up to 10 degrees to ensure that rainwater will quickly clear from the roof. The fall can be provided by either laying the joists at a pitch or by using long tapered wedge-shaped firring pieces on top of each joist.

○ The structural deck, which is fixed to the joists or firring pieces, is normally a manufactured sheet material such as plywood or chipboard. These should be of a moisture resisting grade and sold as suitable for use as flat-roof decking. Decking sheets may be either square-edged or T&G, and are also available pre-covered with a layer of felt to be initially weatherproof.

○ The decking is normally weathered by a seamless covering of either rolls of layered bituminous felt bonded to the decking with cold or hot applied bitumen, or mastic asphalt hot applied in layers on sheathing felt. In order to reflect some of the sun's heat, both types may be protected with a heat-reflecting paint or covered with a layer of pale-coloured stone chippings.

○ Other weatherproofing can be done using lead or copper, and various profiled sheet materials manufactured in protected metals, translucent plastics and cement/mineral fibre.

Pitched roofs

Timber pitched roofs have a slope or pitch of over 10 degrees and may be divided into two broad, but distinct, categories: traditional framed cut roofs and prefabricated trussed rafters.

○ **Traditional framed cut roofs**: almost entirely constructed by carpenters on-site from loose timber sections using simple jointing methods. The main component parts of traditional framed cut roofs are:

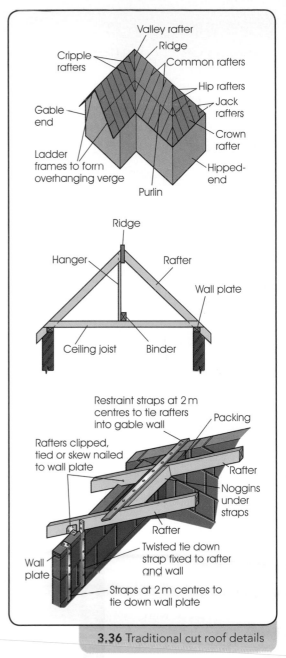

3.36 Traditional cut roof details

Component part	Usage
Common rafters	main load bearers, cut to fit the ridge and birds mouthed over wall plate
Ridge board	backbone of the roof, giving a fixing point for the tops of the rafters, keeping them in line
Wall plates	transfer the loads on the roof uniformly over supporting brickwork and act as bearing and fixing point for the feet of the rafters and ceiling joists
Hip rafters	where two sloping roof surfaces meet at an external angle, they act as fixing point for the jack rafters and transfer their loads to the wall plate
Jack rafters	span from wall plate to hip rafter, like common rafters with shortened tops
Crown rafters	common rafters used in the centre of a hip's ends
Cripple rafters	span from the ridge to the valley, like common rafters with shortened feet (reverse of jack rafters)
Valley rafters	like a hip rafter, but at an internal angle to give fixing point for cripple rafters, transferring their loads to the wall plate
Purlin	a beam providing support for the rafters in their mid span
Ladder frames	or gable ladders, fixed to the last common rafter, forming the overhanging verge on a gable roof. They consist of two rafters with noggins nailed between them.
Ceiling joists	ties for each pair of rafters at wall plate level and give a surface on which the ceiling plasterboard can be fixed
Binders and hangers	stiffen and support the ceiling joists in their mid span, preventing them from sagging and distorting the ceiling

DID YOU KNOW

Wall plates for flat and pitched roofs must be held in place with galvanised metal tie down straps at intervals along the wall. These anchor the wall plates to the walls and prevent movement, especially in windy conditions.

○ **Prefabricated trussed rafters**: normally manufactured off-site under factory conditions and delivered to site ready for erection.

– They are triangular roof frames that consist of rafters, ceiling joists and structural triangulation. They are manufactured using prepared **strength graded** softwood in one plane, with their butt joints fastened with galvanised metal nail plates.

– They are spaced along the roof at between 400 and 600 mm centres and fixed to the wall plate. Unlike common rafters, the trusses simply rest on top of the wall plates and are not birds mouthed over them.

– To provide lateral stability, binders are needed at both ceiling and apex level and diagonal rafter bracing is fixed to the underside of the rafters.

– For stability, the gable wall must be tied back to the roof using lateral restraint straps both up the rafter slope and along the ceiling tie.

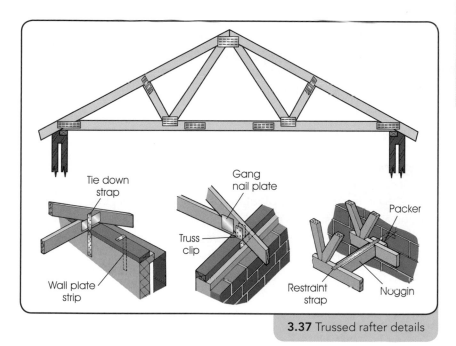

3.37 Trussed rafter details

Pitched roof coverings

Pitched roofs can be weatherproofed using clay or concrete tiles; quarried or man-made slates; wood shingles (normally cedar); thatch (reeds); and various profiled sheet materials manufactured from protected metals, plastics or a cement/mineral fibre mix. In general, as the pitch of the roof lowers the unit size of the covering material must increase.

Pitched roof insulation and ventilation

Insulation is included in pitched roofs to provide the required thermal standards.

◯ It is placed both between and over the ceiling joists to give a total insulating layer of around 300 mm. This is carried over the inner leaf of the cavity wall and well into the eaves.

◯ The eaves must not be blocked with the insulating material, as the roof space must be well ventilated so that warm moist air passing through the ceiling does not form condensation.

◯ A vapour check, such as foil-backed plasterboard, at ceiling level below the insulation will reduce the amount of water vapour passing through the ceiling into the cold roof space.

◯ Adequate eaves ventilation is achieved by:

– leaving a gap between the wall and fascia board to allow a cross flow of air into the roof space. Where eaves are closed with a soffit board, proprietary ventilation strips or discs allow the passage of air.

– proprietary ventilators or timber boards between the rafters prevent the insulation blocking the air path at the eaves.

Stairs

Each step in stairs is a combination of tread and riser., Each continuous set of steps is called a flight. Landings may be introduced between floor levels to break up a long flight, giving rest points, or to change the direction of the stairs. Stairs are classified according to their plan shape or by the material from which they are made. Timber stairs are common in domestic houses, while concrete or steel stairs are more common for other works.

CHECK YOUR UNDERSTANDING

At level 1: K1

◆ Explain what bench marks and datums are used for.

◆ State the purpose of a foundation.

◆ Produce a sketch to show the difference between two types of strip foundations.

◆ State **two** uses of concrete and list the materials used to make it.

◆ State the purpose of DPCs and name two suitable materials that can be used for them.

At level 1: K2

◆ Produce a sketch to show the difference between, stretcher, English and Flemish brick bonds.

◆ State the purpose of wall ties.

◆ State the reason why cavities were originally included in external walls.

◆ State **two** uses of concrete and list the materials used to make it.

◆ Explain what mortar is used for and list the materials used to make it.

At level 1: K3

- ✅ Explain the difference between traditional pitched roofs and modern trussed rafters.
- ✅ State the purpose of wall plates used in roofs.
- ✅ Explain the purpose of firring pieces used in flat roofs.
- ✅ State why felt and battens are used in pitched roofs.
- ✅ Produce a sectional sketch through a pitched roof to show a wall plate, common rafter, purlin and ridge board.

At level 2: K1

- ✅ Explain the difference between live and dead loads in relation to building structures.
- ✅ State the effect of compression and tension in a timber joist under load.
- ✅ Explain the difference between the substructure and superstructure of a building.
- ✅ Name **two** types of internal wall construction and, for each, state **two** alternative methods used to finish them.
- ✅ Produce a sketch to show the difference between solid, cavity and framed external walls.

ASSESSMENT CHECK

Now that you have completed this learning outcome you should now be able to:

At level 1

- ✅ state the purpose of a datum level used in construction
- ✅ list the materials used in concrete foundations and floors
- ✅ state the reasons for the use of DPMs and DPCs
- ✅ explain the need for half-brick bonding
- ✅ state the reason for the use of cavity wall construction
- ✅ state why tie wires and lintels are used in the construction of a building
- ✅ state the methods used for mixing mortar to the required strength/specification
- ✅ list the appropriate roof fixings used in roof construction
- ✅ state the different methods of roof construction
- ✅ state the reason for the use of wall plates and the purpose of wall plate straps
- ✅ state the purpose of different roof components used in roof construction

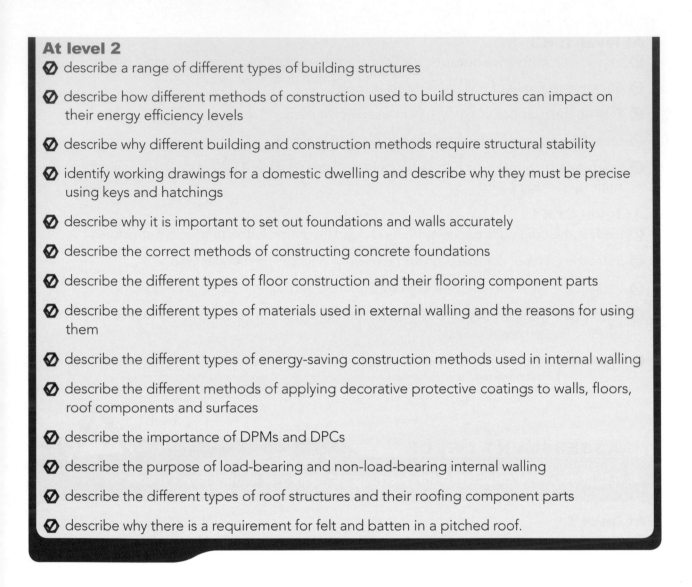

At level 2

- describe a range of different types of building structures

- describe how different methods of construction used to build structures can impact on their energy efficiency levels

- describe why different building and construction methods require structural stability

- identify working drawings for a domestic dwelling and describe why they must be precise using keys and hatchings

- describe why it is important to set out foundations and walls accurately

- describe the correct methods of constructing concrete foundations

- describe the different types of floor construction and their flooring component parts

- describe the different types of materials used in external walling and the reasons for using them

- describe the different types of energy-saving construction methods used in internal walling

- describe the different methods of applying decorative protective coatings to walls, floors, roof components and surfaces

- describe the importance of DPMs and DPCs

- describe the purpose of load-bearing and non-load-bearing internal walling

- describe the different types of roof structures and their roofing component parts

- describe why there is a requirement for felt and batten in a pitched roof.

K2 Principles of internal building work

Material selection

There is a wide range of materials, both natural (timber and stone) and manufactured (bricks, blocks, metals and plastics), available to the building designer. The selection of a particular material for a specific purpose will depend on the following points of consideration.

Materials must:

○ satisfy the client's requirements both functionally and aesthetically

○ satisfy these requirements over the expected life of the building, with little maintenance

○ be readily available at a cost that comes within the client's budget

○ be sustainable, environmentally friendly and energy efficient

DID YOU KNOW

All materials have certain properties and characteristics to be considered when selecting them for a particular use:

○ **Conductivity** refers to the ability of a material to transmit heat, electricity or sound.

○ **Durable** materials will last for a long time; **non-durable** materials will not.

○ **Porous** materials have a surface that contains pores or a body that contains holes; **non-porous** materials do not.

○ **Permeable** materials permit the movement of liquids and gases through them, through pores or holes; **non-permeable** materials do not.

○ **Strength** refers to the ability of a material to withstand a force or stress, such as **compressive**, **tensile** and **shear strength**.

⬡ comply with relevant legislation, British and European standard specifications, codes of practice and other statutory building controls

⬡ blend in with the local environment in such a way that, as far as possible, they are aesthetically acceptable.

Common building materials

The main groups of building materials in common use are considered in the following section.

Aggregates

Aggregates are sands, gravel and crushed rock. They can be used as hardcore in foundations; added to cement as filler material to produce concrete, mortar and screeds; in floors and walls; as insulation and as a filler material in rendering and tar macadam mixes.

Fine aggregate (sand)	All grains are smaller than 5 mm. Those with angular grains are called sharp sands (used in concrete mixes), those with rounded or smooth grains are called soft sands (used in mortar mixes).
Coarse aggregate (gravel and crushed rock)	All grains are a minimum of 5 mm and larger
All-in aggregate	A well-graded mixture of fine and coarse aggregates, also known as ballast
Lightweight aggregate	Low-density fine and coarse aggregates
Natural aggregates	Naturally occurring materials, such as gravel, sand and crushed rock
Manufactured aggregate	Created by some industrial processes often involving heat, such as blast furnace slag
Recycled aggregates	Crushed brickwork and concrete demolition waste

Bricks

Bricks have a standard size of 215 × 102.5 × 65 mm, which gives a modular size including a 10 mm mortar joint allowance of 225 × 75 mm. Handmade brick sizes may vary slightly. Bricks are normally made from either clay or calcium silicate.

○ Clay bricks are usually pressed, cut or moulded and then fired in a kiln at very high temperatures. Their durability, density, strength, colour and surface texture will depend on the variety of clay used and the firing temperature. Frogs and perforations both increase the strength of the bond between the brick and mortar joint.

○ Calcium silicate bricks are pressed into shape and steamed at high temperatures. Pigments may be added during the manufacturing process to achieve a range of colours.

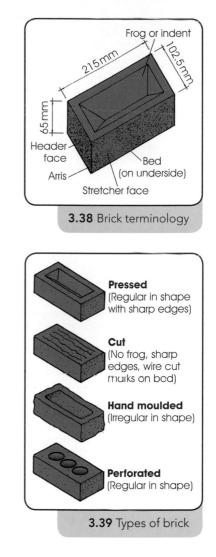

3.38 Brick terminology

The three main types of bricks are as follows:

○ **Common or Fletton bricks**: basic bricks for internal work or covered (rendered or cladded) external work, although sand-faced Flettons are available for use as cheap facing bricks.

○ **Facing bricks**: made from selected clays and chosen for their attractive appearance rather than any other performance characteristic.

○ **Engineering bricks**: have a very high density and strength and do not absorb moisture. They are available in two classes: 'Class A', which are blue in colour, have the highest strength and best resistance to moisture; and 'Class B', which are red in colour, have smooth faces and slightly reduced strength and moisture-resisting properties. Engineering bricks may be used instead of facing bricks, but they are best used in both highly-loaded and damp conditions, such as inspection chambers, basements and other substructure work.

3.39 Types of brick

Careful selection of bricks is required at the design stage as the density and durability can vary widely. Denser bricks can normally carry greater loadings; frost-resistant bricks that are durable should be specified for exposed locations; bricks with a low soluble salt content are less likely to cause **efflorescence**.

Blocks

Blocks are larger than bricks, typically 440 × 215 mm and in a range of widths, giving a modular size when used with 10 mm mortar joints of 450 × 225 mm.

Blocks are normally made from concrete or natural stone.

KEY TERMS

Efflorescence: white powdery deposits on the surface of a wall, caused by soluble salts in the wall, which crystallise as the structure dries.

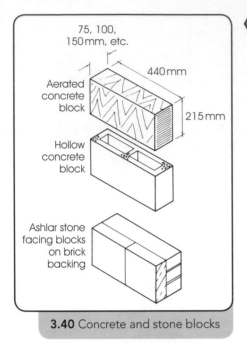

3.40 Concrete and stone blocks

○ **Concrete blocks** can be either dense or lightweight.

– Dense blocks are often made hollow to lighten them.

– Lightweight blocks can use a lightweight or fine aggregate that is aerated to form air bubbles. These are called thermal blocks.

– Concrete blocks are often used for the substructure; the inner leaf of cavity walls and also internal partition walls.

– When used externally, blocks are either rendered or covered in cladding to provide a waterproofing. Internally, they may be plastered, dry lined or painted.

– Hollow concrete blocks are often used in retaining walls, where they are strengthened by filling the voids with wet concrete and steel reinforcing rods.

– The substructure of cavity walls are now often formed using 'Trench' blocks, which have a width equal to the combined width of inner and outer leaves plus the cavity.

– The main advantage of blocks over bricks is they are quicker to lay and the aerated thermal ones provide good thermal insulation.

○ **Stone blocks** are made from a naturally-occurring material such as granite, sandstone, limestone, marble and slate. They are mainly used as thin-dressed stone facings known as ashlar, which are fixed to a brickwork or concrete backing.

Cement

The main types of cement that are used are as follows:

○ **Ordinary Portland cement (OPC)**: for general use. When hardened, its appearance resembles Portland stone.

○ **Rapid hardening Portland cement (RHPC)**: for cold weather use.

○ **Sulphate-resisting Portland cement (SRPC)**: for use underground in high-sulphate conditions.

○ **White or coloured Portland cement**: made using white china clay to which pigments are added to produce a range of coloured cements.

Concrete

Concrete is a mixture of cement, fine and coarse aggregates and water. To refresh your memory about concrete, return to page 212 of this chapter.

Glass

Glass is a mixture of sand, soda, ash, limestone and dolomite that is heated in a furnace to produce molten glass. On cooling, the molten mixture becomes hard and clear. The main forms of glass, which are determined by their manufacturing process, are listed below:

○ **Drawn glass**: molten glass is drawn up between rollers in a continuous flow, cooled in water towers and cut into sheets. Patterned rollers may be introduced to create rough cast and patterned glass. Wire can be incorporated during the drawing to form wired glass, used for increased impact protection and fire-resistant purposes. The surfaces of drawn glass are not perfectly flat, giving a distorted view. This means that large sheets of glass for shop fronts have to be ground and polished perfectly flat and this is known as polished plate glass.

○ **Float glass**: molten glass is floated on to the surface of liquid tin and allowed to cool. This is also known as annealed glass and is the most common type of glass in general use. When looked through, it gives an undistorted view without the need for polishing.

○ **Safety glazing**: 'at risk' areas of glazing, such as fully-glazed doors, patio doors, side panels, low-level glazing and other large glazed areas, should use a safety glazing material or be protected from impact by other screens or barriers.

– **Toughened safety glass** has undergone special additional heat treatment and a rapid cooling process, known as tempering. It is up to five times stronger than standard glass, but cannot be re-cut after tempering. If broken, it will disintegrate into fairly small pieces with dulled edges, thus preventing serious injury.

– **Laminated safety glass** is a sandwich of two or more sheets of glass interlaid with a plastic film. In the event of an impact, the broken segments of glass remain stuck to the plastic film, again preventing serious injury. Depending on the number of layers, impacts from hammer blows and even gun shots can be resisted.

DID YOU KNOW

Special types of glass are available including tinted glass, back-painted glass to show a solid face colour, mirror glass with a safety backing, glass with increased thermal insulating properties known as low E or low emissivity, and self-cleaning glass. These are produced using additional ingredients or surface treatments during and after manufacture.

Insulation

Insulation materials are incorporated into a building for thermal, sound and fire-protection purposes. Many are capable of performing more than one of these roles at the same time.

Thermal insulation materials are used to reduce heat transfer by **conduction**, **convection** or **radiation**. They can be used in varying combinations to achieve thermal comfort within a building, coupled with reduced energy consumption.

Heat is transferred through an element of construction by a combination of all three processes. Warmth from one side is conducted through and heats the structure, the heated structure then radiates heat on the cool side, which is dispersed into and warms the air with the assistance of convection currents. The rate of heat transfer from the warm to cool side in a structure is dependent on two main factors:

- **The density and thickness of the material**: low-density materials that trap air within their structure are poor conductors and thus good insulators; denser materials containing little or no trapped air are good conductors and thus poor insulators.

- **The temperature difference between the two sides**: small differences result in a slow rate of transfer; large differences result in a rapid rate. For example, an unheated house in cold weather conditions would have very little heat transfer, as there will be little difference between the inside and outside temperatures. However, when the heating is switched on, the inside temperature rises causing the rate of heat transfer to rise rapidly.

Types of thermal insulation

Thermal insulation materials can be called bulk insulation or reflective film insulation.

- Bulk insulations are low-density materials containing many small pockets of trapped air, which preventconductive heat transfer and convective flow. There are various types:

   - Mineral wool/fibre or rockwool/fibre is made by heating and spinning rock or iron ore blast furnace slag, to produce a product that is a mass of fine intertwined fibres.

It comes in sheets known as 'batts' for cavity wall insulation, in quilted roll form for floor, loft and n wall insulation or as loose fill for lofts and blown cavity wall insulation. In addition, as mineral wool is non-combustible, it is often used in a sheet or sprayed form as a fire protection of structural steelwork.

– Glassfibre or fibreglass is made in the same way as mineral wool/rockwool, but uses molten recycled glass. Available in the same forms and for the same uses as mineral wool.

– Polystyrene is an air-expanded plastic resin made in sheets or as a loose fill for floors, walls, partitions and lofts.

– Polyurethane is formed by a reaction between two chemicals that expand when mixed together. Available as rigid foam insulation panels used in floors and walls and as a spray foam for gap-filling under rafter installation and cavity walls.

⬡ Reflective film insulation is normally made using aluminium foil. Used in an airspace, it creates a barrier that reflects radiated heat back into the airspace rather than it being absorbed or passing through. There are various types:

– Reflective pads that can be positioned behind central heating radiators, used to prevent heat passing into the structure.

3.41 Insulation materials

DID YOU KNOW

Other bulk forms of insulation include: vermiculite, a mineral that is expanded at high temperatures to form a loose fill material; cellulose, made from recycled paper and available as a loose fill, batts and rolls; flax or hemp plant fibres in batts or rolls; recycled glass batts or rolls and treated sheep's wool.

DID YOU KNOW

Thermal insulation's effectiveness is also dependant on its moisture content. It must be stored in dry conditions and kept dry in use. If it is allowed to become wet, water, which is a good conductor, will replace the insulating air.

- Foil backing to plasterboard, polystyrene and polyurethane sheets, which acts as both a heat reflector and a vapour barrier.

- Foil encapsulation of mineral or rock wool quilts, for increased thermal performance, itch-free installation and moisture protection.

- Double foil-faced bubble pack, used for insulating the underside of rafters and coldwater pipework and also as a vapour barrier.

Metal

All metals are classified as being either ferrous or non-ferrous. Ferrous metals are extracted from iron ore with varying amounts of carbon added to them, such as wrought iron and high-tensile steel. They will corrode rapidly when exposed to air and water, until they are completely rusted. Chromium and nickel may be added to form a stainless-steel alloy that is resistant to rusting. Non-ferrous metals do not contain iron, but consist of other principal metals, such as zinc, copper, tin, lead, aluminium and magnesium that corrode or dissolve very slowly when exposed to sulphur-containing gases or solutions and carbon dioxide, which are present in the air. This corrosion forms a film on the surface, which can protect the metal against further corrosion. In general, the principal non-ferrous metals are rather soft and are often mixed in their molten form to produce harder alloys. Zinc and copper are mixed to form brass; copper and tin form bronze; tin and lead form solder; aluminium and magnesium form aluminium alloys.

Steel is commonly used as beams and columns or portal frames of industrial and commercial buildings, as well as wall cladding and roof coverings. It is used as binders in timber floors, joist hangers, roof truss fixings and restraint straps, and as lintels in domestic and other solid structures. However, to prevent the risk of corrosion they require a secondary finishing process, such as painting, powder coating or galvanising. Although more expensive, the use of stainless steel for vulnerable items, such as wall ties, helps to overcome corrosion risks. Non-ferrous metals are used for water pipes, fittings and window frames, as well as decorative wall cladding, roof covering and DPCs.

Mortar

Mortar is the gap-filling adhesive that holds bricks, blocks or stonework together to form a wall. It takes up the slight difference in shape and provides a uniform bed to transfer the loads from one component to the next. The four main types of mortar are mixtures of the following with water (typical mix ratios are shown in brackets):

- Cement and soft sand mortar (1:3).

- Lime and soft sand mortar (1:3).

- Cement, lime and soft sand mortar often called compo mortar (1:1:6).

- Cement, soft sand plus plasticiser mortar (1:6).

Paint

Paint is a thin, decorative and/or protective coating, which is applied to a surface in a liquid or plastic form and later dries or hardens to a solid film. Paints consist of a film former, known as the vehicle; a thinner or solvent (water, spirit, oil, etc.) to make the coating liquid enough; and a pigment suspended in the vehicle to provide covering power, colour and other additives, which improve the paint's production, storage, application and other performance properties.

Conventional paints are generally classified into two main types.

- **Solvent-based paints**: also known as 'oil-based' or 'alkyd' paints contain high levels of organic solvents, which give them the strong smell noticeable in buildings that have been freshly painted. They are flammable, potentially hazardous to human health and have a toxic impact on the environment. Disposal of cans and surplus paint can also be troublesome as it's considered to be hazardous waste.

- **Water-based paints**: also known as acrylic or latex paints and emulsions are less toxic and its odour fades much faster than solvent-based paints.

DID YOU KNOW

The strength of mortar used for a particular job is determined mainly by the strength of the bricks or blocks being used. It should be about the same strength as the brick or block but never stronger.

- Cement mortars are stronger and more resistant to moisture than lime mortars.

- Lime can be added to cement mortar to prevent it cracking while improving workability and bonding properties.

- Plasticisers are used as an alternative to lime for improving the workability of mortars.

- Sulphate-resisting cement can be used in mortars, particularly for underground work with high levels of sulphate.

DID YOU KNOW

Equipment used with solvent-based paints needs to be cleaned with white spirit or turpentine. Equipment used with water-based paints can be cleaned using warm, soapy water.

Traditionally, virtually all paint used on wood or metal was solvent-based; however, high-quality acrylic paints are increasingly replacing solvents across a wide range of paint applications. In general, solvent-based paints are preferred for external use as they last longer when exposed to the environment. They are also good for internal use in high traffic areas such as entrance hallways, etc. as they can be washed and scrubbed clean with less risk of damaging the surface. In other areas, acrylic paints are increasingly popular because they are easier to apply, can offer excellent durability, have a quicker drying time and are less toxic.

Paint can be applied by brush, spray or roller. One or more coats of the same paint may be required, or a build up of different successive coats, each having their own function (primer, undercoat and finishing coat).

Paint Types	Uses
Emulsion	water-thinned paint for use on walls and ceilings, with a matt or silk finish.
Primers	form a protective coat against moisture and corrosion, or act as a barrier between dissimilar materials. They also provide a good base surface for bonding subsequent coats.
Undercoats	used on primed surfaces to give a uniform body and colour, ready for a finishing coat to be applied.
Finishing or top coats	seal the surface, give the final colour and provide the desired surface shine level such as eggshell or gloss. Gloss paints are best for surfaces that have to be repeatedly cleaned without the risk of damage.
Masonry paints	suitable for external walls, including bricks, blocks, concrete, cement rendering and pebble-dash finishes.
Solvent paints	based on rubber, bitumen or coal tar and used for protecting metals and waterproofing concrete floors and walls, etc.
Preservative	protective coat applied to wood, which increases the wood's resistance to biological attack.
Varnish	paint without a pigment, used for clear finishing of decorative timbers.

FAQ

What is meant by matt, gloss, eggshell, silk and satin paint finishes?

They mainly refer to the level of sheen, shine or reflection of a finish, but they are also associated with the type and use of the paint.

Matt – a low-sheen emulsion finish for walls and ceilings.

Gloss – a glass-like, high-sheen finish for woods and metals.

Eggshell – a soft-sheen finish for woods and metals.

Satin – a mid-sheen finish for woods and metals.

Silk – a high-sheen emulsion finish for walls and ceilings.

Plaster

Plaster is applied on internal walls and ceilings to provide a smooth, easily-decorated surface. Plaster is a mixture that hardens after application. It is based on a binder (gypsum, cement or lime) and water and may include aggregates. Depending on the surface being plastered, plastering schemes may require the application of either one coat, or several undercoats to build up a level surface followed by a finishing coat.

- **Gypsum plaster** is for internal use only and different grades are used according to the surface and coat. For undercoats, **browning** is generally used for brick and blockwork or **bonding** for concrete; for finishing coats, **finish** is used on an undercoat and **board finish** for plasterboard.

- **Cement-sand plaster** is used for external rendering, internal undercoats and water-resistant finishing coats.

- **Lime-sand plaster** is mostly used for undercoats, although lime can be added to other plasters to improve their workability.

Plasterboard

This consists of a gypsum plaster core sandwiched between sheets of heavy paper. Plasterboard is used for wall and ceiling

DID YOU KNOW

External plastering is normally called rendering.

linings and can be either dry finished, known as dry lining, where the joints are filled and taped, or wet finished using a skim coat of plaster.

- ⬡ **Tapered-edge** boards are used for dry lining and **square-edge** board for plastering over.
- ⬡ **Foil-backed** boards are used as both a vapour barrier and as a reflective insulation.
- ⬡ **Composite** panels are also available. These consist of plasterboard bonded to either polystyrene or polyurethane sheets. Single-sided boards are used as insulated wall and ceiling linings and double-faced boards for proprietary partition wall systems.

Plastic

Plastics are synthetic (man-made) materials, which come mainly from petroleum and coal. Plastic products are formed into their required shape while the solution is still soft . This might be done by forcing through a shaped die, film blowing into a tube, sheet casting on to a cooled surface, and injection or vacuum forming into a mould. There are two distinct groups of plastics:

- ⬡ Thermoplastics can be softened by heat and will re-harden on cooling. In general, they tend to be soft, easily scratched and have little resistance to loading, although they have good moisture-resistant properties. Typical examples used in building are as follows:
    - **Acrylic**: for baths, basins, showers, in flat sheets for glazing and also used in paints.
    - **Nylon**: for door and window fittings.
    - **Polythene**: for DPCs and DPMs, waste pipes, water pipes and tanks.
    - **Polyvinyl chloride (PVC)**: for electrical insulation, sheets and floor tiles. A rigid version of PVC, known as uPVC or PVCu, is used for soil and waste pipes, gutters and fittings, and door and window frames.
    - **Polyvinyl acetate (PVA)**: used in adhesives, acrylic paints and as a bonding agent in plasters, mortars and floor screeds.
    - **Polystyrene**: used for tiles and insulation.

⬡ Thermosetting plastics undergo a chemical change when setting and cannot be re-softened by heat. In general, they are harder and stronger than thermoplastics. In addition, they have good electrical insulation properties. Typical examples used in building are as follows:

- **Phenol, resorcinol, urea and melamine formaldehyde resins**: used for adhesives and electrical fittings.

- **Polyester reinforced with a glass fibre to form glassfibre-reinforced plastic (GRP)**: used for claddings and mouldings.

- **Polyurethane**: used in surface coatings, adhesives, insulation and gap-filling foam.

Timber

Timber is sawn or planed wood in its natural or processed state:

⬡ **Softwoods** are from relatively fast-growing coniferous trees, in cooler temperate climates. In general, they are lighter, less decorative and tend to be used for structural work, painted joinery and trim. Typical examples are pine (European redwood), spruce, hemlock and Douglas fir.

⬡ **Hardwoods** are from slower-growing broadleaf trees, which grow in both temperate and tropical climates. In general, they are denser, more decorative, resistant to biological attack and more often used for decorative work, furniture, polished joinery and trim. Temperate examples are ash, beech, oak and walnut, while tropical examples are mahogany, meranti, iroko and teak

All timbers absorb and lose moisture to achieve a balance with their surroundings. This causes the timber to expand and shrink, which can lead to distortion, splitting and cracking. Damp timber used in new buildings will eventually dry out and shrink. This shrinkage will cause joints to open up and cracks to form between elements and components, such as wide gaps between floorboards and cracks between walls and the ceiling line. Damp and wet timber is also highly likely to rot.

DID YOU KNOW

Timber is used to manufacture a wide range of board or sheet materials:

○ **Plywood** usually consists of a number of thin layers, known as veneers, which are glued together with their grains alternating for strength and stability. Used for flooring, formwork, panelling, sheathing and cabinet construction.

○ **Laminated boards** consist of strips of timber that are glued together, sandwiched between two plywood veneers. Blockboard has core strips up to 25mm wide and in laminboard they are up to 8mm. Both types are used for panelling, doors and cabinet construction.

○ **Particle boards** use small wood chips impregnated with a synthetic resin adhesive and bonded together under pressure. Chipboard uses small wood chips and flakes; wafer-board and flake-board use larger wood flakes, wafers and shavings; oriented strand board (OSB) uses large wood strands in three layers. All are widely used for flooring, furniture and cabinet construction.

○ **Fibreboards** are made from pulped wood, mixed with an adhesive and pressed forming hardboard, medium board, medium density fibreboard (MDF) and insulation board. They are used for floor, wall, ceiling and formwork linings, insulation, display boards, furniture and cabinet construction. MDF is also available in moulded sections for use as skirting and architraves and other trims in place of solid timber.

○ **Veneers** are very thin sheets or 'leaves' of real wood cut from a log for decorative or constructional purposes.

Wallpaper

Internal wall and ceiling surfaces are often finished using wallpaper. Wallpaper can be self-finished, painted over with an emulsion or used to hide minor surface defects.

○ **Lining paper**: is used to cross-line walls and ceilings to provide a smooth surface before hanging a finishing paper on top. Alternatively, it can be painted over.

○ **Wood chip**: is a budget paper, which consists of small pieces of wood sandwiched between two layers of paper and is painted over after hanging.

DID YOU KNOW

The standard sheet size for manufactured boards is 2440 × 1220mm.

○ **Relief or embossed paper**: is imprinted with a raised pattern in lots of different designs and provides a good coverage over rough surfaces. They are available in printed patterns for use as a finished paper or in plain finish for painting over.

○ **Printed or patterned papers**: are a cheap finish paper for general use on walls, but are usually difficult to clean, thus best suited for use in low traffic areas. Washable versions, which have a thin plastic coating, are good for hallways, stairs, etc. where there is quite a lot of traffic.

○ **Vinyl coated wallpaper**: is a very durable finish paper that has a top PVC, which enables the walls to be washed or scrubbed. It is also very good for kitchens and bathrooms as it is resistant to steam and mould.

○ **Textured or blown vinyls**: have a deep embossed surface pattern that makes them ideal for use on uneven wall and ceiling surfaces. They are hard wearing, making them suitable for heavy traffic areas such as hallways and children's bedrooms. They may be used either as a finished paper or painted over.

○ **Wallpaper paste**: is used to bond the paper to walls and ceilings. More often the paste is applied to the back of the paper, while others require the paste to be applied directly on to the wall surface. Some wallpapers are pre-pasted and require soaking in water prior to hanging.

DID YOU KNOW

Each type of wallpaper will have a recommended type of paste to use. For example, when hanging vinyl papers you should use a fungicidal paste to prevent mould growth.

Effects of the environment on buildings and materials

Apart from the natural aging process of all buildings during their anticipated life, early deterioration of buildings and the materials used in their construction can be attributed directly to one or more environmental factors.

Water/dampness
This can be the biggest single source of trouble. It causes the rapid deterioration of most building materials, can assist chemical attack and creates conditions that are favourable for biological attack. Dampness can arise from different sources:

Rain penetration through the external structure, will appear on the inside of the building as damp patches.

○ After periods of heavy rain, these patches will spread and then dry out during prolonged periods of dry weather. They will, however, never completely disappear.

○ In some cases, efflorescence will be left on the surface.

○ Mould growth may also occur in damp areas, particularly behind furniture, in corners and other poorly ventilated locations.

○ Over time, the water resistance of brick and stonework and their mortar joints will deteriorate. This deterioration can be accelerated by the action of frost. Rainwater may gather below the surface and freeze. Ice expands causing the brickwork and stonework and their mortar joints to flake and crumble away.

○ Chemicals can be applied to **friable** wall surfaces to increase their moisture resistance and provide a sound base for decoration.

Rising damp is moisture from below ground level rising and spreading up walls and through floors by **capillarity**. This often occurs in older buildings. Many of these were built without DPCs and DPMs or, where they were incorporated, they have broken down possibly with age. (For example, slate, once a popular DPC material, is not flexible and will crack with building movement, so allowing capillarity.)

○ The visual result on the walls is a band of dampness and staining spreading up from the skirting level, wallpaper peeling from the surface and signs of efflorescence.

○ The skirting, joists and floorboards adjacent to the missing or failed DPC are almost certain to be subject to fungal attack.

○ Solid floors may be almost permanently damp causing considerable damage to floor coverings and adjacent timber, furniture, and so on.

Condensation can also cause damp patches, staining, mould growth, peeling wallpaper, efflorescence, the fungal attack of timber and generally damp, unhealthy living conditions. **Leaking plumbing** and heating systems are also significant causes of dampness.

Chemicals

Chemical pollution in the atmosphere can have an effect on a material's surface finish. This includes the corrosion of metals and the sulphate attack of cement.

- Corrosion causes metals to expand and lose strength. Corrosion of steel beams can lift brickwork causing cracks in the mortar joint. Corroded wall ties may cause bulges in cavity brickwork. Metals can be painted in order to seal the surface against corrosion. However, galvanised steel and iron should be used in vulnerable locations.

- The sulphate attack of cement occurs either in the ground or through products of combustion in chimneys. The sulphate mixes with water and causes cement to expand. Sulphate resisting Portland cement (SRPC) should be used in conditions where high levels of sulphate are expected.

- Smoke containing chemicals is given off into the atmosphere from many manufacturing processes. This mixes with water vapour and rainwater to form weak acid solutions known as acid rain. These solutions corrode iron and steel, break down paint films and erode the surfaces of brickwork, stonework and tiles. Acid rain also attacks decorative non-ferrous metals and plastic finishes causing the surface to dissolve and discolour. Regular cleaning to remove the contamination can help these materials to last longer.

- Pre-mature ageing of materials can also be the result of exposure to sunlight, which can cause bleaching, colour fading and even decomposition owing to solar radiation, especially ultra-violet light. Particularly affected are bituminous products, plastics and painted surfaces.

DID YOU KNOW

Galvanised steel and iron goes through a chemical process to prevent corrosion. This involves coating the metal with layers of zinc, which is non-corrosive for protection. When steel and iron are submerged in melted zinc, a chemical reaction takes place that permanently bonds the zinc to the surface and provides what is called galvanic protection. Unlike painting, which provides a surface seal, galvanising actually becomes a permanent part of the metal.

3.42 Cracking due to thermal movement

Movement

The visual effects of movement in buildings may not seem serious, such as windows and doors that jamb or bind in their frames; fine cracks externally along mortar joints and rendering; and fine cracks internally in plastered walls, along the ceiling line. However, they can be the first signs of serious structural weakness. Movement in buildings takes two main forms:

Ground movement will cause settlement in the building. When it is slight and spread evenly over the building, it may be acceptable. However, when ground movement is more than slight or differential (more in one area than another), it can have serious consequences for the building's foundations and load-bearing members.

○ Ground movement is caused mainly by the ground's expansion and shrinkage near the surface, owing to wet and dry conditions. Compact granular ground suffers little movement, whereas clay ground is at high risk.

○ Tree roots cause ground shrinkage owing to the considerable amounts of water they extract from the ground.

○ Frost also causes ground movement. Water in the ground expands on freezing. Where this is allowed to expand on the undersides of foundations, it has a tendency to lift the building (known as frost heave) and drop it again on thawing. This repeated action often results in serious cracking.

○ In addition, overloading of the structure beyond its original design load can also result in ground movement.

Movement in materials is due to temperature changes, moisture-content changes and chemical changes. Provided the building is designed and constructed to accommodate these movements, or steps are taken to prevent them, they should not lead to serious defects.

○ Temperature changes cause expansion on heating and shrinkage on cooling; particularly affected are metals and plastics, although concrete, stonework, brickwork and timber can be affected also. Large areas of brickwork, stonework and concrete may start to show cracks due to thermal expansion and contraction.

⬡ Movement joints should be included during the construction or can be retro fitted. These are straight joints filled with a compressible board, such as bitumen-impregnated fibreboard, with the outer surface sealed with polysulphide to prevent water penetration.

⬡ Moisture changes cause expansion when wetted and shrinkage on drying. This is known as moisture movement. The greatest amount of moisture movement takes place in timber, which should be painted or treated to seal its surface.

⬡ Moisture movement can also affect brickwork, cement rendering and concrete. Rapid drying of wetted brickwork in the hot sun can result in cracks, particularly around window and door openings.

⬡ Movement in older concrete can be caused by an alkali silicate reaction (ASR), which is a chemical process where alkalis in the cement combine with certain types of silica in the aggregate when moisture is present. This reaction produces a gel that expands to cause surface cracking and disruption of the concrete, which can lead to serious structural faults and subsequent demolition of the structure. Concrete structures most at risk are bridges, exposed frames and foundations.

Biological agents

Biological agents affect all types of timber and are caused by fungi and infestation by wood-boring insects. Given the right conditions, an attack by one or both agents is almost inevitable. Dry rot and wet rot are the two main types of fungi that cause decay in building timbers.

⬡ **Dry rot**: this is more serious and more difficult to get rid of than wet rot. It is caused by a fungus that feeds on the cellulose found mainly in sapwood (the outer layers of a growing tree). This causes timber to lose strength and weight, develop cracks in brick-shape patterns and, finally, become so dry and powdery that it can easily be crumbled in the hand. Two initial factors for an attack are damp timber in excess of about 20 per cent moisture content (MC) and bad or non-existent ventilation.

DID YOU KNOW

Infestation of wood-boring insects is commonly called woodworm, after the larvae that bore into, feed on and digest the substance of wood. It is easy to distinguish between an attack of wood-boring insects and other forms of timber decay by the presence of holes that appear on the surface. Also, when a thorough inspection is made below the surface of the timber, the tunnels or galleries bored by the larvae will be found. It is these tunnels that seriously reduce the strength of structural timber.

3.43 Galleries and flight holes clearly visible on surface of floorboards

3.44 Dry rot

3.45 Wet rot

○ **Wet rot**: this does not spread to the same extent as dry rot. It feeds on wet timber (30–50 per cent MC) and is most often found in cellars, neglected external joinery, ends of rafters, under leaking sinks or baths and under waterproof floor coverings. During an attack, the timber becomes soft, darkens to a blackish colour and develops cracks along the grain. Very often, timber decays internally with a fairly thin skin of apparently sound timber remaining on the surface.

To reduce biological attack, timber used in building should be preservative treated with a toxic liquid that poisons the food supply. New timber is best treated by pressure impregnation before use. This is the most effective form of timber preservation, as almost full penetration is achieved. Suppliers with specialist compressed air or vacuum equipment carry out this process before the timber is distributed. Timber in existing building can be treated with a preservative applied by brush or spray, but the effect is more limited as little more than a surface coating is achieved. Timber affected by biological attack should be cut out and replaced with new preservative treated timber.

Fire/heat

Extended exposure to fire can cause damage to a building's structure and the different materials used in its construction. Just because a material is non-combustible it does not mean that it will not be affected.

○ Bricks, blocks and stone are non-combustible but will expand in extremely high temperatures, causing cracking, spalling and buckling.

○ Concrete is non-combustible but can crack, flake and even explode when subjected to prolonged high temperatures in a building fire. This is due mainly to the heating up of the steel reinforcement that expands and forces off the surface concrete.

○ Metal is non-combustible but rapidly conducts heat, expands, buckles and will lose its structural strength at fairly low temperatures. This may cause damage to other structural elements, such as walls where a steel beam or lintel has been built in, leading to structural collapse in the worst cases. Metals can be protected to some extent from fire by coating with an **intumescing paint** or by encasing with a non-combustible material, such as plasterboard or brickwork.

○ Timber is combustible but large structural sections have a slow rate of burning and the charring caused helps to insulate it from the heat. Eventually, after extended exposure, it will lose its structural integrity, leading to collapse. Increased fire protection can be given by coating with an intumescing paint; pressure treating with **fire-retarding chemicals**; or by encasing with a non-combustible material such as plasterboard.

○ Plastics will buckle and melt when exposed to fire and may give off toxic fumes.

REMEMBER

○ **Combustible materials** are solid materials that are able to catch fire and burn.
○ **Non-combustible materials** are solid materials that are not able to catch fire and burn.

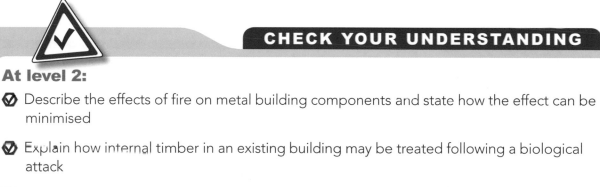

CHECK YOUR UNDERSTANDING

At level 2:

✓ Describe the effects of fire on metal building components and state how the effect can be minimised

✓ Explain how internal timber in an existing building may be treated following a biological attack

✓ Describe the principles behind the workings of bulk and reflective film insulation

✓ State the effect that freezing temperatures can have on concrete and brickwork

✓ State two factors, in addition to the levels of thermal insulation, that could reduce the thermal efficiency of a building.

ASSESSMENT CHECK

Now that you have completed this learning outcome you should now be able to:

- describe a range of different types of materials used internally for the construction of domestic dwellings.

- describe the key properties of timber, brick, blocks and insulation materials.

- describe where a range of different materials are used in the construction of domestic dwellings.

- describe the key characteristics of a range of materials used internally in a domestic dwelling.

- describe the effects of water, frost and chemicals on a range of building materials.

- describe the effects of heat and fire on masonry, concrete, timber and metal building components.

- describe the different types of paint coverings used on internal surfaces and their advantages and disadvantages.

- describe the reasons for treating a range of building materials with suitable chemicals.

- describe the different methods used to rectify deterioration to masonry and concrete, timber and metal building materials.

K3 Delivery and storage of building materials

Site protection

Fences and hoardings are the best means of preventing unauthorised access to a construction site. Entrances and exits should be kept to a minimum. The reception area for site visitors and delivery drivers should be located at the main gate and may be operated by a security guard on larger sites. Other considerations include the following:

- Display of warning notices around perimeter that state 'Security precautions are in force around the perimeter of this site'.

- CCTV cameras and alarm systems to protect the perimeter, compounds, stores and offices.

- Light the perimeter and access gates out of working hours; by sensors if necessary.

Compounds and stores

Large valuable items, such as frames, pipes, drainage fittings and items of plant, should be stored in a fully fenced security compound within the main perimeter hoarding.

Smaller valuable items, such as portable power tools and equipment, carpenters' Ironmongory and fixings, plumbers' copper pipe, fittings and appliances, electricians' wire and fittings, and decorators' paint, wallpaper, paste and fillers, should be kept secure in one or more lockable site huts or containers, depending on the size of the site.

- Stores should have as few windows as possible, which must include mesh grills or lockable shutters.

- Similar items should be stored next to each other on shelving or in a bin system, as appropriate.

- Each shelf or bin should be clearly marked with its contents, and each item entered on a tally card or computerised stock control system.

- The giving out of stores should be by a store person or supervisor against an authorised requisition.

- If unused materials are returned back into stock, they should be put back in the correct place and the stock control system amended accordingly.

- Heavy items should be stored at low level.

- Many construction materials, such as cement, plaster, adhesives and paint, have a limited storage or shelf life and may be marked with a use by date.

- New deliveries should be put at the back of existing stock. This ensures stock is used in rotation and does not become useless through deterioration or hardening.

- To discourage theft, all company property, plant and equipment can be permanently marked, using paint, engraving or ultraviolet security markings.

Delivery of materials

Phased deliveries of material should be considered in line with the planned construction programme. This will prevent the need for both unnecessarily long periods and large areas of site storage.

Physical size, weight and delivery method

This will determine what plant (such as a crane) and labour is required for off-loading and stacking. Non-durable materials should be delivered in closed or tarpaulin-covered lorries that protect them from both wet weather and moisture absorption from damp or humid atmospheres.

Taking delivery of materials

When materials are delivered to a site, the driver will normally present a delivery note to the security guard or other authorised person. They will check that the delivery is due and that it is being delivered to the correct site. The site foreman is required to sign the driver's delivery note after undertaking a careful check to ensure all the materials are there and undamaged. Any missing or damaged goods must be clearly indicated on the delivery note and followed up by a letter to the supplier.

DID YOU KNOW

Many suppliers send out an advice note before delivery, stating details of the materials and the expected delivery date. This allows its unloading and storage to be arranged. Some material suppliers use a paperless system when making deliveries. Details of the delivery are stored on an electronic hand-held notebook, which the receiver of the goods will sign for on a digital screen.

Protection of materials

Many materials are destroyed by extremes of temperature, absorption of moisture or exposure to sunlight.

⬡ Stores should be maintained as far as possible at an even temperature of about 15°C (59°F). High temperatures cause adhesives, paints, varnishes, putties and mastics to dry out and harden.

⬡ Flammable liquids, such as white spirit, thinner, paraffin, petrol, some paints and varnishes, some timber preservatives and some formwork release agents, must be stored in a cool, dry, lockable place. Fumes from such liquids present a fire hazard and can have an overpowering effect if inhaled. Stores of this type should always have two or more fire exits and be equipped with suitable fire extinguishers in case of fire.

⬡ Water-based materials, such as emulsion and acrylic paints and formwork release agents, may be ruined if allowed to freeze.

⬡ Non-durable materials, such as timber, cement and plaster, require weather protection to prevent moisture absorption.

⬡ Bagged powdered materials, such as cement and plaster, will start to set if they are allowed to become damp. This will make them unusable.

⬡ Boxed or canned dry materials, such as powder adhesives, wallpaper paste, fillers, detergent powders and sugar soap, quickly become useless if exposed to any form of dampness.

⬡ Dampness will rust metal containers, which may result in leakage and contamination of the contents.

⬡ Where materials are stored in a building under construction, ensure the building:

- has dried out after so-called 'wet trades' are finished, such as brickwork and plastering
- is fully glazed and preferably heated
- is well ventilated – this is essential to prevent the build up of high humidity (warm, moist air).

LINK

For more information on how to handle/lift items correctly and safely, see page 14 of Chapter 1.

For more information on what PPE you should use, see page 79 of Chapter 1.

Handling and hygiene

Careless or unnecessary repeated handling will result in increased costs through damaged materials and even personal injury.

Manual handling should be the last resort after considering all mechanical means and aids available such as:

- **wheelbarrows**, which are the most common form of handling aids used for moving a variety of materials on-site

- **pallet trucks**, used for moving palletised loads

- **bag trolleys**, used for moving bagged materials and paving slabs

- **mini skips**, used for moving mixed concrete, mortar and plaster in conjunction with forklifts or pallet trucks

- **wheeled plastic tubs**, used for moving mixed concrete, mortar and plaster

- **panel carriers**, used in pairs to allow large sheet materials to be more easily carried around site.

3.46 Manual handling aids

Handling and storage requirements

The following table gives an overview of the handling and storage requirements for a range of common building materials.

Material	Handling and storage requirements
Aggregates Fine aggregate / Coarse aggregate Each bay marked with aggregate size 40mm Hard base slopes for drainage	Aggregate is normally supplied in bulk by tipper lorries. Each size of aggregate should be stored separately, next to the mixer. Stockpiles should be on a hard, concrete base, laid so that water will drain away, and separated into bays by division walls. Stockpiles should be sited away from trees to prevent leaf contamination and kept free from general site and canteen rubbish. Tarpaulins or plastic covers can be used to protect stockpiles from leaves, rubbish and rainwater. In severe winter conditions, the use of insulating blankets is recommended, to provide protection from frost and snow. Smaller amounts of aggregate are available either in one tonne bulk bags, which are off-loaded by the lorry's mechanical arm, or in waterproof 25 kg bags, normally as a palletised load for off-loading via a forklift truck. Bagged aggregates can help to reduce waste and avoid the need for storage bays.
Bricks	Bricks may be supplied loose or banded in unit loads, shrink-wrapped in plastic and sometimes on timber pallets. Loose bricks should be off-loaded manually and never tipped; they should be stacked on edge in rows, on level, well-drained ground. Do not stack too high – up to a maximum of 1.8 m high. Careless handling can chip the faces and arrises (corners) and lead to fractures, making the bricks useless for both face and hidden work. Poor stacking creates an untidy workplace and unsafe conditions for those working or passing through the area. Banded loads of up to 500 are off-loaded mechanically using a lorry-mounted arm, a forklift truck or a crane. Bricks stacked on pallets will be protected from the absorption of sulphates and other contaminants from the ground, which could later spoil the finished brickwork. To protect bricks against rain, frost and atmospheric pollution, all stacks should be covered with a tarpaulin or polythene sheeting weighted at the bottom.
Blocks Blocks stacked on edge / Tarpaulin or plastic cover Six to eight courses high	Blocks may be either supplied loose, banded in unit loads, shrink-wrapped in plastic and sometimes on pallets. Loose blocks should be off-loaded manually, never tipped; they should be stacked on edge in rows or columns, on level, well-drained ground. Do not stack too high – six to eight courses maximum. Banded or palleted loads are off-loaded mechanically using the lorry-mounted device, a forklift truck or a crane. To protect blocks against rain, frost and atmospheric pollution, all stacks should be covered with a tarpaulin or polythene sheets weighted at the bottom. Stone blocks are often stored in straw or other similar soft packing to protect arrises from impact damage.

Material	Handling and storage requirements
Bagged cement and plaster  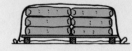 	Bagged materials may be supplied loose in individual bags or in unit loads shrink-wrapped in plastic on pallets. Individual bags should be off-loaded manually, with the bag over the shoulder as the preferred method. Palleted loads are best off-loaded mechanically using the lorry-mounted device, a forklift truck or a crane. Bags supplied in shrink-wrapped loads are best stored in these until required for use. Care must be taken not to damage the plastic. Bags should be stored in ventilated, waterproof sheds or containers on a sound, dry floor, with different products preferably having their own shed or container to avoid confusion. Bags should be stored clear of the walls and no more than eight to 10 bags high. This is to prevent bags becoming damp through a defect in the outside wall, causing the contents to set in the bag. It also reduces the risk of compaction ('warehouse setting') of the lower bags due to the excessive weight of the bags above. Bags should be used in the same order as they were delivered, known as 'first in, first out' (FIFO). This is to minimise the storage time and prevent the bag contents becoming stale or 'air setting'. Where small numbers of bags are stored and a shed or container is not available, they may have to be stored in the open. Stack no more than six to eight bags high on timber pallets and cover with tarpaulins or polythene sheets weighted or tied at ground level.
Glass  No gap between sheet Felt pads Firm wall or partition Timber blocks 	Glass is supplied individually in single sheets or in banded timber packs. Sealed double and triple units and cut sizes may be supplied in shrink-wrapped plastic packs for specific purposes. Glass should be stored in dry, wind-free conditions. Never store glass flat as it will distort and break. Sheets should be stood on one long edge, almost upright at an angle of about 85 degrees. Timber and/or felt blocks should be used to prevent the glass coming into contact with rough surfaces, which can result in scratches or chips. Always stack sheets closely together and never leave spaces as, again, this can lead to distortion and subsequent breakage. When manually handling glass, use laps to protect your palms. In addition, gauntlets may be worn to protect your lower arms and wrists.
Paint	Paints are mainly supplied in 1, 2.5 and 5-litre containers, and more rarely in bulk or trade 25-litre containers. These should be stored on shelves in a secure store at an even temperature. Each shelf and container should be marked with its contents. Large containers should be placed on lower shelves to avoid unnecessary lifting. Remember, paints have a limited storage or shelf life and may be marked with a use by date. New deliveries should be put at the back of existing stock. This ensures stock is used in rotation and does not deteriorate, set or harden, making it useless.

Material	Handling and storage requirements
Plasterboard Cross-bearers	Plasterboard is supplied either as individual sheets, taped face-to-face in pairs, in banded bundles or unit loads on pallets, they may also be supplied in shrink-wrapped plastic packs. Individual sheets should be off-loaded manually. To avoid damage, they should be carried on edge, which may require a person at each end. Banded bundles or palleted loads are best off-loaded mechanically using the lorry-mounted device, a forklift truck or a crane. Sheets supplied in shrink-wrapped plastic packs should be stored in them until required for use. Care must be taken not to damage the plastic. Sheets should preferably be stored in a warm, dry place, ideally stacked flat on timber cross-bearers, spaced close enough together to prevent sagging. Alternatively, where space is limited, sheet material can be stored on edge in a purpose-made rack, which allows the sheets to rest against the back board in a true plane. Leaning sheets against walls on edge or end is not recommended as they will take on a bow, which is difficult to reverse.
Roof tiles and slates Tarpaulin or plastic sheet; End tiles flat and taper stacked; Four to six rows high; Cappings stored on end	Roof tiles and slates may be either supplied loose, in banded packs, in shrink-wrapped plastic packs or in unit loads on timber pallets. Loose tiles should be off-loaded manually, never tipped; they should be stacked on edge in rows, on level, well-drained ground. Do not stack too high – four to six rows maximum; and taper the stack towards the top. End tiles in each course should be laid flat to prevent toppling. Ridge and hip cappings should be stored on end. Banded, packed or palleted loads are off-loaded mechanically using the lorry-mounted device, a forklift truck or a crane. To protect tiles against rain, frost and atmospheric pollution, all stacks should be covered with a tarpaulin or polythene sheet weighted at the bottom.
Thermal insulation materials	Thermal insulation materials are supplied in rolls, batts or larger sheets. Rolls are best stored on end and sheets flat. Both must be kept dry in storage as any moisture will adversely affect their insulation properties and quilted rolls may disintegrate entirely.

Material	Handling and storage requirements
Timber and timber-based manufactured sheet material 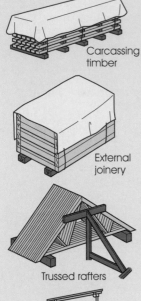Carcassing timber External joinery Trussed rafters Trim and planed sections 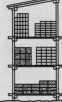Cross bearers 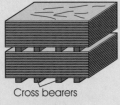Board material	Timber may be either supplied loose in individual lengths, in banded packs or in shrink-wrapped plastic packs. Individual lengths should be off-loaded manually; long lengths and large sections may require a person at each end. Banded or wrapped loads are best off-loaded mechanically using the lorry-mounted device, a forklift truck or a crane. Timber supplied in shrink-wrapped plastic packs should be stored in them until required for use. Care must be taken not to damage the plastic. Carcassing timber and external joinery should be stacked on bearers clear of the ground using piling sticks between each layer or item and covered with waterproof tarpaulins. Stacks must be covered to provide protection from rainwater, snow and direct sunlight. Care must be taken to allow air circulation through the stack, thereby preventing problems with condensation that could form under the covering. Trussed rafters can be racked upright and covered with a waterproof tarpaulin. Alternatively, they could be laid flat on bearers. Internal trim and other planed sections may be stored horizontally in open-ended covered racks. Priming or sealing of trim and planed sections should be carried out on receipt, if it has not been done prior to delivery. Internal joinery items should be stacked in a dry, preferably heated store, using piling sticks where required. As far as practically possible, the conditions in the store (humidity, temperature, etc.) should be equal to those in which the material is to be used. If the materials are stored in the building under construction, it should be fully glazed, heated and ventilated. The ventilation of the building is essential to prevent the build up of high humidity, which could increase the moisture content of the timber. Individual sheets should be off-loaded manually. To avoid damage, they should be carried on edge, which may require a person at each end. Banded bundles or palleted loads are best off-loaded mechanically using the lorry-mounted device, a forklift truck or a crane. Sheets supplied in shrink-wrapped plastic packs should be stored in them until required for use. Care must be taken not to damage the plastic. All sheet materials should preferably be stored in a warm, dry place; ideally stacked flat on timber cross-bearers, spaced close enough together to prevent sagging. Alternatively, where space is limited, sheet material can be stored on edge in a purpose-made rack, which allows the sheets to rest against the back board in a true plane. Leaning sheets against walls on edge or end is not recommended as they will take on a bow, which is difficult to reverse. Veneered or other finished surfaced sheets should be stored good face to good face, to minimise the risk of surface scratching.

CHECK YOUR UNDERSTANDING

At Level 2:

- ✅ State the reason for planning phased deliveries of materials in accordance with the building programme

- ✅ Explain the abbreviation FIFO in relation to the stock rotation of materials

- ✅ Describe the effect on cement and plaster if stored in damp conditions

- ✅ Explain why is it recommended that veneered or other finished surfaced sheets are stored good face to good face

- ✅ List the checks that should be made when materials are delivered to construction sites.

ASSESSMENT CHECK

Now that you have completed this learning outcome you should now be able to:

- ✅ describe the importance of building material delivery times and stock rotation.

- ✅ describe the different range of materials affected by stock rotation.

- ✅ describe the potential effects of bad weather on a range of building materials.

- ✅ describe different methods and equipment used to protect building materials correctly.

- ✅ describe the correct process for checking deliveries of building materials to construction sites.

- ✅ describe the different equipment used to transport a range of building materials safely.

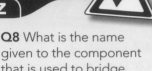

From this chapter you should have a good understanding of:

At level 1:

K1 Foundations, walls and floor construction

K2 Construction of internal and external masonry

K3 Roof construction

Level 1

Q1 The type of foundation mainly used for low-rise domestic structures is:

a Raft

b Pile

c Pad

d Strip

Q2 What is the name given to the roof member that provides intermediate support for the common rafters of a pitched roof?

a Wall plate

b Purlin

c Ridge board

d Fascia board

Q3 Common rafters in a pitched roof are fixed at either end to:

a Sole plate and purlin

b Wall plate and ridge

c Soleplate and crown

d Wall plate and soffit board

Q4 Wall ties are used in which one of the following types of wall?

a Solid brick walls

b Stud partition walls

c Cavity brick and block walls

d Solid block walls

Q5 A roof having a fall or pitch of up to 10 degrees is called a:

a Mono-pitched roof

b Flat roof

c Lean-to roof

d Pitched roof

Q6 Datum pegs and marks are where:

a All site levels are taken from

b The building line is set out from

c The walls of a building intersect

d Stepped foundations are required

Q7 What is the main difference between DPCs and DPMs?

a Their purpose

b Their location in a building

c The material they are made from

d There is no difference

Q8 What is the name given to the component that is used to bridge openings in walls?

a Joist

b Binder

c Lintel

d Sleeper

Q9 What is the main purpose of bonding brickwork?

a To provide a surface that plaster or rendering will bond to

b To spread the loading evenly throughout the wall

c To provide a decorative finished effect

d To minimise the use of materials

Q10 What type of aggregate is normally used in a brickwork mortar mix?

a Soft sand

b Sharp sand

c Coarse aggregate

d All-in aggregate

REVISION QUIZ

Level 2

Q1 What does the term 'galvanic protection' refer to?

a The painting of timber and metal to protect them from moisture

b The chemical treatment of steel and iron with zinc to prevent corrosion

c The pressure treatment of timber with a fire-retarding solution that when heated gives off a vapour that will not burn

d The treatment of walls with a chemical to increase their moisture resistance

Q2 The type of bonding used in cavity walls is known as:

a Cavity bond

b English bond

c Stretcher bond

d Flemish bond

Q3 The type of foundation that covers the whole footprint of a building and is used In poor soil conditions is:

a Raft with edge beam

b Deep strip or trench fill

c Reinforced pad and beam

d Reinforced wide strip

Q4 Phased deliveries of building material in accordance with the programme will:

a Increase costs

b Reduce costs

c Increase storage requirements

d Reduce storage requirements

Q5 Profile boards are used on-site when:

a Laying off plaster

b Pointing brickwork

c Setting out foundations

d Sealing expansion joints

Q6 What part of a building does the following definition refer to: 'All of the structure up to and including the ground floor slab and damp-proof course'?

a The foundations, walls and floors

b The walls, floors and roof

c The substructure

d The superstructure

Q7 A paint that seals a surface from moisture or corrosion and provides a good surface for subsequent coats is known as:

a Sealer

b Primer

c Preservative

d Undercoat

Q8 What type of subsoil is most likely to be affected by seasonal moisture changes?

a Rock

b Gravel

c Clay

d Sand

Q9 What method of applying preservative treatment to timber gives the best protection?

a Hand brushing

b Pressure spraying

c Hand roller

d Pressure impregnation

Q10 The chalky deposit that may be left on the surface of brickwork after drying out is called:

a Efflorescence

b Spalling

c Staining

d Leptospirosis

From this chapter you should have gained a good understanding of:

At level 2:

K1 Principles of building methods and construction technology

K2 Principles of internal building work

K3 Delivery and storage of building materials

Glossary

Acute illness
Extremely serious, severe or painful illness.

Agenda
A document listing the main topics and order of discussion. This is sent out prior to the meeting to allow people to prepare.

Approved codes of practice (ACoP)
A published document that contains guidance, examples of good practice and explanations of the law.

Archive
The term given to both a collection of records and documents, as well as the place in which they are located.

Asphyxia
Suffocation caused by a blockage of the airway or inhalation of toxic gases.

Biological agent
Relating to living organisms that can cause detrimental heath effects.

BODMAS
Brackets, then the Order is Division, Multiplication, Addition and Subtraction

Bonding
The overlapping of vertical joints in brickwork and blockwork.

Brownfield
Previously developed land that is now vacant or derelict, and also land currently in use with a potential for redevelopment.

Capillarity
Or capillary action is the phenomenon whereby water can travel against the force of gravity in fine spaces, between two surfaces that are close together or in porous materials.

Carcinogenic
Capable of causing cancer.

Carded scaffolder
A person who holds a recognised skills card or certificate showing that they have been trained and assessed as being competent in the erection, alteration, dismantling and inspection of tubular scaffolding.

CE mark
Indicates that it has been manufactured to European standards.

Cladding
Cement rendering and tile hanging, which are all used to either weatherproof or give a decorative finish to external walls.

Combustible
A solid material that is able to catch fire and burn.

Commercial
Shops and offices, etc.

Competent person
Someone who has the experience, knowledge and appropriate qualifications, which enable them to identify the risks arising from a given situation and the measures that are required to mitigate the risks.

Conduction
The transfer of heat within a material from hotter to cooler areas.

Conformity
The following of a fixed standard.

Contaminated
Land (often brownfield) that contains concentrations of hazardous waste or pollution that requires cleaning up before building work can start.

Contamination
The presence of an unwanted harmful substance that pollutes a material, physical body, natural environment or workplace, etc.

Convection
The transfer of heat within liquids and gases, including oxygen in the air.

Corrosive
A substance that can destroy or damage another surface or substance on contact.

Deafness
The temporary or permanent impairment or loss of hearing, caused by prolonged exposure to noise over many years or caused immediately by sudden, extremely loud noises.

Denominator
Means how many parts the whole is divided into.

Designer
A person who designs things.

Dislocation
The displacement of a bone from its normal fitting in a joint.

Double insulation mark
Indicates that the motor and other live parts are isolated from the user.

DPC (damp-proof courses)
Built into the horizontal course of brick and blockwork walls, positioned at least 150 mm above the exterior ground level to prevent dampness rising up from the ground through the wall and penetrating into the building.

DPM (damp-proof membranes)
Used under the concrete in ground floors to waterproof them against ground moisture.

Duty
Something that a person or organisation is expected or required to do.

Efflorescence
White powdery deposits that are seen on the surface of a wall, it is caused by soluble salts in the wall, which crystallise as the structure dries.

Employee
A paid worker.

Employer
Pays one or more employees.

English bond
Consists of alternate rows (courses) of bricks laid lengthways along the wall (stretchers) and bricks laid width-ways across the wall (headers).

External flashings
Weatherproof joints between elements.

Facilities for transport
Roads, bridges, railways, harbours and airports, etc.

Fire-retarding chemical
A chemical that penetrates deep into the timber and, when heated, gives off a vapour that will not burn.

Flammable
A gas or liquid that quickly and easily sets on fire and burns.

Flashover
The simultaneous ignition of flammable vapours from a number of sources, causing an intense fire involving all the contents of a room or building.

Flashpoint
The lowest temperature at which a flammable material will give off enough vapour to ignite when exposed to a flame.

Flemish bond
Consists of alternate stretchers and headers in the same course. In both, the quarter lap is formed by placing a queen closer (brick reduced in width) next to the quoin (corner brick).

Floors
Horizontal ground and upper levels in a building, which provide a walking surface.

Foundations
Part of a structure that transfers loads safely onto the supporting ground.

Friable
Refers to surfaces that are easily crumbled or reduced to powder.

Greenfield
Undeveloped land that has never been built on. The term should not be confused with 'greenbelt', which refers to land around urban areas left permanently open or largely undeveloped to restrict further expansion.

Harm
Can vary in its severity, some hazards can cause death, others illness or disability or maybe only cuts or bruises.

Hazard
Something with the potential to cause harm.

Hazardous
Something or a situation that is potentially very dangerous to people, animals or the environment.

Hazardous substances
Substances that can cause ill health.

Hypothermia
Dangerously low body temperature caused by prolonged exposure to cold.

Ignition temperature
The lowest temperature at which a combustible material will give off enough vapour to ignite when exposed to a flame.

Industrial
Factories, workshops, mills and warehouses, etc.

In-situ cast concrete
Concrete that is poured in its liquid form directly into position on-site. It can be mixed either on-site or be supplied to site in a ready-mixed form.

Internal trims
Skirting, architraves and coving or cornices, which mask the joint between adjacent elements.

Intumescing paint
A surface coating, which, on heating in a fire, bubbles and expands to form an insulating layer that cuts off the fire's oxygen supply.

Landslip
Movement of ground down a slope.

Legislation
A law or set of laws written and passed by parliament.

Manufacturer
A person, factory, or company that produces finished goods from raw materials.

Minutes
A document that lists the issues to be resolved arising out of a meeting and actions for individuals.

Musculoskeletal disorder (MSD)
Joint, muscle, tendon, ligament, nerve or repetitive strain injury, which develops over time from years of moving too heavy items, awkward or bulky shapes or using poor procedures and postures.

Natural water table
The underground depth or level at which point the ground is totally saturated with water.

Non-combustible
A solid material that is not able to catch fire and burn.

Non-flammable
A gas or liquid that is not able to catch fire and burn.

Non-notifiable project
Work for a domestic client or where it is expected to last less than 30 days and less than 500 person days of work.

Notifiable project
Work that is expected to last for more than 30 days or involves more than 500 person days of work.

Numerator
Shows how many parts you have.

Obligation
Something that you must do because of a legal or moral duty or responsibility.

Omission
Something that has been deliberately or accidentally not been done or has been left out.

Oversite excavation
Removal of topsoil and vegetable matter prior to starting building work. Depth is typically between 150 and 300mm. The excavated topsoil can be used later for landscaping. If it is not required later, additional labour and transport costs may be offset by selling the soil.

Paramount
Greatest in importance or significance.

Personal protection equipment (PPE)
Personal protective equipment equipment, additions or accessories designed to be worn or held by a person at work to protect against one or more risk.

Pit excavations
Deep rectangular holes in the ground, normally for column base pad foundations. Larger holes may be required for basements etc. Sides may be battered or timbered, depending on depth.

Plant
Describes all industrial machinery and vehicles used on a construction site, such as cranes, excavators, earth-moving equipment, forklifts and dumper trucks and power access equipment.

Portable appliance testing (PAT)
Testing in addition to in-house testing and inspection, which is normally carried out on an annual basis but can be varied depending on the frequency of use.

Potable
Liquid that is suitable for drinking because it's clean and uncontaminated.

Pre-cast concrete
Concrete that is poured into a mould and allowed to cure before being moved to its final location.

Proprietary system
One that has been designed and manufactured by the owner of the patent, brand name, or trademark associated with the system.

Radiation
The transfer of heat from one object to another in the form of heat rays.

Radon
A natural radioactive gas, which enters buildings from the ground and can cause lung cancer.

Ratio
Used in scale drawings to show the relationship between the drawing and the actual object a 1:5 ratio means that 1 unit on the drawing represents 5 units in the actual object.

Reduced level excavation
Carried out after oversite excavation on undulating ground. It consists of cutting and filling operations to produce a level surface, called the formation level.

Regulations
Orders issued by a government department or agency that has the force of law.

Residential
Houses and flats, etc. that are termed dwellings.

Residual current device (RCD)
Monitors the flow of electricity in the live and neutral wires of the circuit. In the event of a fault, an imbalance in the flow occurs causing the device to trip, cutting off the electrical supply almost instantaneously.

Resuscitation
To revive someone from unconsciousness.

Risk assessment
The process of identifying hazards in the workplace or a particular work activity, assessing the likelihood of any harm arising and deciding on adequate precautionary control measures.

Risk
Concerned with the severity of harm and the likelihood of it happening.

Roofs
Uppermost part of a building that spans the walls and protects the building and contents.

Scale
A way of reducing an object in size to fit on a drawing sheet.

Self-employed
A person who earns a living by working independently of an employer, either freelance or by running a business.

Stairs
Series of steps that divide a vertical space into smaller rises so that they can be walked up and provide floor to floor access.

Standing ladder
A ladder that has to be leaned against a surface for support, such as a wall or scaffold.

Stepladder
A ladder that has a folding back frame, which acts as a prop to enable it to be used free-standing without the need to lean it against something.

Stress
When a body is subjected to a force.

Struts
Bracing members that are mainly in compression.

Sub-contractor
A self-employed person or a specialist company that is hired by a main building contractor to carry out a specific part of the building work.

Subsidence
The sinking or downward movement of ground.

Substance abuse
The general term used to refer to the taking of and dependence on an addictive substance, such as drinking alcohol, the taking drugs or the inhaling of solvents.

Substructure
Comprises of structure below ground up to and including the ground floor. Its purpose is to receive the loads from the main building superstructure and its contents and transfer them safely down to a suitable load-bearing layer of ground.

Superstructure
Comprises all of the structure above the substructure, both internally and externally. It encloses and divides space, and transfer loads safely on to the substructure.

Supplier
A person or company that provides goods, materials or services.

Ties
Bracing members that are mainly in tension.

Tinnitus
A ringing in the ears caused by exposure to loud noises.

Toxic
A poisonous substance that is capable of causing an injury, ill health or death.

Toxin
A harmful substance that accumulates in the body.

Trench excavations
Long, narrow holes in the ground made to accommodate strip foundations or underground services. Deep trenches may be battered or timbered to prevent the sides from caving in.

Walls
Vertical enclosing and dividing elements of a building.

Well-being
A good, healthy, or comfortable state.

Index

3:4:5 rule 144

abbreviations 103
accidents and injuries 24
    business implications 27
    key risks/hazards 36, 74
    prevention 32
    reporting 8–10, 22–3
    trends 17, 25–6
acute illness 24, 264
A-frames 67
agenda 187, 264
aggregates 213, 232, 257
air bags 69
alcohol 46–7
Approved codes of practice
   (ACoP) 2, 264
architraves 151–2
archives 95, 264
area, calculating 131, 138–41
arithmetic calculations 122–8
asphyxia 24, 264
assembly drawings 111
authorised persons 27–8

balustrades 204
bar charts 116–18
barge 150
battens 68
bench marks 208–9
bill of quantities (BOQ) 113–14
biological agents 24, 249–50, 264
block plans 109–10
blocks 233–4, 257
blockwork 156–7
BODMAS rule 128, 264
body language 166, 189–90
bonding, walls 215–16, 264–6
bricks 153–5, 232–3, 257
brickwork 153–5, 217–18

brownfield sites 210, 264
building operatives 171–2
buildings and structures 197
    building elements 204–5
    classification 198–9
    finishing elements 205
    loading 201–3
    structural forms 199–201
building teams 170–3
bump caps 79, 81
burns 36, 47, 74

calculations
    approximate answers 128–30
    arithmetic methods 122–8
    BODMAS rule 128, 264
    common errors 128–9
    conversions 141–2
    formulae 137–41
    fractions 121, 128
    money 133
    percentages 135–6
    powers/roots 136–7
    ratios/proportions 134–5
    rounding up 129–30
    triangles 138–9, 143–4
    volume 142–3
    see also measurements
capillarity 246, 264
carcinogenic 52, 264
CDM 11, 22
CE marks 72, 264
cement 212, 234, 239, 247, 257
chemicals, handling and storage
   36–9
circles, calculations formulae
   139–41
cladding 205, 264
clothing, protective 46, 79, 90
commercial buildings 198, 265

communication
    body language 166, 189–90
    building teams 170–3
    company policies 4, 168
    documentation 173–82
    electronic 167–8, 184
    importance 188, 191
    meetings 186–7
    message taking 185–6
    methods 166–7
    positive/negative 169
    telecommunications 183–5
    verbal 166, 183–5
    visual 167, 186
    written 167, 173–82
company policies 4, 168
competent persons 13, 16–17, 27,
   265
concrete 213, 234–5
    in-situ 158, 212, 266
    pre-cast 212, 268
condensation 246
conduction 236, 265
confirmation notices 176
conformity 119, 265
Construction (Design and
   Management) Regulations 2007
   (CDM) 11, 22
Construction Skills 15–17
contaminated land 210, 265
contamination 40, 265
contract documents 95, 119, 191
Control of Substances Hazardous
   to Health Regulations 2002
   (COSHH) 10–11, 43
convection 236
corrosion 40, 247, 265
COSHH Regulations 10–11, 43
costing, labour and materials 161–3
craft operatives 171–2

dado rails 152–3
daily reports 177
damp, effects of 245–6
damp-proofing 219, 265
data protection 95
datum pegs and levels 208–9
deafness 41, 265
death, reporting 10
decibels 41
deliveries 179–80, 254
dermatitis 46–7
designers 3, 5, 11, 265
dimensions 98, 101
diseases, reporting 8–10, 22–3
dislocation 24, 265
doors 204
double insulation marks 72, 265
drawings 95
    abbreviations and symbols
      102–3
    alterations 191
    dimensions 98, 101
    equipment and paper 108
    line styles 98–101
    perspective 106–7
    plans 109–10
    projections 104–7
    scales 96–7
    schedules and specifications
      112–13
    types 106–7, 109–11
drugs 46–7
dry rot 249
duties see employees; employers'
  duties

ears 42–3, 79, 81
efflorescence 233, 265
electrical equipment 76
electricity
    codes and marks 74–6
    key risks/hazards 36, 72, 74
    safe practices 72–3
    supply and voltages 74–5
elevation 104
e-mail 184
emergencies
    evacuation 29–30, 85
    first aid 28–9, 74
    records 22–3
    reporting 22–3
    see also fire

employees 3, 265, 267
    duties 5, 8, 11, 14, 33, 81
    emergency procedures 30
    facilities for 40–1
employers 3, 265, 267
employers' duties 3–4, 92
    accident reporting 8–11
    data protection 95
    facilities, providing 40–1
    fire prevention 84
    first aid 28
    hazardous substances 11–12,
      45–6
    manual handling 14
    noise 41–3, 81
    personal protective
      equipment 13, 78, 80–1
    risk assessment 32–3
    working at height 14–15
English bonds 215, 265
environmental impacts
    biological agents 249–50
    fire/heat 250–1
    ground movement 248
    material movement 248–9
    pollution 246–7
    water 245–6
equipment 108
    fire fighting 86–7
    first aid 28–9
    maintenance 73, 80
    see also personal protective
      equipment
estimates 162
evacuations 29–30, 85
excavations 55, 206, 267
eye contact 189–90
eyes 47, 79

facial expressions 189
facilities, for employees 40–1
falls 69
fascia 150
fax 183
fibreboards 244
finishing elements 205
fire
    building damage from 250–1
    evacuation 85, 90
    fire fighting 85–7
    fire-retarding 251, 266
    fire triangle 83
    prevention 84–5

    risks from 36, 41
    safety signs 85, 89–90
first aid 27–9, 74
flammable substances/materials
    37–9, 73, 255, 266–7
flashings 205, 265
flashover 83, 266
flashpoint 83, 266
Flemish bonds 215, 266
floors 204, 266
    ground floors 220–1
    measuring and quantities
      144–5
    upper floors 221–3
footwear, protective 79
foundations 204, 209–13, 266
fractions 121, 128
framed structures 199–200
frames 204
friability 246, 266
frost 210, 248

Gantt charts 116–18
glass 235, 258
gloves 79
greenfield sites 210, 266
ground movement 248

hand-arm vibration syndrome
    (HAVS) 8, 36, 47, 73
hand gestures/signals 90, 190
harm, meaning 1, 266
harnesses 69
hazard books 35
hazardous substances 10, 266
    control regulations 10–11,
      43–55
    hazardous waste 52
    health monitoring 45
    injury prevention 43–5
    risk assessment 43–4
    safe handling 37–9
    safety signs/labelling 44, 52
    storage 37–8
hazards 1, 36, 266
headwear, protective 79–81
Health and Safety at Work Act
    1974 2–5
Health and Safety Commission 15
Health and Safety Executive 6–8
health and safety, generally
    accident and injury trends
      17, 25–6

Health and Safety *continued*
    authorised persons 27–8
    company policies 4, 168
    enforcement 17
    and housekeeping 32
    importance 1
    method statements 35
health risks 46–8
hearing 42–3, 79, 81
height, working at
    fall protection 69
    key risks/hazards 36, 70
    ladders 56–60
    regulations 14–15, 55
    scaffolding 62–6
    stepladders 56, 60–1
    working platforms 66–8
helmets, safety 79–81
housekeeping 32, 84
hypothermia 24, 266

ignition temperature 83, 266
improvement notices 6
incident contact centres (ICC) 10
induction visits 18–20, 90
industrial buildings 198, 266
injuries *see* accidents and injuries
insulation
    handling and storage 259
    roof 224, 227–8
    types 236–8
internet 184
intumescing paint 250, 266
investigations 6

jointing 217
joists 146–7

labelling *see* safety signs
labour, costing 161–3
ladders 56–61
laminated boards 244
landslips 212, 266
lanyards 69
letters 181–2
lime 239
linings 204
lintels 218–19
loading 201–3
    foundations 209–10
    overloading 247
maintenance, of equipment 73, 80

manual handling 256
    key risks/hazards 36
    regulations 14
    risk assessment 49–50
    safe practices 50–2
manufacturers 3, 5, 11, 16, 188, 267
materials
    costing 161–2
    delivery 254
    handling 248–9, 256–60
    measuring and quantities
      144–61
    storage 253–60
measurements
    area 131
    length 130–1
    mass/weight 132
    money 133
    perimeter 131
    units of 129
    volume/capacity 131–2
    see also materials,
      measuring
meetings 186–7
memorandum 181
metals 238, 247
method statements 35
minutes 187, 267
mortar 153, 156–7, 218, 239
musculoskeletal disorder (MSD)
    47, 267

noise
    employers' duties 41–3
    key risks/hazards 36, 47
    personal protective
      equipment 42–3, 79, 81
notifiable projects 11–12, 267

omissions 5, 267
Ordnance Survey bench marks
    (OBM) 208–9
orthographic projections 104–5
overheads 163

paint 239–41
    handling and storage 258
    intumescing paint 250, 266
    quantities 159–60
panel structures 200
particle boards 244
paving slabs 159
pegs 207

percentages 135–6
perimeter, measuring 131, 139–41
personal hygiene 46
personal protection equipment
    (PPE) 4, 267
    clothing 46, 79
    employers' duties 13, 78, 80
    for hazardous substances 45
    headwear 79–81
    importance 78, 81
    for noise 42–3, 81
    storage 80
perspective 106–7
pests, damage by 249
pictorial projections 106–7
picture rails 152–3
plant, meaning 2, 267
plan views 104
plaster 241
plasterboard 241–2, 259
plastics 242–3
platforms 66–8
plywood 244
pointing 217
pollution 246–7
portable appliance testing (PAT)
    73, 267
posture 189
powers, calculating 136
profile boards 207
prohibition notices 6–7
projections 104–7
proportions 134–5
proprietary systems 64, 268
Pythagoras' theorem 143–4

quantities, calculating 113–14,
    144–61
quotations 162

radiation 236, 268
radio communications 184
radon 211, 268
rafters 148–50, 225–7
ratios 96, 134–5, 268
rectangles, calculations formulae
    139, 141
recycling 53–4
rendering 241
residential buildings 198, 268
residual current devices (RCD) 73,
    268
respiratory diseases 46–7, 79

rest facilities 41
resuscitation 24, 268
RIDDOR 8–10, 22–3
rising damp 246
risk assessment 191
    duties 32–4
    fire hazards 84
    hazardous substances 43–4
    meaning 1, 10, 268
    method statements 35
    procedures 33
roofs 268
    coverings 227
    flat roofs 224–5
    insulation 224, 227–8
    pitched roofs 225–8
    roof elements 223–4
rounding up 129–30
Royal Society for Public Health 16
Royal Society for the Prevention of
    Accidents 16

safety data sheets 44
safety nets 69
safety signs/labelling 52, 85,
    89–90, 186
scaffolders, carded 19, 264
scaffolding 62–6, 68
scale 96–7, 268
schedules 112–13
section views 104
security 253
self-employed 3, 268
setting-out 207
sheet materials 151
shock, electrical 74
signs see safety signs
site diaries 177
site investigation 210–11
site plans 109–10
site rules 168
sketches 109
skin diseases 46–7, 79
skirting 152–3
slates 259

sofits 150
specifications 112
square roots 137
stairs 204, 228, 268
standard form of contract 114–15
standing ladders 56–60, 268
steel 238, 247
stepladders 56, 60–1, 268, 269
storage
    building materials 253–60
    equipment 76, 80
    hazardous substances 36–8
    personal possessions 40
stress 48, 269
    loading 202–3
string lines 207
structures see buildings and
    structures
struts 202–3, 269
stud partitions 147–8
sub-contractors 5, 170, 269
subsidence 211, 269
substance abuse 46–7, 269
substructure 201, 269
superstructure 201, 269
suppliers 3, 5, 11, 16, 269
surface structures 200–1
symbols 102

telephone communications 184–5
Temporary bench marks (TBMs)
    208
tenders/tendering 162–3
ties 202–3, 269
tile battens 227
tiles 159, 259
timber
    handling and storage 260
    materials made from 244
    measuring 242–3
    quantities 144
    types 243
timesheets 173
tinnitus 41, 269
toilets 40

toolbox talks 20, 87
toxic substances 40, 269
toxins 24, 269
transport buildings 198, 265
triangles, calculations formulae
    138–9, 143–4
trims 151, 205, 266
tripping and slipping 36

underground work 239

vanishing points 106–7
variation orders 175
veneers 244
ventilation 38, 40, 45
vibration 8, 36, 47, 73
volume, calculating 142–3

wallpaper 160–1, 243–5
walls 204, 269
    bonding 215–16, 264–6
    cavity 214–15
    external 213–18
    framed 215
    internal 219–20
    jointing/pointing 217
wall ties 218
washing facilities 40, 46
waste, classification 52
waste disposal 53–4
water
    drinking/potable 40, 213,
        268
    effects of 245–6, 248–9
    and electricity 73
    natural water table 210, 267
welfare facilities 40–1
wet rot 250
windows 204–5
wood preservation 249
Work at Height Regulations 2005
    14–15, 55
work programmes 115–18
work restrictions 191